Maaike Voorhoeve is a Humboldt fellow at the Europe in the Middle East – The Middle East in Europe (EUME) Program of the Forum Transregionale Studien and the Re-configurations Programme at Philipps Universität Marburg. She is also associate researcher at the Amsterdam Center for Middle Eastern Studies. Her PhD dissertation (University of Amsterdam, 2011), was published under the title *Gender and Divorce Law in North Africa: Sharia, Custom and the Personal Status Code in Tunisia* (I.B.Tauris, 2014).

'A must-read for those interested in the law and gender issues in the Middle East.'
Ruud Peters, University of Amsterdam

'Indeed, *Family Law in Islam* proves that there is still considerable space for scholarly work and hope for new insights ... The volume represents an impressive collection of sound research on contemporary issues regarding Islamic family law. Its strength lies in providing cohesive information in fields which are not easily accessible, even for specialists. It was also a wise decision by the editors and authors to refrain from a normative approach and instead present legal–anthropological work in great detail ... A remarkable collection of research conducted by both experienced and by promising young scholars who are ready to enter into time-consuming and challenging fieldwork.'
Mathias Rohe, Friedrich-Alexander-Universität Erlangen-Nürnberg

'These chapters are informative and sophisticated studies, and they advance our knowledge of how family law in several Muslim countries is debated as well as how it actually works.'
Kenneth M. Cuno, University of Illinois Urbana–Champaign

FAMILY LAW IN ISLAM

Divorce, Marriage and Women in the Muslim World

Edited by
Maaike Voorhoeve

Paperback edition published in 2016 by
I.B.Tauris & Co. Ltd
London • New York
www.ibtauris.com

First published in hardback in 2012 by
I.B.Tauris & Co. Ltd

Copyright Editorial selection and Introduction © 2012 Maaike Voorhoeve

Copyright Individual Chapters © 2012 Susanne Dahlgren, Baudouin Dupret, Esther van Eijk, Christine Hegel-Cantarella, Arzoo Osanloo, Massimo Di Ricco, Nadia Sonneveld, Sarah Vincent-Grosso and Maaike Voorhoeve

The right of Maaike Voorhoeve to be identified as editor of this work has been asserted by the editor in accordance with the Copyright, Designs and Patents Act 1988.

All rights reserved. Except for brief quotations in a review, this book, or any part thereof, may not be reproduced, stored in or introduced into a retrieval system, or transmitted, in any form or by any means, electronic, mechanical, photocopying, recording or otherwise, without the prior written permission of the publisher.

ISBN: 978 1 78453 626 8
eISBN: 978 0 85773 240 8

A full CIP record for this book is available from the British Library
A full CIP record for this book is available from the Library of Congress

Library of Congress catalog card: available

Typeset by Newgen Publishers, Chennai

CONTENTS

Notes on Transliteration   vii

Acknowledgements   ix

Introduction
Baudouin Dupret and Maaike Voorhoeve   1

DISCOURSES ON THE LAW

1. 'She brings up Healthy Children for the Homeland':
   Morality Discourses in Yemeni Legal Debates   13
   Susanne Dahlgren

2. Reclaiming Changes within the Community Public Sphere:
   Druze Women's Activism, Personal Status Law and the
   Quest for Lebanese Multiple Citizenship   31
   Massimo di Ricco

3. What a Focus on 'Family' Means in the
   Islamic Republic of Iran   51
   Arzoo Osanloo

4. Rethinking the Difference between Formal and Informal
   Marriages in Egypt   77
   Nadia Sonneveld

DISCOURSES OF THE LAW

5   Waiting to Win: Family Disputes, Court Reform, and
    the Ethnography of Delay   111
    Christine Hegel-Cantarella

6   Divorce Practices in Muslim and Christian
    Courts in Syria   147
    Esther van Eijk

7   *Maktub*: An Ethnography of Evidence
    in a Tunisian Divorce Court   171
    Sarah Vincent-Grosso

8   Judicial Discretion in Tunisian Personal Status Law   199
    Maaike Voorhoeve

Contributors   231

Index   234

NOTES ON TRANSLITERATION

Consonants

b = ب	t = ط
t = ت	z = ظ
th = ث	' = ع
j = ج	gh = غ
h = ح	f = ف
kh = خ	q = ق
d = د	k = ك
dh = ذ	l = ل
r = ر	m = م
z = ز	n = ن
s = س	h = ه
sh = ش	w = و
s = ص	y = ي
d = ض	

Vowels

Short: a = ́ ; i = ؍ ; u = ́
Long: a = ا ; i = ي ; u = و
Diphthong: ay = اي ; aw = او

ACKNOWLEDGEMENTS

This publication would not have been accomplished without the help of professors Baudouin Dupret, Ruud Peters and Léon Buskens. We also want to thank Maria Marsh at I.B.Tauris, and Peter Barnes for editorial support, as well as the University of Amsterdam for financial support.

INTRODUCTION

Baudouin Dupret and Maaike Voorhoeve

In this introduction, three issues are addressed. First, emphasis is placed on the necessity of addressing the law and its practice in the Middle East and North Africa in a descriptive, non-interpretive way. Second, clarification is sought in the meaning and uses of several frequently-used words and concepts in this field of inquiry. And third, a suggestion is made to draw a distinction, within this domain, between the study of the discourse *on* the law and the study of the discourse *of* the law – that is, how the law is formulated and then referred to.

I

Since they were mainly considered an offspring of the jurisprudential corpus called 'Islamic law', the many legal systems of the Middle East and North Africa (MENA) used to be treated in terms of their relationship to Islam. The direct outcome of this tendency was to ascribe overarching importance to Islam in the inception and organisation of the law, and to minimise those specificities of each country which had proceeded from the historical and social circumstances of their recent development. In other words, Islam's influence was overemphasised, while the impact of socio-political transformation was neglected.

The main symptom of this tendency is the exclusive attention given to family law. Because it is by far the sole domain where the inspiration of the Sharia and the *fiqh* (doctrine) is still obvious, family law is the focus of most of the research. Per se, this does not constitute a problem, and the present volume testifies to the relevance of this theme. However, two things must be kept in mind. First, the domain of family law represents only a tiny minority of these countries' body of regulations. Second, family law, although often presented as the 'last bastion' of Islamic law, has in fact been transformed from 'divine' into 'man-made law' (Peters): it has gone through the process of 'positivisation' that followed the specific evolutions of every country's legal system.[1]

Focusing on the theme of Islamic law, researchers forgot to consider that the law is a daily and ordinary activity, with litigants trying to settle their problems and professionals carrying out their jobs. Legal activities are performed for all practical purposes, and therefore their study must primarily consist of the description of what people do when using legal provisions and institutions. To put it bluntly, law is first of all a conflict-resolution or guarantee-setting device, not the symbolic reflection of society's unconscious. Contrary to 'mirror theories' (Tamanaha), which do not consider the law for what it *does* but for what it *symbolises*[2], a realistic approach to the law in MENA countries is interested in what is in practice achieved by the many protagonists. In that sense, it does not look for *interpretation* – at least in Geertz's 'thick' sense – for this would mean that what is said and done by these protagonists cannot be accessed, and therefore needs some additional explanation drawn from the researchers' knowledge of the underlying culture. Rather, the realistic approach assumes that the observer does not understand the observed activities better than those he/she observes performing them. They share the same world of meaning, which is fundamentally made up of the 'technicalities' and 'practicalities' of everyday life, including legal life.

The prime benefit of such a realistic, pragmatic description of legal practices is that, contrary to an ironic stance *vis-à-vis* people and what they say and do when engaged in their actual life – assuming for instance that they behave irrationally because of some hidden cultural pattern – it details the ways in which they act to realise their goals. In other words, it replaces the question of *why* people do something by asking *how* they seek this realisation. In this process, we might have lost some understanding of metaphysical issues, but returning to law as an object of analysis in its own right, looking to the empirical as the only object of research, and paying attention to practice as the only area where the law is to be seen at work, represents a step towards understanding the workings of our mundane world.

II

The second aim of this introduction is to clarify the meaning and use of terms which traditionally occupy a central place in research on so-called Islamic law. Once a descriptive approach is chosen, these terms lose their theoretical and scholarly weight and 'thickness': they tend then to correspond to what 'lies open to view' (Wittgenstein), not to the depths of a mysterious world that needs to be overseen by scholars for its interpretation.[3]

Among these terms, 'Islam' and its adjective 'Islamic' occupy a central role. Since these countries and societies are assumed to be mainly characterised by their adherence to a specific religion, the inner and essential nature of the latter becomes paramount. From this point of view scholars must define *what Islam is* in order to understand what happens in this cultural framework. By contrast, the descriptive approach is not interested in any substantive definition, but restricts itself to the task of examining *how* Islam is invoked and referred to by those people who, at some point in their daily life, orient their talk and actions towards it. In that sense, Islam cannot be found outside its practice, and describing something as 'Islamic' is to ascribe to it the quality of being closely related to Islam, whatever the 'something' in question. Thus 'Islamic law' corresponds to what people consider as specifically Islamic in the law, independent of any consideration about the truth of such a claim.[4]

One observes the frequent use of terms imported from other languages which remain untranslated because of the ineffable meaning they are supposed to carry. This implies that cross-cultural communication is impossible, since languages are impervious to each other. If we take this one step further, people would not be able to talk to one another at all, since the meaning one person attributes to a word would never exactly correspond to the meaning the interlocutor attributes to it. This gives language a metaphysical dimension that any proper attention paid to the workings of the social world directly contradicts. Words are vehicles of communication, and the meanings they convey are the object of constant, pragmatic adjustments for the practical purpose of mutual understanding.

A frequent problem with the use of foreign-language terms is that, instead of keeping the denotative sense they have in that language, they acquire a connotative dimension in the cultural context into which they are imported. Thus, the usage of words like 'Sharia' testifies to the slippery process which necessarily characterises the referral to supposedly alien cultures. Per se, there is no reason not to speak of 'law', 'leader' or 'God'. Of course, it can be convenient at some point to know the terms used 'on the ground', although not in order to give them any non-translatable sense. Here again, the descriptive approach we advocate tries to understand how people refer to concepts and use words in action, independently of the abstract sense native and non-native scholars ascribe to them on the basis of doctrinal sources and outside any real-life context. In that perspective, for instance, Sharia would be what people refer to as such in context and in action, notwithstanding its orthodox (or deviant) use with respect to the Grand Tradition.

In a slightly different way, there are other terms where caution is indicated – for instance concepts in the social sciences which, although having their origins in ordinary language, have acquired a theoretical dimension to which the social world is assumed to conform. There is a strange looping process at work here, where ordinary notions are invested with a theoretical load that eventually gives them their meaning. The problem is that often these concepts are not deduced from close observation of what is going on in action and context, but are assumed *a priori*, and therefore serve as the lens through which further observations are interpreted. This is the case, for instance, with terms like 'patriarchal' and its extension 'patriarchalism'. The patriarchal nature of some legal relationships might be derived from empirical data concerning divorce in (for instance) Iran. However, some researchers 'know' *in advance* that the Iranian legal system is patriarchal instead of deducing it from their observations, although the latter offer a much more nuanced picture. The net result of this process is that research imposes its interpretations on the world, rather than the world finding in research an adequate description.

III

People address the issue of Sharia for very different purposes. When demanding its implementation in a country, activists address a legal theme for political purposes. When assessing whether a law is in conformity with Article 2 of the Egyptian Constitution, which stipulates that 'the principles of Sharia are the main source of legislation', the Egyptian Supreme Constitutional Court deals with the same theme for judicial and constitutional purposes. And when the heading of a Western newspaper states that the stoning of an Iranian woman 'is a symbolic issue, but it is at the same time the whole Sharia that is questionable' (*Le Soir*, 28 August 2010), it is clear that the journalist's purpose is related to the ongoing debate in Europe on the so-called 'clash of civilisations'. An adequate description of how different people address the issue of Sharia shows that the latter is not seen in the same light – or as 'the same thing' – simply because the same word is used. To put it in a different way, people are oriented towards the notion of Sharia in a way that is sensitive to the context in which it is used and to the practice in which they are engaged.

Such contexts are, broadly speaking, of two types. On the one hand there is the context of ongoing public debates, where the issue of law is a theme and a resource for addressing a matter that is not specifically legal. On the other hand, there is the legal context as such, where law is a textual source, an achievement and a practice. In other words, there is a discourse *on* the law and a discourse *of* the law, i.e. law as a *topic* and law as a *performance*: and there is a huge gap between these two conceptions of law. This gap is not related to a difference in the substance of what is at stake, but to a difference in the goal-orientation of the protagonists, i.e. what we call their practical purposes. Doing politics is very different from adjudicating; writing an open editorial aims at something other than formulating a plea; claiming that Sharia is a kind of Pole Star of a regime's legitimacy is technically and consequentially different from the search for *fiqh*-based solutions in the formulation and implementation of a ruling; and so on. When not taking these fundamental differences into account – an omission that comes about merely by sticking to the words people utter without looking at what they are doing when they utter them – research misses the phenomenon it purports to explore. It remains fascinated by the power of terms endowed with an intrinsic, essential meaning, independent of their practical uses. Thus, for instance, the Arabic word *tashri'* is supposed to convey a reference to the divine[5] on the sole basis of its etymology – 'referring to Sharia' – while a competent look into contemporary legal systems shows that the word has the direct, obvious sense of 'legislation'. Similarly, it is supposed that the Islamic state is intrinsically instable, because the etymology of the Arabic word used to capture this institution (*dawla*) conveys the notion of a cyclic change (see Bernard Lewis)[6]. Phrased in an anthropological way, the same cultural concept has resulted in attributing intrinsic meanings to words such as *haqq*, which are deemed to convey the power of their supposed linguistic 'origins' (see Geertz)[7], instead of simply expressing ideas related to the context of their uses (e.g. the 'right' to do this or that, or one of God's names, or the 'truth' of a statement).

Instead of deriving the meaning of words from assumptions about their etymology, research should arrive at a description of what people do in actual contexts. However, this does not mean that words are devoid of any importance, that talk is opposed to action, or that, in the sphere of law, there is a conflict between 'living law' and state law. Indeed, there is a classical dichotomy in socio-legal studies that opposes the law set out in codes, rulings and jurisprudence to the law as it can be observed in action, that is, when performed by flesh-and-blood human beings. Although this distinction stems from a positive intent – that one should not merely stick to legal formulations in order to study the law – it queers researchers' pitch by artificially severing legal practice from one of their main resources, i.e. legal texts. The law is mostly performed through direct or indirect references to formal sources, which protagonists use to orient themselves in choosing a way forward. This issue of rule-following, which has been much debated in philosophy, can be dealt with, when turning to more empirical contexts, through the notion of 'instructed action'.[8] Instead of considering that legal rules and legal practice each work autonomously, it suggests that they can indeed be distinguished analytically, but empirically function in an interdependent way: a rule is always a rule-instructing-an-action (since a rule alone has no existence but on paper) and the action is always an action-as-constrained-by-a-rule (since an action cannot be characterised as legal if it has no connection to a rule). This mode of describing the law has the double advantage of doing justice to the teleological formulation of legal rules – i.e. which aim at being implemented – and to the legal protagonists' systematic referencing of them – whether to apply or evade them.

IV

This book resulted from a wish to bring together academics working on family law and its practice in the Middle East and North Africa. The same motive led to the organisation of two panels at the World Congress for Middle East Studies (WOCMES, Barcelona, 2010), where the idea for this publishing project emerged.

All contributors to this volume address the topic of family law in the MENA from different angles. First, on the geographical level – contributions range from Tunisia to Syria and from Lebanon to Iran. Second, on the disciplinary level, as some contributors have a legal background, whereas others are specialists in anthropology or political science. Third, the contributions differ as to the perspective from which the topic of family law is addressed. Discourses *on* the law are addressed by discussing public, political and religious debates, while discourses *of* the law are described by examining the practices of judges, lawyers and litigants.

Part one of this volume is made of contributions which try to capture discourses on the law. Dahlgren, in chapter one, describes the discourses on morality in Yemen against the background of the family-law reforms that took place in the southern part of the country in the 1970s and 1990s. Specifically, she looks at how Islam is played out as a discourse both to promote and to limit women's rights. The analysis of these debates is conducted in the light of the difficult unification of the tribal North Yemen and the modernising South Yemen.

In chapter two, Di Ricco addresses public debates on Druze family law in Lebanon, focusing on the ways in which Druze organisations for women's rights go about enhancing the protection of those rights in the field of personal-status law. In the autumn of 2006 the Lebanese Druze community introduced important reforms in its institutions; inspired by these reforms, a group of Druze women started to claim changes in the Druze personal-status law. This article analyses the claims, forms of actions and achievements of these activists.

In chapter three, Osanloo examines the contemporary legal, social and religious (jurisprudential) debates over the current revisions to Iran's Family Protection Act. By highlighting the varying tenor of these debates in different sectors of Iranian society, she reveals the tensions over women's status and rights, the role of law in shaping that status 'from above', and finally the disparate groups claiming authority to define women's roles in the Iranian social order. The chapter will connect such debates to the broader contests over legitimacy and authority in governance, in an Islamic republic that is moving closer to a consolidation of power within particular groupings.

In chapter four, Sonneveld contrasts discourses on and discourses of the law, in this way linking part one of this volume to the second part. Focusing on informal marriages in Egypt, Sonneveld contrasts public images of informal marriages with everyday practices observed in Cairo. Publicly perceived as a means for young people to have premarital sex without the knowledge of their parents, in this chapter, Sonneveld shows that informal marriages are also practised by men who do not have the financial means to marry, and by women who hope that marrying an already married man will enable them to keep their freedom and independence. As such, she argues that informal marriages are reflective of changing gender roles.

In chapter five, Hegel-Cantarella analyses court delay as a particular object of concern in recent court-reform initiatives in Egypt. Although delay is often configured as a failure to progress and as an inert temporal space in which something is *not* happening, Hegel-Cantarella posits that it is productive to see the ways in which delay draws litigants into peripheral and focal legal spaces that provoke specific types of interaction and enable participant-observation in/of the work of law. Socio-legal and anthropological theory is used to analyse ethnographic data (collected in Port Said) that focuses on litigants' experiences of court delay in two primary peripheral legal spaces: lawyers' offices and the Office of the Experts (an office under the administration of the Ministry of Justice that provides technical expertise to judges on evidentiary matters).

In chapter six, van Eijk draws a comparison between Catholic and Muslim family courts in Syria, focusing on divorce practices. She studies judicial practices in these courts from the viewpoint of 'reconciliation', as judges in the different religious courts generally aim to reconcile the disputing parties.

In chapter seven, Vincent-Grosso addresses judicial practices in Tunisia, focusing on evidential requirements in divorce cases – since evidence plays a crucial role in enabling litigants to access their divorce rights when the law is translated into practice. This is especially true in cases of divorce on the grounds of harm (*darar*). Vincent-Grosso's chapter draws on one particular case study to illuminate how evidence underpins the litigant's experience of such divorces.

In chapter eight, Voorhoeve examines how Tunisian courts deal with their discretionary powers in so-called 'delicate fields of law'. On the basis of court decisions, Voorhoeve finds that the law concerning some delicate topics is applied in a very consistent way by the various Tunisian courts, while the application of other topics is characterised by casuistry. Voorhoeve examines how both the uniformity and the casuistry can be explained, describing the factors that curtail judicial discretion but are allowed under the legislation.

Notes

1 Peters, 1988.
2 Tamanaha, 1997.
3 Wittgenstein, 1967.
4 Dupret, 2011.
5 See the Encyclopaedia of Islam, 2nd edition.
6 Lewis, 1988.

7 Geertz, 1983.
8 Livingston, 1995, and Dupret, 2011.

References

Dupret, Baudouin, *Adjudication in Action* (Aldershot, 2011).
Geertz, Clifford, *Local Knowledge: Further Essays in Interpretive Anthropology* (New York, 1983).
Lewis, Bernard, *Le langage politique de l'Islam* (Paris, 1988).
Livingston, Eric, *An Anthropology of Reading* (Bloomington and Indianapolis, 1995).
Peters, Ruud, 'Divine Law or Man-Made Law ? Egypt and the Application of the Shari'a', *Arab Law Quarterly*, iii/3 (1988), pp. 231–253.
Tamanaha, Brian Z., *Realistic Socio-Legal Theory: Pragmatism and A Social Theory Of Law* (Oxford, 1997).
Wittgenstein, Ludwig, *Philosophical Investigations* (Oxford & Cambridge, 1967).

DISCOURSES ON THE LAW

1

'SHE BRINGS UP HEALTHY CHILDREN FOR THE HOMELAND': MORALITY DISCOURSES IN YEMENI LEGAL DEBATES*

Susanne Dahlgren

In this chapter, I will discuss the morality discourses in Yemen against the background of the family law reforms that took place in the southern part of the country in the 1970s and 1990s. I will look at the rhetorical tools used in the law debates dealing with women, the family and the state from the perspective of the southern women who entered the 1990 unification of Yemen from a privileged position compared to that of northern women, who were soon to lose many of the earlier gains. In this analysis, I will look at how Islam is played out as a discourse both to promote and to limit the rights of women. I will argue that by the turn of the millennium, Islam has emerged as the decisive factor in defining woman's 'place' in society, sidestepping the discourses of 'modernity' and 'tradition' that earlier characterised such debates. This change has also been accommodated in the women's rights movement, where the old demands for women's emancipation (*tahrir al-mar'a*) are now voiced as if they originated from Islam. In analysing these debates, I will ask how the difficult unification of the tribal North Yemen and the modernising South Yemen is expressed in the family law debates. These elaborations provide a background to the debates in the Arab countries at large. While particular legal codes are referred to as 'family laws', what is at issue tends to be women's rights and the contested question of how much modernity, understood as personal freedom from a kin bond, a state can afford to grant its women.

Each country naturally has its own peculiarities. Characteristic of the family law debates in Yemen in the 1990s and 2000s is the labelling of the previous Southern Yemeni Family Law (Family Law, law no. 1 of 1974 in Connection to the Family) as having 'deviated from Sharia', while the current law (Personal Status Law, law no. 30 of 1992 as amended) allegedly follows 'the Islamic perspective'.

Sixty Years of Women's Struggle

At the end of 1989, when Northern and Southern Yemeni political leaders announced that the two countries were to unite, a heated debate began in the newspapers of the Southern Yemeni capital, Aden. The border between the two countries had been opened the year before for people on both sides carrying their identity cards to visit the 'other side of the homeland', and Adenis tended to have no illusions as to the kind of society they were about to join. Rumours circulated of how police on the northern side of the border randomly practised rigid morality rules; one such story told of an Adeni woman who was arrested on charges of indecency in the Northern capital of Sana'a for simply sitting in the same car as her brother. In the South, such stories belonged to the past; only older women could remember similar stories from their youth in the rural South. In some areas, a woman was discouraged from leaving her home to the extent that her father or brother had the right to shoot her if they encountered her in the wrong place. At the weekends, the roads were filled with Northern cars full of men going to spend a jolly evening in a nightclub in the cosmopolitan port town of Aden; they returned home to tell stories about the 'immorality' in the South.

On whatever criteria, the future of Southern women's emancipation (*tahrir al-mar'a*) was thought to be over. At the end of the 1980s, the official women's organisation, the General Union of Yemeni Women (GUYW), was in trouble in their attempt to defend the reforms that had taken place during the leftist regime in South Yemen (then called the People's Democratic Republic of Yemen (PDRY)). But there was also a sense of fatigue concerning women's rights among the Southern male elite. As a high member of the judiciary told me, women had too many rights and he was prepared to put a stop to that.

After Southern independence in 1967, and after the introduction of the government's policy of women's emancipation two years later (in the leftist turn of the so-called 'Corrective Move' of 1969), political leaders often raised the question of women's status in their public speeches. As the country's second leader, Salim Rubaya 'Ali, affirmed, during the colonial era not only society at large, but a woman's own father, brother or husband, practised absolute authority over her, a system that denied all her basic rights. According to Rubaya 'Ali, it was not enough that women gain economic independence – she also needed society to guarantee her rights within the family. The government's policy of woman's emancipation was put in place to transform the family and to make her contribution as valuable as a man's in the eyes of society at large.[1] Sometimes male leaders used folklore as evidence of how women's inferiority had hitherto been an everyday phenomenon; but men were also addressed in such speeches, and instructed to correct their language when talking about women. Proverbs such as 'Whoever listens to women is one of them' or 'When a woman shows her teeth she isn't smiling' were presented as evidence. Thus the policy of female emancipation not only aimed at inviting women to join in education and the labour force, but also to instruct men to treat every woman 'as his sister'.

In 1970, a committee was established to draft a family code, the first ever on the Arabian Peninsula. The committee consisted of experts on Islamic law such as the *qadi*s and lay people who had not earlier been in a position to be consulted about legal questions in mass organisations. The bill was distributed for public debate in 1971 and for four months, the committee members toured the country and held mass meetings where the proposed provisions were discussed.[2] Finally the parliament ratified the law in 1974 under the name Law no. 1 of 1974 in Relation to the Family. The most important provisions included stipulating that a marriage be a relationship between a man and a woman (thus excluding the role of the woman's 'guardian', §2), forbidding out-of-court repudiation (Part II, §§25–30), limiting the practice of polygamy (§11) and excessive dowers (*mahr*, §18) and making the burden of meeting the expenses of marital life apply to both men and women according to their respective means (§17).[3]

In the constitution, the GUYW was assigned a semi-official role in promoting women's advancement in society.[4] In the first national Women's Union conference, held in 1974 in Sayun, women's situation was discussed in a complex way; one point of criticism was that Islam itself was abused by relegating women to an inferior position. The conference documents explain that the system called 'priestly feudalism' also imposed the veil on women. In some areas of the countryside, this ideology forced a woman to wear a veil, even in her own home, in front of her in-laws.[5] While it was understood that society could not suddenly remove the veil, the way it was earlier practised was criticised. The rhetoric was formulated anew – woman had emerged from the confines of 'four walls' to participate 'alongside her brother' in building society and creating a 'happy family'. In the constitution enacted in 1970, women were called 'half of society' (*al-mar'a nusf al-mujtama'*), and in line with the government's modernising approach, the task of the entire society was to eradicate 'backward customs' detrimental to women, such as early marriage.[6]

These government measures echoed the demands raised during the colonial era, when various intellectual circles and women's groups had promoted modernisation as a key to improving women's situation; their discourses referred to 'negative traditions' and 'bad customs' as the main obstacles to women's advancement. The new constitution constructed a double role for women, in 'building society' alongside men and in acting as mothers of a new, enlightened generation. The contrast to earlier times was explained by referring to how a woman was now a rational being (*'aqliyya*) whose education would guide the family alongside her husband. Thus the Socialist government continued and expanded the scope of modernisation first initiated by the British in the Colony of Aden (1839–1967), which had in fact marginalised women in the very attempt at modernising, given the British colonial rulers' reluctance to touch 'religion and custom' (Dahlgren 2010).

Unification and New Demands on Women

Following the unification of Yemen in 1990, the gains women had made in the erstwhile South, including in education, health care and women's rights, became discursively 'forgotten', as though they did not exist. Government propaganda presented the situation as if unification had kick-started a whole new era for women, in both parts of the republic. For instance, schools were renamed and given new founding dates, to give the impression that the present government was busy in 'introducing' education to the South. In the International Women's Day festivities held in March 2008 – and organised by the reformed Adeni Women's Union, which was now being run by the ruling party's femocrats – women's access to jobs in the police was celebrated as a new accomplishment and as a sign of an advancement that only unification had brought to women. This was criticised by those women activists who knew that female officers had a long history in the police force during the PDRY era.

The result of these changes was that women were no longer considered men's partners in building society, but were treated as part of the *harim*, the sacred 'private' area, where the male is sovereign and the state has no role to play, as has always been the case in the North. One female reader expressed the disillusionment of Southern women in her opinion piece in the governmental *al-Thawra* newspaper in the winter of 1991. She wrote: 'Many Yemeni men seem to think the oriental man is governed by customs, traditions and religion. But what about the oriental woman? By what is she governed? The oriental woman, and the Yemeni woman in particular, is governed by religion before she is governed by tradition.'[7] The author of this article also described the shift in argumentation on the women's question that was taking place around that time. Now it was no longer a question of 'traditions' being replaced by 'modernity' but a choice between the 'Islamic way' and the 'non-Islamic way' of organising society, including woman's role in the family and in society at large.

The 'Islamic way' and the 'non-Islamic way' became labels that also began to appear in the law-reform debates. One of the first of these took place a year after unification, when the constitution was to be accepted in a referendum. At this time, the crucial question became, thanks to the recently formed 'Islamic party' – the Congregation for Reform (Islah) – whether the basic law should consider Islam to be the 'main source' or as the 'sole source' of all laws. The first of these formulations was in the draft, and it was adopted by a clear majority, while the Islah boycotted the referendum. Nonetheless, it took only four years for it to be 'corrected', establishing Islam as the sole source of all laws, as a concession to the Islah party for its role in siding with the Northern forces in the 1994 civil war between the North and South.

'Islam Guarantees Women all their Rights'

During the 1990s, different strands of an 'intolerant' Islam, such as Wahhabism and Salafism – which had previously been suppressed by the state – became openly active in the South. The message delivered from the mosques, headed by Salafists, was that a woman's proper, Islamic place is at home raising a happy family.[8] In some neighbourhoods, residents tried to complain about prayer calls and sessions that were broadcast too loudly, but the local authorities remained helpless. Such broadcasts created an entirely new atmosphere in those quarters of Aden where Salafi-run mosques were operating. As a consequence, women no longer wished to go out when the prayer time was approaching.

At the same time, in the North, a leading politician of the Islah party, Shaykh Abdulmajid al-Zindani, was busy building a network of religious schools (*ma'ahid 'ilmiyya*); and women's public roles then became a target for hostile arguments among the controversial issues discussed in the classes conducted for young men. In the South, women's rights activists feared that such intolerance would spread throughout the country, and influence young people at large. Zindani's *fatwa* in support of 'tourist marriage', that he chose to call *zawaj al-frind* ('girl-friend for marriage'),[9] was also heavily criticised among Adeni people. Partly, Zindani wanted to encourage Yemeni men to contract temporary marriages while studying abroad. He also wanted to please Saudi Arabia and the Gulf States, whose male citizens arrive in the Northern town of Ibb in the summer months specifically to contract a temporary marriage with a young local woman for the purpose of enjoying sexual relations with her. After the lapse of the agreed time, these men disappear without a trace back to their countries.

A call to 're-Islamise' the South was issued in the early years of unity. These attempts followed earlier discourses of 'othering' that prevailed in both parts of the divided country. The Southerners tended to call the Northerners 'uncivilised *badus*' or '*dahbash*',[10] while the Northerners called the Southerners 'unbelievers' and the Southern women 'morally loose'. The latter themes were also paraded before unification in the anti-PDRY propaganda broadcast from neighbouring Saudi Arabia. Women's rights in South Yemen were to help prove how 'un-Islamic' the country was.[11] Many women reacted spontaneously to this atmosphere by adopting the 'Islamic costume', thus avoiding the harassment in the streets practised at the time by young boys. Transfer of the government and its offices from Aden to the new capital Sana'a spread moral anomaly and strengthened the people's sense of having no regime present. In such historical moments of uncertainty, attention tends to turn to women and their 'morality'.

In order to safeguard the legacy of women's activism in the South, the Southern women's organisation GUYW joined forces with the Northern Women's Union, and together they formed the Yemeni Women's Federation in Sana'a, the new national capital. For the Adeni Women's Union (AWU), the changes meant losing most of its neighbourhood club houses, as the government introduced a policy of privatising hitherto state-owned property. In fact, the buildings were then often distributed not to their previous owners (if there were any) but to the members of the new elite. Thus, the Adeni Women's Union had dramatically to narrow the scope of its activities. The early years of unity also brought about economic problems for those families who had previously relied on subsidised food and housing, and women had less and less energy to engage in activities outside the home in the same way as before.

In the Adeni women's movement, these changes were not ignored. It was understood that in this new atmosphere advancement in women's rights would only be possible within the Islamic framework. At the beginning of the new millennium, the Adeni Women's Union – now part of the unified Yemeni Women's Federation – was suddenly taken over by a group loyal to the People's General Congress (PGC), the ruling party. These loyalists overthrew the previous leadership, who represented both independent women and those from different political parties, including the PGC, the Yemeni Socialist Party (the former ruling party in the South) and Islah. The new leadership consisted of 'femocrats', i.e. wives of the ruling elite and prominent women in different semi-official and official positions. The ousted activists regrouped in 2004 to form the Arab Association for Supporting Women's and Juvenile Issues (AAFSWJI) but this association had far fewer resources than the AWU had ever had.

Within the AAFSWJI, women from different backgrounds – whether independent, Socialist or Islamic activists – strove to continue the legacy of the Adeni women's rights activism, with its roots in the early 1950s. The same goals, however, were now promoted through Islamic rhetoric, by explaining that women's cause would not be in contradiction with Sharia. In the AAFSWJI discussions, the then-current family legislation was said to contradict Sharia, as it contained paragraphs referring to women negatively, and such provisions could be traced to customs prevalent in the North. Furthermore, these women refused to see women's questions uniquely within the family paradigm – in a patriarchal society, the family is viewed as the source of women's subjugation and of male domination. To fight the negative understandings claimed to originate in Islam, activist women started to read Islamic texts, including the Quran and hadiths, and works of literature written by progressive Islamic thinkers and members of the *'ulama*. Among these is Muhammad Saif 'Abdallah Khalid al-'Adani, a graduate of a religious institute in Saudi Arabia, where he also spent his youth. Born in 1952 in a village in the Northern governorate of Ibb, he is the father of 11 children and a respected scholar.

'Adani's book, *'ashara 'awa'iq amama huquq al-nisa' fi-l-islam* ('ten obstacles to women's rights in Islam'), was published in 2004 by a Ta'izz-based human rights organisation, the Women's Forum for Research and Training; this is headed by a young Ta'izz-born woman, Su'ad al-Qadsi, who works in close cooperation with the Adeni women's movement. Among the 'ten obstacles' 'Adani discusses are the influence of folk customs within Islam; weak hadiths that according to him have contributed to a negative understanding of women's rights; the role of classical jurists in formulating rights negatively with respect to women; and the contradiction in the *tafsir* (Quranic exegetics) between women's half-share and their full capacity as Muslims. He also advocates women's rights regarding marriage, such as the right of a woman to contract a marriage without her guardian's consent, and discusses the issue of *jabr*, or compulsion in marriage, in the light of the different Sunni schools.[12]

Putting Women's Rights in Perspective

After the establishment of a united Yemen the government began the process of unifying legislation and of drafting laws for the new republic. It became clear that one of the most urgent law reforms concerned family law. A committee with legal experts from the North was formed to review a draft already prepared in the North prior to unification; this draft was a slightly more moderate bill than the one issued there in 1978. Fearing of what was to come, widespread public debate started in the South, both on the street and in newspapers. Debates on the family code seemed to crystallise larger concerns: the country's future was said to be based either on a 'modern family code' that allowed women their rights or on a 'code based on Sharia', with both camps having their supporters. In retrospect, this polarisation symbolised how unification was to develop during the next 20 years. What remain under debate are those aspects of the 1974 Family Law or of the present Personal Status Law (1992) that are derived from the *fiqh* (Islamic jurisprudence) and which according to some are customs wrongly identified as Islamic.

Both men and women participated in these debates. The Adeni Women's Union organised several public meetings during the years 1990 and 1991 to discuss questions such as whether Islam mandates a woman to cover her hair (with a Sudanese Islamic studies professor from Aden University); women's role and rights in Islam (with an Egyptian Imam and two local Muslim intellectuals); and the family-code bill. The last mentioned of these meetings was held in November 1991, when the draft of a new family code was distributed only among a limited number of people in Sana'a and most of the participants in the meeting had only hearsay evidence of what was proposed. In a critical news report on the meeting, entitled 'Woman against woman', reporter Taha Ghalib from the governmental *14th October* newspaper, stated: 'In today's Yemen, a fierce battle is being fought against women in order to limit their rights in work, education and politics. Still, it is noteworthy that women, and the Yemeni Women's Union, are not in a position to fight such tendencies.'[13] Instead of giving a voice to women to speak up for their rights, the reporter went on to praise a Northern Yemeni activist woman and compared her to the women present in the meeting: 'She [the Northern Yemeni activist] was dressed in a proper manner, she was modest and simple both in appearance and in nature. She spoke in perfect language and her intellect and strong personality gave the impression that her self-esteem is at a high level. She is the kind of woman every Yemeni woman should be.'

In his eagerness to judge women on the basis of their appearance, the reporter – who himself had not been able to read the draft law – condemned women who were chiefly concerned with the introduction of the new law of unlimited polygamy, and with out-of-court repudiation (*talaq*). In this way, the reporter touched on a sensitive issue that was common in the early years of unity: what is the legacy of women's emancipation in the South, and how much of that legacy should the new state embrace? As noted above, there was a tendency to make the advancement in women's rights in both parts of the previously divided country appear as if they existed on the same level. Many voices were also raised against the 'overly free' Southern woman.

In a similar vein, many of the articles published on the same debate in the Adeni newspapers dealt with the question of whether the Southern woman, who had gained her rights during the leftist government, would be able to retain them. Some authors backed up their demands for the rights of women by citing the latter's role in the struggle for independence, in working life and in politics, while others went on to describe them in a more abstract, idealised way. Few participants in the newspaper debates demanded outright that women should return home and leave their jobs or studies.

One author, Abdul Aziz Bin Buraik, describes the woman in her double role: 'A woman is active in all spheres of life and creates trust in her children, thus playing a double role over her life span. One role is that for the nation (*watan*) and the other is at home. She brings up healthy children for the homeland, who will then serve the nation and continue the work of the previous generations.' Challenging 'the other side [i.e. reactionary forces in the North] who want the woman to continue in the darkness of the past', the author claims that such reactionary forces would prefer women to live in the era of the harem, when 'men's animal lust competed for her'. The author concludes that such forces will never be overcome, as the woman already acts alongside the man in 33 ministries and 'that is where her place is, next to the man'.[14]

In a similar tone, the female author Salwa al-Sana'ani addressed women's situation in a column published on the occasion of the upcoming Women's Day in 1990, the day that before unification was celebrated as a national holiday in the South. Salwa stated:

> They [Northern reactionary men] alternate between marriage and divorce and change wives as easily as a shirt. They want to spread their kind of decent costume and the *hijab* [to the South] and reintroduce the golden era of Ottoman rule. With these measures they believe women's honour (*sharaf*) and chastity (*'iffa*) will be protected.

She concludes by asserting that equity and justice guarantee a happy family and that the coming unity of the country should not be allowed to cause the dissolution of the family. 'Divorce and polygamy are traditions (*taqalid*) that do not serve social and economic development; on the contrary, they destroy all hope in society.'[15]

In these two opinion pieces, women's rights are supported by using similar vocabulary to that of the presumed opponent, namely the qualities of a happy family and a chaste woman. While during the PDRY era the woman was ascribed the double role of a builder of society (alongside men) and the mother of the new generation, her social and political roles were always emphasised more than her role as a mother.[16] In the above pieces, Southern gender culture involving women's rights is contrasted with an imagined Northern culture described either as the 'era of the harem' or as 'the golden era of Ottoman rule'. Even though neither of these characterisations is historically accurate (the Ottomans did not succeed in reigning over the Northern Yemeni area, nor is there evidence of large ruling courts with harems), they are meant to refer to the all-concealing women's dress that the Yemenis believe came with the Ottomans. Such quasi-historical argumentation in these articles also served the purpose of discussing modernity and women's advancement in society, and juxtaposing these issues with women being tied to the *harim* as targets of 'men's animal lust'.

As the early years of debates prior to and immediately after unification focused on linking women's advancement and rights to a modern society, the shift to 'Islamic' discourse brought forward arguments that treated women's rights by reference to the Quran and the Prophetic hadiths. When I looked through the newspaper archives in the *14th October* editorial house in January 1998 I noted how active the debate on women's role in society was at the turn of the 1990s, with both male and female participants supporting the women's cause, and how such debate had ceased entirely by 1993, when the situation in the South was worsened and the 1994 civil war approaching. After 1994 through to the end of the 1990s, newspapers in Aden no longer published articles, columns or even readers' letters on the women's rights issue. This was the period when Southerners started to talk about the 'Northern occupation' – the South being now under the political, economic and cultural domination of the North.

Fighting for Women's Rights in Legislation

Political developments during the 1990s and 2000s further narrowed the scope in which women's rights could be discussed in the new republic, with the unified Yemeni Women's Federation struggling to establish a national voice after having lost the official support that it had previously enjoyed in the South. Internally divided, the Federation had problems presenting a common front against the 1991 draft law of personal status. Partly it was a question of the different expectations for women's rights in the two parts of the previously divided country, but partly also a question of heavy propaganda against the 1974 Southern law, which characterised it as 'deviating from Sharia', while the 1992 PSL was considered to be in accordance with it. As a National Women's Committee report on *The Status of Woman in Yemen* (1996) expressed the latter notion: '[...] the present Law of Personal Status has considered the rights and obligations of the wife and the husband as well as the rights of the child from an Islamic perspective.'[17]

Such misconceptions as these were also debated in the press. A prominent Northern intellectual, university professor and author, Abu Bakr al-Saqqaf, wrote a long article entitled *The Personal Status Law project and the future of social development*, in which he supported the 1974 law and argued against the 1991 draft:

> Those beautiful words in the Quran describing marriage have been sacrificed [in the draft law] and instead marriage is addressed only as sex. By focusing on sex, the notions of *nushuz* (rebellion by the wife) and *bayt al-ta'a* (house of obedience) have entered the law. Because of these two notions, the value of marriage is degraded and it is transformed into a relationship that is void of beauty, humanism, Islamic comportment and solidarity. It becomes merely a sexual relationship that is a misconception of Sharia.

The political rationale behind this law, the author explained, is the same as in politics and economics in the country at large: take the worst option and explain to the people that this is the best choice.

'It is a logic (*mantiq*) that makes illogic into logic.'[18] According to al-Saqqaf, it was wrong to describe the 1974 Family Law as being at odds with Sharia, as that law was the result of a long struggle by men and women in the South to obtain political and economic freedom, and to put in place secular rule; but this secular rule was not established to act against Islam, asserted al-Saqqaf. The article was published on 25 March 1992, i.e. during Ramadan, and a few days before the law was enacted by presidential decree. The parliament never debated the bill and was not in session when the enactment took place.

It took Southern women's activists some time to rally their forces in the struggle against such misconceptions. After studying the Quran and the Sunna, the activists defended the 1974 law as being fully compliant with Sharia. Naturally, all this came too late, as by August 1992 the new law had replaced the old. The 1994 civil war destroyed morale in the South, and as a consequence further deteriorations in the 1992 PSL encountered little resistance; these included, in 1998, discontinuing the payment of compensation to the wife following an unjust divorce in 1998 (§71 1992 PSL), or tying the marital age to the provision that allows the guardian of a minor to marry her off (*zaffa*[19]), merely on the condition that she is fit for sexual intercourse (§15, as amended in 1999[20]).

More legal battles were to follow in the course of the 2000s. Women's rights activists felt that they had gained an important victory in 2000–01 when a draft law was secretly prepared in the parliament, initiated by the Islah, to introduce new provisions on *bayt al-taʿa* ('house of obedience', i.e. the husband's authority over his wife). The formulation of this legal principle of obedience to the husband, included provisions on the husband's right after a disagreement to send the police to bring back a wife who has taken refuge in her father's home. Women's activists labelled this as violence against women, a popular slogan that in the 1990s had spread from international NGOs to Yemeni civil society. As a result of their appeals to the Yemeni president and to the embassies of some foreign donor-countries, President Salih decided not to sign the proposed law. This entire incident created a feeling of optimism among women's rights and human rights activists, a sentiment that was soon to fade as new controversies emerged, including the war in the northern Saʿada province, attempts to introduce a morality police, and the spreading in the southern provinces of general dissent towards the Sanaʾa regime.

In July 2008, the Salafi Shaykh Abdulmajid al-Zindani referred to above was a leading figure in launching the 'Committee for Promoting Virtue and Combating Vice', together with a large number of conservative clerics and tribal dignitaries.[21] It was announced that this committee, which was designed to establish a morality police in line with a similar institution in Saudi Arabia, was mounting an urgent response to the alleged deterioration in morality and spread of vice in the republic. The streets were to be combed to eradicate targeted 'vices': to find unrelated couples, to reprimand women dressed 'immodestly' and to fight 'indecent' Arab pop singers such as the Syrian Asala Nasri (whose concert in Aden conservative forces had tried to prevent some time earlier). The government, however, was quick to declare that all executive power lay with the state authorities, and that it had no plans for such a police force. Women's rights activists were shocked to hear about the committee, and the leadership of the Yemeni Women's Federation declared that it 'undermined women and the fundamental role they play in building Yemeni society'.[22] After much dispute, the morality police remained only a proposal, but a dramatic example of what conservative forces intend to introduce in Yemen, as women's rights activists contended.

A more recent debate on raising the legal age for marriage was sparked by the case of the ten-year-old Nugud, discussed internationally, who managed on her own to get a divorce from a marriage her father had contracted for her with a much older man. In order to placate Western audiences, the government decided to discuss in parliament an old proposal put forward by the National Women's Committee, the official body recognised by the state as representing women, to establish an age limit for marriage of 18, for both men and women.[23] After the first round of plenary talks, the limit was set at 17, with the Islah party's MPs being divided and some claiming that any age limit would run counter to Sharia. After the plenary discussion, the law was sent back to a parliament sub-committee, where it has not been discussed for over a year.

Conclusions

In this chapter I have presented some of the most heated debates on women's rights and the law over a 40-year period of women's activism in the southern part of the Republic of Yemen. As has become evident, political platforms where women have engaged to voice their demands have dramatically changed, while the ruling elite's support for such demands has also altered. In Yemen women have taken part in the nationalist project of building a centralised state only in one part of the unified state, the South, and their activism has left a legacy that the advocates of traditional, kin-based roles for women have been busy fighting against. One of their methods has been to invoke traditionalist views and to claim that they are in accordance with Sharia; Amal al-Ashtal (2009) has referred to such views as acts of 'arbitrary Shariaism'. Still, as the discursive field where the women's question is now debated has moved from an approach characterised by an engagement with modernity to an Islamic framework, Southern women have had to acquire new strategies to regain a more hegemonic role for women's issues.

As the Yemeni case shows, advocates of women's rights need to adjust to rapid changes not only in political platforms, but also in political arguments. As Muslim communities within and outside the Middle East increasingly debate questions of morality and of women's proper roles in society, speaking in favour of modernity is no longer sufficient to guarantee the promotion of women's rights in the family and in society at large. In the Arab countries, the unholy union of the proponents of tribal customs, conservative clerics and state power-elites persists even in the era of modernisation. Against this trend, the women's movement in Yemen has planted a small seed to help women-friendly Sharia interpretations flourish in the future.

Notes

* This chapter is based on ethnographic fieldwork carried out in the Southern Yemeni town of Aden during the course of the late 1980s, 1990s and 2000s, altogether some three years.

Morality Discourses in Yemeni Legal Debates 29

1 Speech by Salim Rubaya 'Ali to the first congress of Yemeni women, in *Documents of the General Union of Yemeni Women* 1977: 4.
2 See 'Freedom takes time', *Middle East* (February 1983), p. 47.
3 Family Law (1976); see also Dahlgren 2010.
4 Constitution of the People's Democratic Republic of Yemen 1970, Ch. II, Art. 58 (1971: 25) states: 'The Women's Organisation shall unite women and girls so as to develop political awareness amongst women to enable them to play a productive role in society for the realisation of educational and cultural tasks within the family, and to assist women to benefit from their rights as laid down in the Constitution on the basis of equality with men.'
5 A study on conditions of Yemeni women in *Documents of the First General Congress of Yemeni Women* (1977).
6 *Constitution of the People's Democratic Republic of Yemen* 1970, Ch. I, Art. 34 (1971: 19).
7 Op-ed piece by Arwa Muhammad published in *al-Thawra* (winter 1991), as translated and reprinted in *Middle East Times* (Yemen edn.) (February 1991), p. 2.
8 Such messages were also disseminated via audio-cassettes, distributed in all the main markets in Aden. Some of the recorded sermons also gave instructions on how to wear proper Islamic dress and on women's rights in marriage. The preachers included Shaykh Sa'id Masfar, Shaykh Muhammad al-Muhayisni, Abu Bakr al-Mashtud and Abu Bakr al-Haddad.
9 The idea is to contract a marriage that is from the very outset a temporary relationship.
10 A pejorative name that refers to a comical character in a popular TV series, shown on Sana'a TV.
11 After unification such propaganda was spread in pamphlets and in books such as al-Wad'i (n.d.), available in bookshops and from street peddlers.
12 Al-'Adani 2004.
13 *14th October* (a governmental newspaper), 25 November 1991.
14 'Women's Corner' in *al-Ayyam* (an independent newspaper), 15 July 1992.
15 *14th October*, 7 March 1990.
16 See note 5 above.
17 *The Status of Women in Yemen* (1996), p. 19.
18 *Al-Ayyam* newspaper, 25 March 1992.
19 In Yemen, *zaffa* means wedding party, which culminates in the bride's penetration.
20 *Al-jumhuriya al-yamaniyya, wizarat al-shu'un al-qanuniyya* (Personal Status Law no. 20 of 1992).
21 This committee echoes the striving in many Muslim-majority countries to address the doctrine of 'commanding right and forbidding wrong' (*al-amr bi-l-ma'ruf wa-l-nahy 'an al-munkar*). See Cook 2000.
22 <http://www.adnkronos.com/AKI/English/Religion/?id=1.0.2348087523>, accessed 23 August 2010.

23 The criterion for a legitimate marriage is that the bride is capable of sexual intercourse (Personal Status Law § 15, as amended in 1999).

References

Al-'Adani, Muhammad Saif 'Abdallah Khalid, *'ashara 'awa'iq amāma huquq al-nisa' fi-l-islam. Dirasat huquq al-insan* 5. Multaqa al-mar'a li-l-dirasat w-al-tadrib (Women's Forum for Research and Training) and Deutsche Gesellschaft für Technische Zusammenarbeit (s.l., 2004).

Al-Ashtal, Amal, 'Does Sharia oppose the state law on marriage?', *Yemen Today* (April 2009). At <http://www.wluml.org/english/newsfulltxt.shtml?cmd[157]=x-157-564272>, accessed 15 October 2010).

Cook, Michael, *Commanding Right and Forbidding Wrong in Islamic Thought* (Cambridge:, 2000).

Constitution of the People's Democratic Republic of Yemen Enacted in 1970 (Aden, 1971).

Dahlgren, Susanne, *Contesting Realities: The Public Sphere and Morality in Southern Yemen* (Syracuse, NY, 2010).

Family Law, Law no. 1 of 1974, official English translation, issued by the Information Department of the Ministry of Information (Aden, 1976).

'Freedom takes time', *Middle East,* February 1983, pp. 47–8.

General Union of Yemeni Women, *Documents of the General Union of Yemeni Women*. First General Congress of Yemeni Women in Saiun, 15–16 July, 1974 (Aden: 14 October Corporation, 1977).

Al-jumhuriya al-yamaniyya, wizarat al-shu'un al-qanuniyya, *al-qirar al-jumhuri bi-l-qanun raqm (20) li-sanat 1992 bi-sha'n al-ahwal al-shakhsiyya* (Aden: 14 October Corporation, 1992).

Middle East Times (Yemen edn.) (February 1991), p. 2.

Al-Wadi'iyy, Muqbil bin Hadi, *al-suyuf al-batirat li-l-hadi al-shuyu'iyyat al-kafirat* (s.l., n.d.).

Women's National Committee, Republic of Yemen, *The Status of Women in Yemen* (No place of publication: Women's National Committee, 1996).

2

RECLAIMING CHANGES WITHIN THE COMMUNITY PUBLIC SPHERE: DRUZE WOMEN'S ACTIVISM, PERSONAL STATUS LAW AND THE QUEST FOR LEBANESE MULTIPLE CITIZENSHIP

Massimo di Ricco

Family Law in a Communitarian System

From a tenth-floor apartment facing the Druze Community Council in the Verdun district of Beirut, Roula recounts her matrimonial experience. A young Druze woman (21 years old), she has two children and no husband; he divorced her suddenly and for no apparent reason, leaving her with only a small amount of money to cover the children's education, and without considering other, related expenses and the difficulty of raising two children alone. The judge presiding over the case did not even call her into court to hear her claim or the reasoning behind it.

Roula recounts her story to a small group of activists in the weekly gathering at the apartment of Anissa Al-Najjar, who from 2006 to

2007 made her home the temporary headquarters for a group of Druze women to discuss their status within their community; from there they started to lobby publicly for changes by addressing communal authorities on the need to reform the personal status law, which they consider discriminatory towards women.

In the Middle East, the revision or discussion of family law generally concerns the state, or is presented as a struggle between the state and a specific community. In Lebanon, however, family law is in the hands of sub-national communities.[1] Uniquely, both in the region and internationally, the Lebanese political structure has a form of state governance based on a mixture of collective rights and a compulsory double identity – communal and national – for its citizens; the country's political system allows religious communities in Lebanon to manage the personal status issues of their own constituents. Under the auspices of the family law, the connection between the communitarian system and the family sheds light on the importance of family as one of the main features of the Lebanese political system, and explains its strong influence on Lebanese society.

The Druze are one of the institutionally-recognised religious communities comprising the Lebanese state, and this chapter analyses the claims, forms of action and achievements of these Druze women activists. For this, it engages with the idea of 'a community public sphere', and with the role of Lebanese individuals within their community. Women's situation in society is regulated by both national laws and laws of personal status, and this study aims to highlight the importance of what could be defined as 'communal activism'. Family law in Lebanon is a useful tool for understanding the relationship between the community public sphere and the national Lebanese public sphere.

Family Law in Lebanon: Communities' Prerogatives and the State

Lebanon is a constitutional parliamentary republic that has adopted the shape of a multi-communal state.[2] It is composed of 19 recognised religious communities, each of which is subject to a personal status code, applied by religious courts[3]; there are 16 such codes in total.[4] The French High Commissioner first officially recognised such communities on 30 March 1936, in Legislative Act No. 36. The Christian and Jewish communities organised themselves on 2 April 1951 and since then have also been recognised by the state. In 1955, the Sunni community followed with its own judicial system, based on Hanafi law. In 1962, the Druze joined with a draft of a law dating back to 1930; and finally, on 16 July 1967, the Shia community followed with a judicial system based on Jaafari law.[5]

Each of the 19 religious communities enjoys legal authority in the personal status law of its members. The state has a presence in the higher courts only of the three main Muslim communities, represented by a civil judge to ensure that rulings are in accordance with the laws of the state.[6] Christian religious courts are institutionally entirely independent of the Lebanese state, while Catholic courts come under the religious authority of the Vatican.

Articles 9 and 10 of the Lebanese constitution stipulate that the confessional communities can enjoy certain privileges of the state. Article 9 allows communities to judge their members on issues concerning personal status, among which marriage, inheritance and paternity are the most important. Article 10 grants the communities the right to their own schools and educational programmes. What must be underlined here is the almost complete absence of the state within such community affairs, as well as a complete ban on the state making decisions with respect to personal status of community members. Family law, in the specific and peculiar case of Lebanon, is a powerful tool in the hands of religious communities, and an important component of the struggle over configuration of citizenship and over gender equality.

Each Lebanese community enjoys political quotas, along with the management of their own personal status laws, thus making these communities the intermediaries between the individual and the state. State institutions place confessional affiliation before national citizenship, necessarily assigning individuals to their respective confessional community.[7] As a consequence, the system does not allow the individual any exemption from membership of such a community, which remains the primary national identity. In effect, Lebanese citizens do not have the option of being subject to a civil status law.

The Druze and their Personal Status Law

The Druze community comprises approximately 7 per cent of the Lebanese population, and is characterised by strong internal cohesion and by isolation. The strength of the community and its internal cohesion are mostly derived from two main community 'practices', or precepts. The first is the wide practice of endogamy which, although diminished over the last decade, has always been strong and takes the form of marriage between first cousins, and by clan and lineage. The second practice is the belief in reincarnation of the soul in the bodies of other Druze.[8] Besides, the history of the Druze cohesion comprises the histories of Druze leaders and of families going back centuries; this reinforces the maintenance of traditional political representation as well as the division of power in community institutions among the major families. Community solidarity also goes hand-in-hand with the image of the Druze as a minority under threat. Internal cohesion and a refusal to allow internal criticism to become public are also characteristic of the sect. In other words, the community configuration makes it difficult to bring about structural changes and internal institutional reforms.

During the Ottoman Empire, the Druze community enjoyed autonomy in matters of divorce, marriage and succession. By creating independent communal courts in 1930, the French mandate authorities gave the Druze management of their personal status issues.[9] The current Druze personal status law was institutionalised on 24 February 1948, drawing its inspiration from the family law established by al-Amir al-Sayyid in the fifteenth century. It comprises 172 articles, divided between 19 chapters, and covering the law of marriage, dissolution of marriage, custody of children, maintenance of relatives, guardianship, appointment and duties of executors, interdiction, missing persons, paternity, testate and intestate succession, and *waqf*.[10] Personal status issues not covered by the law come under Article 171, which provides that 'on any of the subjects that are not under the competence of the judge and that are not considered by this law, the judge will apply the dispositions of Hanafi law and the other laws that are not in contradiction with Islamic law.'[11] This provision is controversial, and the activists in this case study address their claims to it, as will be discussed later.

The Druze personal status law authorises religious courts to handle the relevant issues raised by community members. Although officially they represent the Ministry of Justice, the courts handle such cases almost entirely independently.[12] Besides the establishment of the Druze personal status law in 1948, three laws that regulate the Druze judiciary system were promulgated between 1960 and 1962. These concern the organisation of the Druze courts, the Druze Council and the election of the spiritual head of the community.[13] Druze courts are located in six different areas in Lebanon in which Druze inhabitants are dominant: Aley, Chouf, Metn, Rashaya, Hasbaya and Beirut. The Druze judiciary is comprised of the six judges of these courts, the head of the Supreme Court, two consultants and a representative of the public attorney. The public attorney, who ensures the maintenance of public order, represents the Lebanese government; this attorney must be a civil judge and Druze, though formally working for the state.

Judge Noed Hariz, head of the Druze Supreme Council, calls attention to the civil character of Druze personal status, and discusses the privileged legal status of women within the Druze community, especially when compared to other, Muslim communities:

> Our personal status law is very good, very close to civil status law. We differ from other Lebanese communities. Marriage and divorce are contracted by a judge and not by a religious figure. The wife can ask for divorce just as the husband can. Everyone takes his share of responsibility, and the status of men and women is very egalitarian.[14]

Druze family law has often been presented as both very modern and very egalitarian with respect to women and men. A considerable part of this law concerns roles and duties, specifically the position of women with respect to men within the community; it provides the right to self-determination for adults in marriage and divorce; it clearly enunciates the husband's duties in cases of divorce; it bans polygamy; it includes compensation for divorce and bans repudiation; and it considers that the male guardian has no absolute authority over the adolescent girl.[15] Druze women have always been depicted as having special roles within the community and the family, as pillars and as guardians of morality. Azzam discusses how literature on the Druze community, either by Druze or non-Druze authors, sketches idealised images of Druze women, sometimes exaggerating their role in the public and political life of the community.[16]

Such descriptions of women are reinforced by a strong egalitarianism imbued in the original Druze doctrine concerning gender relations within the community. The reinterpretation of the scriptures by the Emir Tanukhi in the fourteenth century forms the foundation of the contemporary Druze personal status law (established in 1930 and institutionalised in 1948).[17] However, it is argued that the original textual egalitarianism of the Druze doctrine differs both from the 1948 law and from daily reality for Druze women within the community, for many members of which this difference is of particular concern. Activists and scholars claim that the law continues to discriminate against women, and goes against the egalitarianism outlined in the Druze doctrine.[18] Such daily reality is related to the structure of the communal institutions and to the maintenance of traditional social practices in the community.

Time for Change: The Reform of the Druze Community Institutions

In the aftermath of Hariri's assassination there was uproar over the reform of the main communal Druze institutions. The formation of the new cabinet ruled by the '14 March' majority bloc, acted as a catalyst in addressing the issues with which the reform was concerned. In the June 2005 elections the Druze quota in the national parliament was completely filled by representatives of the Progressive Socialist Party, led by Walid Jumblatt.[19] The public debate concerning the reform of Druze institutions focused on the reform of the Druze Council (*al-majlis al-madhhabi l-al taifa al-durziyya*) and the election of a new Shaykh al-'Aql, two functions that are related to one another. Founded in 1962, the Council, in theory, has legislative authority; it also manages the economic and administrative affairs of Druze organisations, particularly the incomes of the *waqf*, community proprieties, as well as shrines and sanctuaries. The Shaykh al-'Aql is the highest-ranking position in the Druze court, and is also the head of the Druze Community Council. The Shaykh acts as an intermediary between the state and the Druze community; he is, however, not the highest Druze religious authority, as that position is reserved for the Shaykh al-Masheikh. The Shaykh al-'Aql is in fact a political appointee, whose election can cause controversy among the different Druze factions.[20] Traditionally and historically, he has close ties to one of the powerful families. Before Rafik Hariri's assassination, the elections and the successive changes in the law of the Druze community, there was a stalemate in Druze institutions and a dispute with regard to the Shaykh's role, which led to immobility in the Council.[21]

In December 2005, the Druze bloc gathered around Walid Jumblatt, who proposed a draft law that would change the internal community law. The law proposed that all Druze in Lebanon elect the Druze Council, instead of it being decided upon by the highest Druze religious authority. The following autumn, the Druze officially reformed the institutions of the community and the new Shaykh al-'Aql, Naim Hassan, took his seat at the beginning of November. The new *majlis al-madhhabi* now comprised 88 members, an arrangement based on the criteria of profession and regional provenance.

Community members displayed clear signs of hope concerning the newly reformed Community Council, believing that the Council would introduce change in the community and ameliorate the use of community property. Many Druze were aware of the importance of such an institution, in that it would be possible for the Council to form a space for debate within the community, and to become an institution where claims could be put forward – developments ruled out in the previous *majlis* due to its immobility.[22] In this chapter I argue that the presence of these new and genuinely functioning institutions, and the recognition of an approachable figure in the person of Naim Hassan was one of the main factors in the start of lobbying for change in the personal status law.

The Call for Reforms Within the Community: Lobbying for Equality

Anissa Al-Najjar is a '94-year-old young lady' (as she used to call herself at the time of the research) and a very active figure in both the national and communitarian scene. The widow of a former Lebanese Minister of Agriculture, she lobbied on a national level in the early 1950s to achieve women's suffrage, and is still very active, especially as head of the Village Welfare Society. The organisation does not have a defined Druze communal stance, though it works to create awareness amongst women in mountain areas. Al-Najjar's work focuses on women's rights and empowerment, and oscillates between a national, inter-confessional stance and a more Druze-specific one. Many Druze women gather around Al-Najjar, especially at her home in Verdun, just in front of the Druze Council building in Beirut, in order to define those issues of women's rights within the community that need to be raised with the Druze authorities and institutions. Such female Druze activism is clearly related to the birth of the reformed Druze Council in 2006: as soon as the new Council and Shaykh al-'Aql had been inaugurated, Druze women were ready to present their claims directly to the highest Druze authorities.

> We think that the new Shaykh al-'Aql is a very wise man, not like the one before who blocked the institutions. Before it made no sense to contact the shaykh in order to reform women's status in the community. No one was really responsible for the community, and so it was impossible to address anyone.[23]

The presence of functioning institutions is important to the activism of Druze women. Before the reform, activists mainly relied on informal private channels to establish contact with community representatives;

they could not address the Community Council, and instead engaged with informal authorities and influential Druze political figures. The relationship between functioning institutions and the election of a legitimate authority for community affairs and for lobbying is a very close one. The legitimacy of the reformed council is in part due to the creation of a committee in charge of women's affairs; and the main focus of women's activism is to claim women's rights from within the community:

> It is necessary to claim rights on a national level, but also on a community level. The main claims concern issues related to the laws and practices of inheritance and divorce within the community. The Druze community has a very progressive law of personal status, but such laws are not working. Their rights exist on paper, but no one applies them. The idea is to stabilise equality within the community with reference to the law that we have.[24]

Al-Najjar's main focus is on the laws of divorce and inheritance. For example, Druze family law does not provide for divorce if there are children of the marriage, meaning that in such cases it is Hanafi law which is applied; this is considered to attach a great deal of importance to the interests of the children, but correspondingly less to those of the wife.[25]

Though Druze women activists are motivated by a general wish to see improvement in the legal and social status of all Lebanese women, they realise that their primary focus should be on conditions within their own community. They gather weekly at al-Najjar's to discuss their claims, and organise meetings and public speeches to raise awareness among members of their community in the mountain regions or in the capital. At these meetings they invite people from within that community to give a lecture, such as judges and other influential members who could help support their cause.

Another prominent female Druze activist is May Abu Hamdan, who heads the Charitable Organisation for Social Enlightenment, which she established to combat injustices and to urge women to claim their rights. In a lecture in Beirut in September 2007 she addressed the main claims and the necessary amendments to the Druze personal status law. The amendments had been drafted by a committee a few years earlier, but were never implemented due to the lack of concern on the part of Druze political and religious authorities. The amendments Abu Hamdan called for are as follows:

1. To develop and update the Personal Status Law in accordance with the jurisprudence and annotations of Druze theological doctrine, to give justice to women with regard to marriage, divorce, inheritance, custody and alimony.
2. To raise the minimum age of marriage for girls to 18 years, to enable them to continue their education and thus to help secure their future.
3. To raise the minimum age of child custody to 13 years for boys and 15 years for girls, to grant judges the authority to raise or lower the age when such action is called for in the interests of the child under guardianship, and to give the mother preference in the decision to grant custody, especially in the case of female children.
4. To ensure that should the father of a daughter die intestate or without having sons, the daughter should inherit – the current law is based on Hanafi law, which gives the paternal uncle the right to appropriate half the estate of his deceased brother.
5. To give the mother legal guardianship of children after the death of the husband, with the judge given the power to determine the identity of the second guardian from among her husband's family.

> I [Abu Hamdan] call upon all young girls and boys to adopt upon marriage a modern contract based on the jurisprudence of *Al-Tawhid*, adding a condition – approved by the couple and registered by the judge on the marriage certificate – stipulating that any wealth acquired after the marriage be equally divided during marital life or upon separation, provided that the amount of the dowry remains low...[26]

One highly controversial issue at the basis of the claims concerns inheritance – the attempt to change the role of the judge in inheritance cases. The Druze have a very dynamic tradition in terms of wills and inheritance; a will is composed freely in the sense that one can donate to strangers and to people outside the community. (This is not allowed in other Lebanese communities, where only wills bequeathing inheritance within the family, or at least within the community, are permitted.[27]) The point is controversial because such 'freedom' could lead to a misuse of inheritance laws, especially by men towards their wives and daughters.[28] Activists claim that although 'injustice depends on the way in which these laws are implemented, they can be used for the benefit of a male society in order to subordinate the woman and humiliate her' and they suggest that: 'Since wills should be registered in their office, judges should not accept those that exclude women from inheritance.'[29]

Another controversial point concerns the absence of a will before the death of a father or husband. In such cases, Druze family law again follows the Hanafi School in reserving one-eighth of the property to the wife, if the couple have children, and one-fourth if they do not – a rule that Druze activists consider unfair to women and not in line with the traditions of their community.[30]

> Can it be that this same woman, in inheriting, forfeits her right, along with her daughters, to the legacy, for her husband keeps it to himself and passes it on to his male children, no matter if they are bad, or already rich? After being the lady of the house, she is abandoned and left to live in the house of the separated, while others enjoy her fortune? Is this the Justice that Allah has prescribed? Some husbands without male heirs even deny their wives and daughters any legacy at all, and leave their estate to other relatives.[31]

Even in those cases where equality is sanctioned on paper, the activists consider that in reality there remains a clear imbalance between the rights and prerogatives of women and those of men. The legal issues taken into consideration in this study show there are notable gaps in the law and in social practice, as well as laws which are 'recognised', but not applied.

Communal Gender Activism: Education and Knowledge

Most women mentioned in this study are active in Lebanese society, both politically and socially, and many belong to or even head associations that help communities in mountainous areas to empower women through education. These activists are not 'everyday' people, so to speak, though they do attempt to connect with 'ordinary' women through public discourse in such areas.

> Most of the women who gather in my house and are working with me are very well educated persons, mainly professionals, teachers and mothers, from the city. Unfortunately there are no 'ordinary' Druze women among us. For example, in October 2007, when we arranged the meeting with the new elected Shaykh al-'Aql, only one of the 40 women who attended the appointment was from the mountains.[32]

Most of the activists that lobby for women's rights within the community are well educated people with professional profiles, and many live in Beirut; among them can be found university professors, philanthropists, teachers, doctoral candidates and intellectuals. In general, there is a division between urban and mountain societies that revolves around issues of education, knowledge and accessibility.

Education and awareness are two key issues that need to be taken into consideration, as these activists are conscious of the need to correct the imbalances within the community in terms of access to education. For this reason, they consider it necessary to confront these issues within the physical territory of the community, by working to creating an awareness of them within it.

> Virtuous mothers, the reason behind the marginalisation we are suffering from today goes back to the wrong way in which we were raised, to the differentiation in upbringing and the

discrimination between boy and girl, not to mention the custom to clip the girl's wings, subdue her and steal from her the freedom to decide. We should change what's in the spirit before changing what's in the texts, enlighten the girl as to her rights and obligations, and prepare her for carrying out the sacred mission of motherhood. It is wrong for a mother to think that the laws alone are sufficient to protect her rights. It is education in the home, based on rightness and faith, that is the true protection of the parents and all members of the family.[33]

Such considerations raise another issue pertaining to knowledge and accessibility – the paucity of knowledge about the community religious doctrine, which Druze activists and scholars consider the principle cause for the lack of equality. Al-Najjar and many other Druze individuals often complain about this lack of specific knowledge, blaming it on the absence of serious teaching of religion in schools and kindergartens. These complaints exemplify how important a knowledge of the religious doctrine is to general awareness – though that doctrine is still shrouded in secrecy.[34]

Conclusion: Individuals, Personal Status Law and the Community Public Sphere

The role of active individuals at the communal level seems crucial in changing the status of women. In order to change community family laws in Lebanon, strong communal activism along with strong and functioning community institutions are necessary. Personal status law is the prerogative of the community, and the decision for change is thus in the hands of communal institutions and leaders. Such considerations highlight the importance of communal activism in terms of participating in the affairs of the community. In such cases, the state has no role in the dynamics of internal change; only individuals within the community can actively participate in changing such conditions, without interference from either communal or state authorities.[35]

It is worth mentioning a case from the 1950s that is directly related to issues of personal status. At the time, Al-Najjar was campaigning for women's rights at a national level, in an inter-confessional group of women headed by human rights activist Laure Moghaizel. The work of this group was instrumental in lobbying for basic laws aimed at changing the status of Lebanese women; it brought about woman's suffrage in 1953, and equality in inheritance law for non-Muslims in 1959, which transferred the relevant prerogatives to the civil courts. Such lobbying thus led to a tangible improvement of women's status at a national level. However, in order to gain equality in inheritance law, the activists had to split into their respective confessional communities; and given the preponderance of Christian activists in the group, they managed to achieve such equality only within Christian communities.

Recalling events of the 1950s in this way leads to considerations on the general political system in Lebanon, and the role of the individual within it. By devolving several prerogatives to the community, the Lebanese system makes it a necessary intermediary between the individual and the state. In doing so, the state is formally delegating legal responsibilities to the main communal institutions. The Community Council is a place, in physical terms, where members of the community or its main representatives could meet, and where communal individuals could give voice to their claims.

The council's latter function is exemplified by the case of Druze women attempting to abolish gender inequality within the community. It was only after the reshaping of a new council and the appointment of a new Shaykh al-'Aql that a group of Druze women decided to present their claims to the reformed communal institutions. According to these activists, the reason for not approaching the institutions earlier was mainly due to the fact that there was a figure missing – many communal individuals considered that the previous Shaykh al-'Aql had not really represented the community – in other words, there was no one to whom their claims might be addressed. This specific case exemplifies that there must be an authority figure within communal institutions for individuals to refer to in lobbying for change, in such cases (as we have seen) the state has no part in the dynamic of internal change where issues of personal status are concerned.

Both the case of family law and the actions of activists suggest that the community sphere is an important site of reform, which should not be neglected. Furthermore, it is also implied that Lebanese individuals need not only to act on a national level but also within the community to have their claims heard. It is difficult to consider change without internal lobbying from directly affected members within a community, as they are the only players able to interfere in communal, but also structural, issues. No national figures or members of another Lebanese community would mingle in the affairs of another community to which they did not belong.

The community public sphere is one where the individuals within it are the only actors able to extend the public sphere and to exert some control over its internal dynamics. Due to the compulsory communal identity, however, individuals need to operate between the spheres, not just in a single one. The idea can be advanced of communal individuals enjoying a sort of 'extended' citizenship, or better yet, a multiple citizenship that needs to function at both communal and national levels. According to Salam, the problem of citizenship in Lebanon does not lie in the absence of the individual, but in the fact that it is not politically recognised;[36] I argue, however, that Lebanese individuals enjoy double or multiple recognitions in terms of their rights and duties as citizens. They need to operate between the spheres and simultaneously engage in several public spheres. Public visibility at the community level is indeed a source of potential power, and needs to be actuated by a consciousness that citizenship also functions at that level. The idea that communal affiliations and citizenship are not compatible should be dismissed. The Lebanese confessional system sanctions multiple identities, and therefore it can well be suggested that it also sanctions multiple citizenships.

Notes

1 For more on the notion of citizens as members of what Suad Joseph defines as 'subnational' communities, see Joseph 1996: 6–7.

2 On the different interpretations of the Lebanese political system, see Hanf 1993; Messarra 2003; Picard 2002.
3 This is a direct consequence of a framework of laws inherited from the Ottoman Empire. On the historical background of family law and religious communities during the Ottoman Empire, see Basile 1993: 24–47.
4 Some of the Christian communities have the same personal status law; see Shehadeh 2004: 86.
5 On the recent history of the personal status law of Lebanese communities, see Basile 1993: 126–44; El Gemayel 2005.
6 Personal status laws, in the Lebanese case, are often in conflict, in respect to competence, with the national judiciary system. Such conflicts concern mixed marriage, change of religion, civil marriage and the status of foreigners; see Basile 1993: 203–9.
7 Salam 1998.
8 The Druze faith (*madhhab al-tawhid*) was established with the *daʿwa* of the Fatimid caliph Hakim, and by the writings of Hamza bin ʿAli in the fifth century of the Hegira, in the year 408/1017. Hamza bin Ali was proclaimed Imam of the movement, and in the same year wrote the epistles in collaboration with Baha al-Din, in which the norms of the new doctrine and the seven principal pillars that shape the Druze dogma were formulated. On the basic principles of the Druze faith, see Makarem 1974; Obeid, 2006.
9 On the formation of Druze personal status law, see Azzam 2007: 101–4; Nissim 2003: 85–96; Betts 1988).
10 Anderson 1952a: 1–9; 1952b: 83–94; Basile 1993: 140–1.
11 Basile 1993: 141; Azzam 2007: 102–3.
12 Khuri 2004: 132; Basile 1993: 192–9.
13 These laws represented an attempt by the state to normalise Druze family law, at that time characterised by strong traditional practices. The amendment of 1962 aimed at strictly linking the Shaykh al-ʿAql to the state. On these issues, see Azzam 2007: 103; Harik 1994: 472–3.
14 Interview with judge Hariz, Beirut, 4 July 2007.
15 Azzam 2007: 104–6.
16 The importance of the Druze woman as a repository of family honour in Druze family life is discussed in Betts 1988: 42; Azzam 2007: 4–8; Layish 1982: 21.
17 On the egalitarian character of the scripture and the perception of gender and patriarchy in the thought of Emir Tanuki, see Azzam 1997: 22–42; 2007: 55–90.
18 Customary rules are still persistent within the Druze community, and concern women's access to education, forced marriage and, in practice, absence of freedom in testacy; see Azzam 2007: 116–7.
19 Former Prime Minister Rafik Hariri's assassination instigated what has been named *Intifada al-Istiqlal*, the independence uprising that sought to expel Syrian troops and security apparatus out of Lebanon and called for as truth

account of the assassination. By the end of April 2005, Damascus had withdrawn its troops from Lebanon, after a presence in the country of nearly 30 years, and elections were held in June. The opposition emerged from these with a large majority.

20 Until 2000, it was possible to elect two persons to the position of Shaykh al-'Aql, unlike in other Druze communities in the region, due to the presence of two main families, Arslan and Jumblatt, within the Lebanese community. In 2000 the law changed, permitting the election of only one. On the controversial figure of the Shaykh al-'Aql and its relation with the state, see Harik 1994: 462.

21 The position of the Shaykh al-'Aql has always been strongly politicised; see Harik 1994. According to many members of the community, the immobility of the Druze institutions until 2005 occurred because the Council no longer had an effective function, being used merely to control the financial affairs of each organisation.

22 Despite important reform and the direct involvement of community members, most of the latter are completely uninformed of the duties and functions of the Council; see Azzam 2007: 202.

23 Interview with Anissa al Najjar, Beirut, 19 October 2007.

24 Ibid.

25 Issues related to divorce and dissolution of marriage are the subject of Ch. 7, Articles 37–49, in the Druze family law; see Anderson 1952b: 83–4.

26 Extract from May Abu Hamdan lecture, Beirut, 21 September 2007.

27 On the freedom of testacy in the Tawhid faith, see Azzam 2007: 40–2.

28 Issues related to inheritance are the subject of Ch. 8, Articles 50–3 in the Druze family law. See Anderson 1952b: 86–7; Basile 1993: 392–7.

29 Interview with Anissa al-Najjar, Beirut, 19 October 2007.

30 Article 168 of the Druze family law states that 'where someone dies without a testament, or with a will which is void, he shall distribute the estate according to the Islamic law of inheritance'; see Anderson 1952b: 93.

31 Extract from May Abu Hamdan lecture, Beirut, 21 September 2007.

32 Interview with Anissa al-Najjar, 19 October 2007, Beirut, Lebanon.

33 Extract from May Abu Hamdan lecture, Beirut, 21 September 2007.

34 One of the main characteristics of the Druze faith is the distinction between *uqqal* and *juhhal*, the initiated and uninitiated members of the community. Until 1965, the holy scriptures of the Druze faith were kept secret, and the publication of a book quoting them represented a point of crisis within the community. After such a controversial move, many other works were published that interpreted the scriptures and Druze dogma. Even if the scriptures were more accessible, religious knowledge within the community is still problematic, and presents many obstacles; see Schenk 2005: 79–80; Azzam 1997: 33–7.

35 The Lebanese system does not offer a refuge for those who do not wish publicly to identify themselves as members of a community, but prefer a national

identity. One of the ways in which this is addressed at the national level is a campaign for the creation of a 'civil-status' community through the institutionalisation of civil marriage; also, most activists claim that a unified personal status law for all communities would support gender equality. See Zalzal: 1997: Shehade 1998: 97.
36 Salam 1998: 64.

Bibliography

Anderson, J.N.D., 'The personal law of the Druze community', *Die Welt des Islams*, ii/1 (1952a), pp. 1–19.
────── 'The personal law of the Druze community', *Die Welt des Islams*, ii/2 (1952b), pp. 83–94.
Azzam, Intisar J., *Change for Continuity: Druze in America* (Beirut, 1997).
────── *Gender and Religion: Druze Women* (London, 2007).
Basile, Basile P., *Statut personnel et compétence judiciaire des communautés confessionnelles au Liban* (Kaslik, 1993).
Betts, Robert Brenton, *The Druze* (New Haven, CT, 1988).
El Gemayel, Antoine, *The Lebanese Legal System* (Washington, DC, 2005).
Hanf, Theodore, *Coexistence in Wartime Lebanon: Decline of a State and Birth of a Nation* (London, 1993).
Harik, Judith Palmer, ' "Shaykh al-'Aql" and the Druze of Mount Lebanon: conflict and accommodation', *Middle Eastern Studies*, 30/3 (1994), pp. 461–85.
Joseph, Suad, 'Gender and citizenship in Middle Eastern states', *Middle East Report*, 198 (1996), pp. 4–10.
Khuri, Fuad I., *Being a Druze* (London, 2004).
Layish, Aharon, *Marriage, Divorce and Succession in the Druze Family* (Leiden, 1982).
Makarem, Sami Nasib, *The Druze Faith* (New York, 1974).
Messarra, Antoine Nasri, *La gouvernance d'un système consensuel. (Le Liban après les amendements constitutionnels de 1990)* (Beirut, 2003).
Nissim, Dana, *The Druze in the Middle East: Their Faith, Leadership, Identity and Status* (Brighton, 2003).
Obeid, Anis, *The Druze and Their Faith in Tawhid* (Syracuse, NY, 2006).
Picard, Elizabeth, *Lebanon, a Shattered Country: Myths and Realities of the Wars in Lebanon* (New York, 2002).
Salam, Nawaf, *La condition libanaise: des communautés, du citoyen et de l'état* (Beirut, 1998).
Shehadeh, Lamia Rustum, 'The legal status of married women in Lebanon', *International Journal of Middle East Studies*, 30/4 (1998), pp. 501–19.
────── 'Coverture in Lebanon', *Feminist Review*, 76: 'Post-Communism: Women's Lives in Transition' (2004), pp. 83–99.

Schenk, Bernadette, 'Druze identity in the Middle East: tendencies and developments in modern Druze communities since the 1960s'. In Kamal Salibi (ed.), *The Druze: Realities and Perceptions* (London, 2005), pp. 79–93.

Zalzal, Marie Rose, 'Secularism and personal status codes in Lebanon: interview with Marie Rose Zalzal', *Middle East Report*, 203 (1997), pp. 37–9.

3

WHAT A FOCUS ON 'FAMILY' MEANS IN THE ISLAMIC REPUBLIC OF IRAN

Arzoo Osanloo

Introduction

In September 2008, the Iranian parliament returned a bill containing proposed amendments to Iran's civil code of marriage and family under the title of 'Family Protection', to the parliamentary commission for further study. Domestic and international women's rights groups celebrated a victory resulting from their mutual efforts to oppose the bill that would further impede women's rights in marriage and other matters of personal status in the context of the family. The bill, introduced by the government's executive branch in August 2007, was then sent to the Legal and Judicial Commission of the Iranian parliament for review. With the commission's approval of the bill almost a year later, on 9 July 2008, the bill was to be sent to the full parliament for a vote that would make it law.

Among numerous controversial articles in the bill were nos. 22 and 23. Article 22 aimed at abolishing the requirement to register temporary marriages (*sigheh*) by suggesting that registration of temporary marriage would be subject to procedures yet to be promulgated by the Ministry of Justice. By removing the existing requirement to register temporary marriages with the Office of the Registrar, the bill would move the jurisdiction for regulating temporary marriages to the exclusive purview of the executive branch. Eliminating the registration requirement would potentially remove any financial or legal protections for women in temporary marriages as well as for any children born into them.

Article 23 sanctioned polygamy for a man based solely on his ability to prove to a judge that he possessed the financial means to support multiple wives and treat them equally. The article, however, did not delineate that parameters of adequate financial resources to support multiple wives, nor did it define the meaning of equal treatment of multiple wives. Indeed, with this provision, the existing requirement to obtain the consent of the first wife in order to enter into a second marriage was excluded, apparently supplanted by the husband's proffer of evidence to the court. For reasons that will become clear at the end, this chapter will deal primarily with these two provisions of the bill, even though there are other problematic articles, including a tax on the dower or bride price (*mahrieh*) and the potential criminalisation of women's marriages to foreign nationals.[1]

In an outpouring of dissent, spanning from Qom to Los Angeles, Western women's rights activists and members of the Iranian Shia *'ulama* criticised key articles within the bill as acting against women's interests, Islamic principles and protection of the family alike. This coalition effectively prevented the bill from moving to a final vote of parliament, and saw it sent back to the commission, which then formed a special committee to further research and review the proposed bill.

While this decision was seen as a victory for women's rights and activism, it was only part of an on-going struggle to define the nature of the Islamic state by regulating women's bodies and lives through legal debates about the concept of family. Since the 1979 revolution that ushered in the Islamic Republic, guardians of the state have made family a central focus of legislation and regulation, having deemed it the foundation of society, and women – *keeyan-e khanevadeh*, or 'crowning jewels' of the family,' would be regulated to preserve the family's honour and dignity.

In this chapter, I will consider how the notion of family and women's roles in it have shaped both reformist and hardline attempts at the consolidation of power since the start of what has come to be termed the reform period (1997–2005). This struggle emerges in the context of a deepening battle to define the nature of governance, and concomitantly, the authority to interpret Islamic guidelines (Sharia) within it. What will become clear is that debates about the status and rights of women take shape in a broader field of struggles for power by groups with conflicting ideas of the Islamic Republic. These disputes reveal the different ideologies of governance that have emerged since the revolution, and concern questions about Islamic principles and their relationship with republican forms of governance.

In what follows, I will re-examine the situation of women as a trope for the post-revolutionary state. In doing so, I will highlight how various state actors characterise this trope differently, at times as 'women's status' and at others as 'women's rights'. I argue that the choice of words here is intentional and carries with it distinct ideological meaning. Next, I trace the shift in language from 'rights' to 'status' as it emerged in revolutionary discourse, especially in 1979. I then consider how the presidency of Mohammad Khatami (1997–2005) placed a different emphasis on women, with the intention of strengthening the participatory institutions of the Islamic republic. In order to do so, I analyse the Centre for Women's Participation, an executive branch office charged with supporting women's rights. In the section that follows, I examine how the 2005 election of Mahmoud Ahmadinejad to the presidency brought about a change in the discourse surrounding women's issues, while maintaining the focus on the same presidential office, now bearing a new name: the Centre for Women and Family Affairs. In the final section, I return to my initial interest, the debates around the proposed changes to the Family Protection Bill, which highlight how the Ahmadinejad administration attempted to make changes to the law consistent with its view of Islamic government as opposed to Islamic republic.

Shifting Discourses: Women's 'Rights' and 'Status'

Women's status has been an important trope in Iran and much of the world, as a measure of modernity and social advancement. Mohammad Khatami's rise to the presidency in 1997 ushered in unprecedented levels of participation by women in the post-revolutionary period, and Iranian women witnessed a change in the emphasis on their status. This shift was characterised by the executive's increased emphasis on women's civil and political participation. This move, I argue, emerged in tandem with Khatami's broader goals of building and strengthening the legal instruments and civil bodies of the state, giving the 'republican' organs of the Islamic Republic some much-needed institutional, structural and procedural expression. Khatami's attention to the rule of law redirected the state's (or at least the executive's) focus on women, as well. Khatami's government moved beyond a concern with women as wives and mothers exclusively to an added interest in them as individuals, citizens and political beings endowed with rights.

This shift is not immediately evident, given the nature of much of the international media's attention to Iran, and the seemingly persistent depiction of the Iranian woman as oppressed. The changes are also difficult to discern and to differentiate from the long history of women's activism and struggles for equality in Iran, particularly in the pre-revolutionary period. Sometimes the most remarkable aspects of this shift appear in ordinary practices – and only once those practices are considered in the context of the immediate aftermath of the Iranian revolution, and women's place therein, can the seemingly routine appear extraordinary. As an anthropologist, I had my first encounter with such 'unremarkable' practices of legal institution-building in the first years of the Khatami presidency, when I encountered a family-law attorney in Tehran and explained to her that I was interested in exploring how women in Iran are finding their 'rights' through Sharia. This was an attorney whose legal career began well before the revolution; she was quite well-known, had authored many articles and books, and her representation was so highly sought-after that her suite of offices was filled with clients right up to the end of the evening. She responded with dismay, telling me:

> This is a law office and I am a lawyer. We have civil codes in Iran and civil courts. I do not deal in Sharia; I deal in the law (*qanun*). If you want to understand how laws work, you need to go to the court to see for yourself. You need to see for yourself how women are getting their rights.

So, where was the 'Islam' in these laws through which women were struggling, as expressed in the many articles I had been reading as a graduate student? This is not to say that Islam was absent, but that there was, here in this lawyer's response and during much of the Khatami period, an emphasis on *qanun* over Sharia, which was quite significant if one had an understanding of the period immediately after the revolution – particularly as far as women's status was concerned – and even more important when considering the unresolved debates over the nature of the state.

Revolution: from Rights to Status

Many know of the 1979 Iranian revolution, where images of women became symbolic of a political and social change. This was a revolution in large part against the excesses of Western societies, aimed to turn the country back to some 'indigenous' values. This struck a chord with a broad cross-section of the population, far from religious groups alone. While the revolution is sometimes called 'Islamic' this is actually a misnomer, as it leaves out this important component of the revolution: the many secular nationalists that came together with religious groups to overthrow a 'monarchy' and establish a representative government through what became ultimately an Islamic *republic*. This was a grand compromise, whose effects continue to until today. Among those effects was the visible politicisation of 'rights talk' and the mobilisation – by both state and non-state revolutionary actors – of the Iranian woman as a symbolic counter to the Western woman.

By 'politicisation' I refer to the deployment of the language of rights by numerous revolutionary factions, which was seen at that time (1979) as redolent of the ills of Western individualism, one which overlooked the fact that that the basis of a healthy society was the family and that individuals' needs had to yield to greater social and familial concerns. Rights talk in this context became a verbal index for a sense of entitlement without responsibility, thought to be the source of much of the ills of Western societies, which were characterised by excess and anomie. The politicisation of this rights talk was most poignantly brought to bear on activists in March 1979, when by the tens of thousands Iranian women and men flooded urban centres to protest the repeal of a Shah-era Family Protection Act (1967, rev. 1975) that had given women some rights in marriage dissolution and child custody, and other possible legal setbacks, including mandatory veiling, which was imposed in the end, and the revocation of female suffrage, which was not. In protest of these actions, women fought back with the help of American activists like Kate Millet, who was their keynote speaker for the protests that coincided with International Women's Day (9 March). They held up signs in Persian and English to make their grievances known: 'Equality' and 'Women's Rights' (Millet 1982). For these actions, the protestors were dubbed 'Western puppets', and attacked. It is here where we first begin to see some of the fissures within the popular struggle to remove a monarchy. Just what was to emerge was as yet uncertain, and the populace was divided. It is also here that we begin to see the association of a language of rights with Western excesses and imperialism, where the language of rights (*huquq*) began to be disassociated from the language of status (*moghaiat*). Thus we see a discursive shift away from an emphasis on women's rights (*huquq-e zan*) to one on women's status (*moghaiat-e zan*), which also signals an important transition in the perceived roles for women – that their roles as mothers and wives should be foremost, and regulated by the state to meet the broader aim of producing a healthy society.

And this was what in part caused my surprise when the lawyer I met in Iran told me to look at the civil codes and laws, and this further inspired my interest in understanding how they operate, because in the initial months after I arrived in Iran, I was again and again surprised to find that my interlocutors, many of them pious Muslim women, many of them supportive of the Islamic Republic, used renewed, post-revolutionary rights talk, referencing as their source of rights not Islamic principles, but law. How did this come about?

In 1979, revolutionary discourse mobilised the Iranian woman as a symbolic foil to the Western woman – we see that for the pious Muslim Iranian woman, the Western woman was objectified, commodified, hyper-sexualised and thus unemancipated and oppressed. The 1983 Veiling Act was legislated in tandem with a discourse of rehabilitating the Iranian woman and restoring her to a place of respect. The *chador* was symbolic, not just of the renewed piety of the Iranian woman, but also of a collective shift among Iranian women, in the name of the whole country – a political shift toward a religio-national idea of Iran that represented the triumph of the revolution over Western values so symbolised by the Pahlavi monarchy. Many are already familiar with this story, and it is not my aim here simply to repeat what has already been said.

Instead, I want to think further about the significance of improving women's status, symbolically and even materially, as a primary revolutionary aim. By placing women's issues in central focus, the resulting government would now, could now, be held accountable for promises to improve women's status and to rehabilitate the population. Soon after the revolution, we saw many scholarly and journalistic accounts of how women in Iran were relegated to the *andaruni*, 'indoor spaces', or to going backwards or to medieval time. The persistence of a language of binary oppositions, referenced and made comprehensible to audiences outside Iran by exiled elites, trained and educated in the US and Europe, offered credible, seemingly objective and generalisable accounts of what was happening. Most importantly, these depictions fit well within the repertoire of orientalised Middle Eastern women: exotic, fundamentalist Muslim, oppressed and in need of saving.

Back in Iran, however, these accounts did not correspond with the visibility of women in public spaces, in civil society, including working outside the home, and in government. Around this time, from the mid-1980s to perhaps the late-1990s, we also saw a shift in scholarship. New depictions of women's lives recognised very different empirical situations. Some of this was attributed to the political situation and material conditions, including the war with Iraq, which was taking a severe political, economic and human toll. As a result, women were performing well beyond the roles prescribed for them as financially-maintained wives and mothers, roles idealised by the leading Shia *'ulama* now holding the reins of governmental control.[2] Some scholarship and journalistic essays on this topic reflected material changes and conditions, but by and large revealed them as a change in women's status brought on by new readings of Islamic texts, even an Islamic feminism that was leading the way. Many scholars, themselves Iranian exiles, would attribute the shifts in status to the work women like them had done, the paths they had paved before the revolution. Some authors, pundits and bloggers credit the successes of the women's movement to the strength of Iranian women – almost as if they possessed some biologically-conferred fortitude that somehow set them apart from women in the rest of the Middle East, or for that matter, the world.

While no one can deny the persistence and strength of Iranian women, both in and outside Iran, here I am interested in understanding the existing means of social change, reform, resistance and dissemination that women and women's advocates are using. That is to say, the literature referred to above provided analyses of governmental and religious prescriptions, both administrative and theoretical, with regard to women's place in family, state and society. However, we also saw and continue to see extensive scholarship unravelling the novel, complex, contradictory, even unpredictable nature of the Islamic Republic of Iran. Yet many of the prescriptive accounts of women's lives and status leave out of consideration the tensions, complexities or possibilities inherent in the indefinite and indeed evolving nature of the state. How could that be? How could our understanding of the state, of government and its institutions, be so rich and textured, and account for changes, opportunities and even possibilities, while our understanding of women's rights or roles or status remains so flat, level, stagnant and unidirectional?[3]

Thus, one of the goals of my work in general has been to make sense of the processes and institutions that shape the spaces for advocacy, legal or otherwise, for women's and human rights. But I have also aimed to place analyses about this novel enterprise, the Islamic Republic of Iran – the first modern religious state – alongside discussions of the status of women. Some of the changes in women's status, roles and rights emerge from the possibilities or opportunities created – unwittingly, perhaps – by the hybrid state institutions. Thus attention to legal processes and institutions can provide important revelations not just about disputes, but about the politics of law, rights and gender relations, and about the operation of power, both legally and extra-legally.

To understand this, it is important to consider the formation and reformation of some legal and political institutions born of this seemingly contradictory form of state, the Islamic Republic. Indeed, it was more than just contradictory, in 1979, it was also an unknown quantity, and what it would become was not clear to anyone. In the mid-1980s Richard Cottam noted, 'after several years of revolution, there is still no accepted developmental strategy for achieving this esoteric end' (1986: 61). There was no certainty about the final nature of the state at the time of its formation, nor is there finality for what it might still become. In my work, situating the shifting meaning of rights talk in social, political and legal contexts has become a methodological concern, since it shapes the nature and consequences of the claims people make on the Islamic Republic, and in only ten years there have been several shifts in the meaning and effect of rights discourses. What was entitled the Islamic Republic of Iran was to some a transitional period before achieving the 'pure' Islamic government of Ayatollah Khomeini. But the institutions and meaning of the 'republic,' which emphasised the popular nature of the revolution, remained a philosophical and academic inquiry for much of the first 20 years of post-revolutionary Iran, in part due to the war and the charismatic leadership of Khomeini.

One important component contributing to the shifts in rights talk is the legislative, law-making body, which in Khomeini's thesis for governance did not exist.[4] There was no need for 'man-made laws' as only God's law would matter, and thus the legislative body was to be dissolved. According to Khomeini: 'The Glorious Quran and the *Sunna* contain all the laws and ordinances man needs in order to achieve happiness and the perfection of his state' (1981: 17). When the provisional government of the new Islamic Republic attempted to 'purify' the laws by repealing legislation and the legal codes, however, confusion over how to adjudicate the laws of God caused such a severe outcry that over time some laws were re-authenticated by the governing bodies of the Islamic Republic, and codified.[5] More importantly, as Zubaida has pointed out,

> codified law is the law of the state, and the judge is a functionary of the state who has to arrive at a judgement from the codes and procedures determined by it rather than by autonomous judgement through reference to sacred sources and the principle derived from them (2005: 134).

The codified form of the law is significant in that it disrupts the historical power of Islamic judges to use a certain level of discretion in assessing the cases before them. Legislative authority, too, was to an extent reinstated, though in a very limited form. For Khomeini, the legislative body constituted one of the three branches of government, but was to act simply as a planning body (1981: 28).

So it becomes important that despite an anti-Western revolution in which a new government dissolved the legislature, disbanded civil courts and repealed civil codes, little by little, the Islamic Republic reestablished civil courts as a venue for adjudication and reinstated civil codes as the formal expression of the law.[6] All of these factors in the legal system have tangible, manifest consequences for the conceptualization of rights. And it was all done after Khomeini had nullified and invalidated code law, including the important Family Protection Act mentioned earlier. The legal blending disrupted the conventional symmetry between Sharia and state-administered law that had existed for many years. Through codification, Sharia was given unambiguous legal force for the first time ever (Mir-Hosseini 1993). If the combining of Sharia and civil law was a reflection of the compromises among these disparate groups, it was also an effect of the final outcome of the revolution: that the entity that came to fruition after the revolution was neither a pure, 'traditional' expression of Islam, nor a copy of the European state model, but something different, something new. In the end, it was Islam that was made to accommodate to the republican state framework, as it did, it produced (and reauthenticated) liberal subjects in various segments of society, especially the legal. Even while the post-revolutionary government made women's issues the grounds on which political disputes over governance were fought, those disputes took shape in discourses and gave way to institutions that were conspicuously liberal, through the nation-state as a republic. The institutions of the state comprise the tangible apparatus of everyday life and shape the patterns of practice, even if the content of such practice is premised on Islamic principles. As apparatuses of a republic, the institutions of the state require subjects to operate in a liberal framework, particularly when interacting with those institutions.

So it was with this understanding, perhaps, that the lawyer with whom I spoke insisted I go to the courts, where it was so apparent that women and men, judges and adversarial parties alike were discussing their rights, not their status. As individuals interacted with these state institutions, they were also gaining expertise in legal matters, sometimes new, sometimes renewed, as they were both regulated by civil processes and yet beholden to Islamic principles. It is here, then, that I redirect the reader's attention to the remarkable unremarkability of the law offices, where the civil processes mediated by lawyers seem very ordinary to observers unfamiliar with this history, and yet are emblematic of this important shift back to a call for rights – now legitimised by Islamic principles.

Khatami's Rule of Law: from Status to Rights

It was not until the mid-1990s, after the war had ended and Khomeini had died, that debates about the nature of the state, legal processes and renewed discourses of rights, no longer blemished by the taint of imperialism, began to enter into newly-emerging public spaces. Such rights talk was nurtured and encouraged during the Khatami presidency. Women were also participating in dialogue and debate, challenging the statist promulgations of their status and roles in numerous arenas, such as newspapers and magazines, but also in venues as diverse as non-governmental organisations, scriptural reading groups, courts, their places of work and even government ministries. These 'dialogical sites', I have argued elsewhere, have emerged as productive effects of the intersection of Islamic guidelines and republican principles.[7]

One such emblematic site is the Centre for Women's Participation. In 1991, then-President Ayatollah Hashemi Rafsanjani suggested the establishment of a centre for women's affairs under the office of the president. Upon approval by Iran's Supreme Council of the Cultural Revolution (SCCR),[8] on 1 December 1991, Rafsanjani appointed the first presidential adviser on women's affairs, who also was also charged with heading the first Centre for Women's Affairs. The Centre's website states the early aims of its mission: 'This office shaped its activities with the aim of enhancing and promoting women's status and improving their capabilities to flourish their talents for the development and growth of Islamic society.'[9]

In 1998, President Khatami elevated the Centre to a cabinet-level portfolio, quadrupled its funding, and gave it a new name, Centre for Women's Participation (CWP). The new mission of the CWP was women's civil, legal and political education. The head of the CWP, Zahra Shojaee, was Iran's representative to the United Nations on women's issues, and among its many projects the CWP worked with legal specialists, experts in both international law and Islamic jurisprudence (*fiqh*), in determining the compatibility of the Convention on the Elimination of Discrimination Against Women (CEDAW) with Islamic principles. The CWP lobbied Iran's parliament to pass CEDAW. In the end, however, Iran's parliament did not ratify the convention because the Council of Guardians, a body that determines whether laws passed by parliament are in conformity with Islamic principles, overrode parliament and rejected the CWP's briefs arguing that CEDAW is in agreement with Islamic principles.

The CWP's pamphlets lay out its aims with considerable attention to the public roles that women could have in addition to their roles in the family. In one of its last pamphlets, published in 2004, the CWP lists its objectives as:

1. Promotion of women's participation in various spheres of human endeavors by expert and technical review of the issue and presentation of recommendations to the Cabinet, Islamic Consultative Assembly, Women's Cultural-Social Council and other legislative bodies for the purpose of formulating legislation and regulations and adoption of policies;
2. Presentation of advisory opinions to the President on the issues relating to women by acquiring precise understanding on the situation of women and drawing up their desirable living situation;
3. Studying practical ways for strengthening the leadership and educative role of women in the family along with enhancement of their leadership role at the higher levels of society;
4. Presentation of proper strategies with a view of raising general awareness and knowledge of women and enhancing their intellectual and reasoning capacity;
5. Presentation of a role model for Muslim women;
6. Understanding of women issues and problems in the society, family and workplace and amendment of relevant legislation [by] proposing new legislation for solving their problems.[10]

A review of the CWP's functions reflects a desire to focus on women's participation and leadership roles in society. Another notable feature of the CWP's aims is its repeated objective of liaising with the legislative and executive bodies of government in support of their aim to improve women's lives. In their stated objectives, the CWP also seeks to bring about change by proposing new legislation. Interesting in all of this is the wording of objective three in which the CWP highlights and distinguishes two realms of participation for women, 'in the family' and 'at the higher levels of society'.

Another example of the CWP's focus on rights and the rule of law is a pamphlet entitled 'Human Rights of Women', in which the CWP lists no fewer than 41 'legal measures and modifications made to the law by the Islamic Republic of Iran', in support of 'raising the issue of human rights [to] help boost sensitivity of people and governments toward discrimination against women and make them not to be negligent.'[11]

Efforts on behalf of women during Khatami's reform period were not only top-down, however. Attention to the effects of legal processes can further clarify how rights talk inevitably re-emerged in the post-revolutionary period. In addition to reformists' attention to the rule of law and to women's political and civil participation, another important component of the relegitimation of rights talk during this period derived from the reinstitution of civil courts and the repackaging of Islamic principles in civil codes. Part of the reason for this, I have argued elsewhere, is that the civil laws which derive from Sharia maintain the right of marriage dissolution as a contractual right of husbands.[12] As a result, a system that requires women to build and prove their legal cases, and thus to convince a judge to delegate the husband's right to dissolve the marriage to them, led women to gain legal understanding with respect to using the system and juridical knowledge in the context of Islamic precepts. The same is not true for men, who did not have to petition the court in order to dissolve their marriages. These legal processes also served to resituate women as individuated citizens, responsive to the state's civil courts, beyond their roles as wives and mothers accountable only to their husbands, as had been imagined for them in the immediate post-revolutionary period.

Ahmadinejad's Backlash: from Rights to Status

Five years after I had started following legal cases and initiatives in various law offices and courts, I asked one of my legal interlocutors how she thought the laws were being adjudicated. This was in 2005, just as Ahmadinejad was starting his first term of office. She responded:

> Five years ago, I thought women did not know their rights. There are laws on the books, good laws, but women just did not know how to use them. Today, I think women know their rights, but they forget their duties.

The successes of women in litigating marriage dissolution cases, alongside increased social and political participation, were leading some social conservatives to call for more regulation. More precisely, hardliners were appealing for more constraints on the adjudication of women's rights in marriage and turning their attention instead to women's status in the family, as they called on women to abide by their duties rather than seeking out their rights.

This shift became readily apparent when, soon after the inauguration of Mahmoud Ahmadinejad, the President's office changed the Centre for Women's Participation to the Centre for Women and Family Affairs (CWFA). The CWFA's redesigned website indicates the shift in concerns from women's rights to a greater focus on their status as wives and mothers. According to the Center's website:

> With the start of the ninth government, Dr Ahmadinejad proposed a broader idea on the social and religious necessities and the central role of women in the stabilization of families. He therefore expanded the centre to the Centre for Women and Family Affairs ... [13]

In what it sees as a historic expansion of its agenda, the CWFA states:

> In addition to the protecting the human dignity of women in Islam and emphasizing on their positive presence in the different social, managerial, political, cultural, economic and scientific fields, it also emphasizes their role as centre of passion and love for nurturing humans and as the main survival factor in for morality in the society.

The website goes on to explain that 'in 2005, the Centre developed its functions from "women participation" to "women and family affairs"', listing its primary functions as:

1. Studying and examining the situation of women and families by conducting research (in cooperation with universities and research

centers) on ways of improving their status in accordance with Islamic principles;
2. Establishment [of a] liaison with all ministries and other stakeholders in planning activities relating to women and families with a view to coordination and improving current and future programs;
3. Planning and coordinating with NGOs and presenting general and common policies for their activities;
4. Liaising with the Commissions of the Islamic Consultative Assembly (Majlis) and its representatives in order to exchange views and to influence legislative trends on women and family issues;
5. Establishment of constant relationships with Women's Cultural and Social Council for the purpose of covering government's efforts with the policies and guidelines of the Council;
6. Following up the efforts to secure fair allocation of resources to various regions of the country with a view to supporting activities and efforts of women and families in different parts of the nation;
7. Establishment of relations with statistical centers in the country and abroad for the purpose of collecting the information relating to women and families as well as of analyzing it for timely and appropriate use;
8. Taking necessary actions for active presence of women in international forums and seminars relating to women and families, as well as taking required actions with a view to enhancing presence of women in cultural and sports activities in Iran and abroad;
9. Presenting advisory comments to the president, governmental and legislative bodies with respect to the issues and problems affecting women and families;
10. Presenting necessary reports regarding the activities of the Center to the President and following up his directives until achieving the [desired] result.[14]

Here it is evident that the CWFA has not altogether abandoned its outreach and its objective of influencing legislation, but has reformulated its primary policy objective, and hence its lobbying mission, from women's participation to a focus on women's status in family affairs.

Each of the ten functions listed above reiterates the aim of supporting women in the context of 'women and families'. The text delineates and defines support for women in the context of their status in families, and through that role, their upholding of the social moral order, but does not see women as individuals outside of this context.

Of course the shift in tone and mission of the women's centre, from political participation to concern with status in families, is just one example of the broader shift away from the individuated discourse of rights. Just after the revolution, such discourses seemed to be proscribed because of their association with the ills of Western society and the Pahlavi era's attempts to emulate them. Then a seeming re-emergence of rights-based strategies for improving women's lives grew alongside a wide-ranging emphasis by the Khatami government on the rule of law and the development of institutions commonly associated with popular governance. Republican institutions grew in tandem with justifications about their compatibility with Islamic principles for guiding the populace and the Islamic Republic's own mission of self-governance.[15]

With the ascendance of Mahmoud Ahmadinejad to the presidency, another seeming shift had taken place. While Iranians continue to employ discourses of rights, such discourses increasingly carry with them grave consequences amidst fraught and often volatile political situations. Indeed, the effects of contemporary discourses of 'regime change' that highlight women's rights in their aims are used by Iran's increasingly authoritarian leaders against what are, on the one hand, domestic, internal reform movements, such as the One Million Signatures Campaign, or on the other hand international calls for Iran to abide by treaties that it has signed and ratified, even post-1979, such as the Convention on the Rights of the Child.[16] This is because as the attacks are framed increasingly in ideological terms, the response is to further delineate and restrict the range of possibilities for women calling for improvements in their lot, a response that is also ideological and binary, and thus not only occludes but even critically shifts the on-the-ground possibilities for women. This leaves us with a backlash against rights groups and with competing calls for improvements in women's status, but not necessarily rights. Indeed, after 12 June

2009, as in 1979, rights activists and the very discourse of rights are characterized by state forces as the indices of such groups' aims of fomenting a type of 'velvet revolution'. The indictments issued by the Islamic Republic against those who protested at the 12 June elections demonstrate this.[17] While many activists felt that the success of the reform period was thwarted by those events, there are enduring socio-legal effects of the attention paid to the rule of law, in particular when we return to the proposed Family Protection bill and the developments after it was sent back to the Legal and Judicial Commission of parliament.

Re-asserting women's 'rights' in the family: on the aftermath of the 2007 Family Protection bill

On 26 November 2009 the rapporteur for the Legal and Judicial Commission issued a statement notable for its legal inefficacy, its jargon and its evasion of specific problematic issues. As reported by the Islamic Student News Association, the spokesman, the MP from the town of Malayar, Amin Hossein Rahimi, stated that the special committee had completed its research on the Family Protection bill and had sent it to the Commission.[18] The special committee was formed in response to the large outcry caused by the bill, Rahimi stated. He went on to explain that the committee had reviewed the bill in consideration of its main aim, that of 'strengthening the family':

> Having considered this paramount aim, the special committee determined that the taking of another wife was not consonant with the express goal of strengthening the family, and thus a second marriage would be prohibited without the consent of the first wife.

He continued:

> Because of the outcry over this article, the special committee issued new regulations for a second marriage without the consent of the first wife, which could be permissible in very limited

circumstances, where special misconduct was found, such as that which would result in five years in prison or in cases where the wife has abandoned the family.

If the wife does not possess any of these difficulties, and the husband marries another woman, there is a punishment of prison that has been rendered for this. In addition, he will not be permitted to register this [second] marriage. That is to say, there are many additional legal consequences in addition to the fact that the perpetrator will be guilty of having committed a crime.

In these two paragraphs, the parliamentary spokesman for the commission decidedly addresses the outpouring of dissent, and even notes the influence of this opposition in reconsidering the provisions of the bill and considerably revising the article, now proposing to make such a second marriage both a crime and a civil legal transgression. The rapporteur then raised the issue of whether in cases like this the marriage contract is invalid or not.

In the Family Protection bill, the debate is procedural and no debate about the substantive nature of the validity of the marriage took place. This issue is a matter of Islamic guidelines and jurisprudence (Sharia and *fiqh*), into which we did not enter. However, if a man marries again without attaining the aforementioned conditions, he will be punished and his wife has the right to petition for dissolution of the marriage.

In this, one of the most interesting parts of the statement, Rahimi defers certain matters of validity, even in the face of illegality, to Islamic jurists. That is to say, even though the commission has proposed to criminalise the taking of a second wife without the permission of the first, he defers to the *'ulama* on the issue of whether the marriage is still considered valid, even while suggesting that the first wife would have the right to ask that her marriage be dissolved. The interesting move here is the distinction made by Rahimi between law and procedure, on the one hand, and jurisprudence on the other. As law-makers, the members of the commission will provide procedures, even while deferring judgment on the substantive issues which the commission is regulating.

The final two paragraphs of the statement from the commission's spokesman refer to temporary marriage, which the Family Protection bill, under Article 22, attempted to deregulate. These two paragraphs will be considered together, since the unstated but clearly related opinions of the commission in the first paragraph are both reiterated and broadened in the second.

> The bill which the judiciary and the executive proposed did not make any mention of temporary marriage, except that it was stated that the registration of temporary marriage would be regulated according to memoranda to be issued by the executive's office. However, the majority of the Legal and Judicial Commission of parliament believes with regard to this issue that such memoranda speaking to the registration of temporary marriage can in no way be used as a basis for the regulations of temporary marriage. In reality, if necessary laws for this must be approved; however, in the debates about the Family Protection bill, for which we are recording law, we understand family as permanent marriage, and in Islam and in our regulations, permanent marriage is foundational and it is that which creates the family. Thus, in the Family Protection bill, with regard to permanent marriage, the type of regulations we considered were those that would offer strength to the family.
>
> In conclusion, the legal and judicial commission in conclusion reflected that temporary marriage is an issue that from the perspective of Sharia is permissible; however, it has specific conditions which are restricted and exceptional. Thus, individuals cannot undertake temporary marriage under any conditions, unless this effort is undertaken clandestinely. Given that temporary marriage is not consistent with a family and is not a part of marriage from the perspective of strengthening the family, it was not an issue of emphasis in Islam, and we did not see any

need to consider making laws for it in this bill. If it does exist, however, only under special conditions is it possibly to carry out. In conclusion, if a man would like to register his temporary marriage, he must follow the laws consistent with the laws of obtaining another wife. To better explain, temporary marriage can only be registered given the consent of the first wife, unless a man clandestinely enters into the temporary marriage.

There are two issues which are important to address here: first, the issue of separation of powers, to which Rahimi very subtly refers when speaking of the governmental authority for regulating temporary marriage. The commission did not, in this bill, consider issuing regulations for temporary marriage because the aim of its proposals is to strengthen the family. Not only does temporary marriage not do that, but according to the statement, a marriage entered into temporarily does not constitute a family. Moreover, the spokesman suggests that the commission had at least considered the executive's proviso (Article 22) that it would issue guidelines for temporary marriage and defiantly states that temporary marriage, while not within the purview of this bill, is something to be regulated. According to him, the majority of the commission's members are of the opinion that such guidelines should come in the form of law from the government's law-making body, and not the executive.

The rapporteur then continues to discuss temporary marriage, even after establishing that it does not fall under the definition of family, let alone family protection, and thus is not a matter for the bill under consideration. He reiterates that while temporary marriage is permissible under Sharia, it is allowable only under very specific and narrow circumstances, here suggesting that even if it is allowable, it is undesirable except under very strict conditions. This is interesting in that in the earlier paragraphs, Rahimi deferred matters of substantive Sharia to the *'ulama*, but here opines quite definitively on temporary marriage.

But it is the final two sentences of his statement that are indeed ground-breaking. Having established that the commission is of the opinion that temporary marriages should be regulated by parliament, and registered, he then concludes by saying that even in the case of temporary marriage, in order for a man to register it, he must follow the laws which cover the taking of a second wife. That is, he must obtain the first wife's consent, effectively putting temporary marriage on a par with second marriage. Presumably, or at least arguably, if the husband does not obtain the first wife's permission, and marries clandestinely – which is the only way it could be done if he does not seek to register it – then she would have the right to apply for dissolution of the marriage were she to find out about either such a clandestine temporary marriage, or a temporary marriage to which she had refused to consent. In the final analysis, however, Rahimi does not suggest any consequences in cases where men do not register their temporary marriages and carry them out clandestinely.

Conclusion

This article was originally published during the Ahmadinejad administration and does not analyze the actions of the current administration of Hassan Rouhani. Rouhani's government has maintained the name of the Center for Woman and Family Affairs, but has appointed a Khatami-era moderate, Shahindokht Mowlaverdi, to head this organization. Like the president, Mowlaverdi has cautiously called for the end to discrimination based on gender. Also like her boss, however, she has been unable to effect serious legal reform. The tensions that exist in Iran do so at the intersection of two primary state ideologies: Islam and republicanism. The laws in question here are a new cultural product, which I refer to as 'Islamico-civil' laws. Understanding how such laws operate helps us to appreciate better the basis of current tensions and indeed of possibilities within Iran. It also leaves us with some new, perhaps slightly discordant results: women are at the vanguard of reform and women's status has improved in some circumstances. Today women have some legal rights that they did not have prior to the revolution. In addition, there are more young women in university, in the workforce, and in higher governmental and administrative positions than before. Some of this, I have argued, has resulted from the discourse of improvement in women's status as an important revolutionary aim, but it is also an effect of new civil and legal institutions, which women, by some measure, have been active in mobilising, as in cases of marriage dissolution and child custody, and even the very public protests against the new Family Protection bill. But it is also in the seemingly small actions, such as the advice given in lawyers' offices or the legal knowledge produced by women using the courts, as well as in informal networks, whether women's reading groups, Quranic or otherwise, or extra-legal work in NGOs, or social workers creating safe-houses for indigent women. These everyday activities in which women are getting on with their lives, when taken together, constitute and shape the field of possibilities for socio-legal changes in women's lives. To be a bit more precise, I return to my earlier statement on the observation of seemingly unremarkable practices: I do not mean to suggest that the 'small actions' are insignificant, but rather, that they are often no more than procedural operations in the laws or knowledge of government regulations through which women and other access their rights and are empowered as citizens.

What I hope to have demonstrated with these examples is that the backlash to reformists, their rights talk and these social movements for change in the Islamic Republic emerged well before the 12 June elections. However, the world came to see the limiting factors of reform in the government's violent crackdown after those elections. Criticisms of rights discourses have again emerged at the forefront of the threat that has now been rescripted from imperialism to 'regime change' and now to 'velvet revolution'. The indictments against persons said to be active in fomenting such revolution are substantiated by claiming that they are involved in women's rights and human-rights campaigns. The deeper issue is a sharp divide and an increasingly violent battle over the nature of governance today: Islamic government (*hukumat-e Islami*) or Islamic Republic (*jomhuri-e Islami*).

Notes

1 Later revisions to the bill changed some of the article numbers referred to here. There are other problematic provisions: Article 25 imposes a tax on the dower paid to the wife. While this amount is legally owed to the wife at the time of

the marriage, women often do not receive it; it is frequently paid only when the marriage is dissolved, and gives a wife leverage against her husband should she have no justiciable grounds for dissolution. Taxation of the dower therefore potentially reinforces a husband's financial power over his wife during their marriage, and hinders her becoming financially autonomous at the time of a divorce. In addition, this provision of the bill imposes on women additional procedural impediments to marriage dissolution. Article 46 criminalises the marriage of a foreigner to an Iranian woman without proper authorisation. The foreign man is subject to imprisonment for between 90 days and a year, and the woman if she married of her own free will, her father, if he gave permission and the marriage officials could all be sentenced as accomplices.

2 Most notable among these was Mutahhari (1981).
3 Interestingly, one scholar, Naghibi (2007), relegates some responsibility for the lack of depth in scholarship to some Iranian exiles who have worked in tandem with neo-conservatives to co-opt feminist work. At the same time, feminist scholars are aware of the ways in which liberal feminists have benefited at home (or in exile) by pitching their lot with the colonial overseer. In this way, feminism has been deployed in the service of colonial enterprises.
4 Not all the Shia *'ulama* agreed with Khomeini's thesis on Islamic governance. While some did agree that a final authority on Islamic guidelines should lead the nation, for others the features of governance expressed in the republican model, with Islamic laws rationalised in codes, were offensive to the essential values of Islam. Similar disagreement existed in Iran's first constitutional revolution, but the thesis of *Velayat-e Faqih* (Guardianship of the Jurist) was intended to address the concerns brought out in the previous era. Debates on this issue persist. See Soroush (2000) and Salimi (2003).
5 Paidar (1995) details the confusion in adjudicating marriage dissolution. Zubaida (2005) discusses the disorder that ensued in drafting penal sanctions.
6 This blended legal system grew out of struggles to determine how to put into operation this unique system where Islam and a republican model of government intersect. Not all of the Shia *'ulama* agreed with Ayatollah Khomeini's thesis on Islamic governance. For detailed discussions see Arjomand (1988).
7 This is the main focus of my book, *The Politics of Women's Rights in Iran* (2009).
8 The SCCR is a governmental body created soon after the revolution to purge social and cultural institutions, and is charged with expanding and promoting Islamic culture throughout society. It is the primary body regulating the universities and other educational and academic institutions in Iran, for the broad purpose of enriching public culture; see at <http://en.farhangoelm.ir/>, accessed 8 October 2015.

9 See at <http://women.gov.ir/portal/home/?generaltext/80564/80591/>, accessed 8 October 2015.
10 'Centre for Women's Participation, at a glance', Presidential Office, August 2004. The pamphlet also lists 15 'functions', all in tandem with the aims of 'presenting practical strategies for increasing women's participation'.
11 Centre for Women's Participation, March 2003.
12 Osanloo 2006.
13 See at <http://women.gov.ir/portal/home/?generaltext/80564/80591/>, accessed 8 October 2015.
14 See at <http://women.gov.ir/portal/home/?generaltext/80564/80591/>, accessed 8 October 2015.
15 Khatami pointed this out numerous times during his presidency, most notably during the first-ever city-council elections of 1999, which were part of a strategy to decentralise power and allow for greater local self-government, as envisioned in the constitution of the Islamic Republic.
16 One commentator provides a similarly political basis for the introduction of the 2007 Family Protection bill: 'There are many speculations about the reasons the bill has been passed at this time. Some argue that it is the Iranian regime's response to an increasingly powerful women's movement in Iran and their battle to change discriminatory laws, including polygamy. Others claim that the threat of a US military strike against Iran creates an environment of uncertainty, which, combined with an economic crisis and political and social repression, provides a fertile climate for the patriarchs in power in Iran to bring the anti-family bill into public discourse' (Amani 2008).
17 Indictments can be read in English at <http://www.qlineorientalist.com/IranRises/the-indictment/> and <http://www.qlineorientalist.com/IranRises/the-complete-text-of-the-indictment-of-the-second-group-of-accused-in-the-project-for-a-velvet-coup/>, both accessed 17 December 2009.
18 Iranian Students News Agency, 9 August 2008, at <http://www.vekalatonline.ir/index.php?ToDo=ShowArticles&AID=866>, accessed 8 October 2015.

References

Amani, Elahe, 'Widespread opposition to Iran's "Family Protection bill": from bad to worse and beyond ...', 15 August 2008, at <http://www.Iran-women-solidarity.net/spip.phP?article430>, accessed 3 October 2015.

Arjomand, Said Amir, *The Turban for the Crown: The Islamic Revolution in Iran* (Oxford, 1982).

Cottam, Richard W., 'The Iranian revolution'. In Cole, Juan R.I. and Nikki R. Keddie, (eds.), *Shi'ism and Social Protest* (New Haven, CT, 1986), pp. 55–87.

Khomeini, Ruhollah, *Islam and Revolution: Writings and Declarations of Imam Khomeini*, trans. Hamid Algar (Berkeley, CA, 1981).

Millet, Kate, *Going to Iran* (New York, 1982).

Mir-Hosseini, Ziba, *Marriage on Trial: A Study of Islamic Family Law. Iran and Morocco Compared* (London, 1993).
Mutahhari, Ayatollah Morteza, *The System of Women's Rights in Islam*. (Qom, 1981).
Naghibi, Nima, *Rethinking Global Sisterhood: Western Feminism and Iran* (Minneapolis, MN, 2007).
Osanloo, Arzoo, *The Politics of Women's Rights in Iran*. (Princeton, NJ, 2009).
——— 'Islamico-civil rights talk: women, subjectivity and law in Iranian Family Court,' *American Ethnologist*, 33/2 (2006), pp. 191–209.
Paidar, Parvin, *Women and the Political Process in Twentieth-Century Iran* (Cambridge, 1995).
Salimi, Muhammad Husayn (ed.), *Islamic Views on Human Rights: Viewpoints of Iranian Scholars* (New Delhi, 2003).
Soroush, Abdolkarim, *Reason, Freedom and Democracy in Islam: Essential Writings of Abdolkarim Soroush*, trans. Mahmoud Sadri and Ahmad Sadri (Oxford, 2000).
Zubaida, Sami, *Law and Power in the Islamic World* (London, 2005).

4

RETHINKING THE DIFFERENCE BETWEEN FORMAL AND INFORMAL MARRIAGES IN EGYPT*

Nadia Sonneveld

Presenting: Anthony and Cleopatra's Love Story

In the film *Memoirs of a Teenage Girl* the issue of informal marriages is represented by a love story resembling that of Anthony and Cleopatra. Gamila, a young schoolgirl from Cairo's wealthy upper-middle class, wonders why people have eliminated romanticism from their lives. Admiring Cleopatra, who she thinks was strong precisely because of her romanticism, Gamila often dreams that she is living the life of the ancient Ptolemaic Queen. In one dream, a knight on a white horse tells her that if they ever meet again, the fame of their love story will surpass that of Anthony and Cleopatra's.

During a school trip to Upper Egypt, Gamila is stunned when she meets the Anthony of her dream in real life, so feeling certain that she has met him before, she calls him Anthony and herself Cleopatra. Gamila and Anthony, whose real name is Raouf, fall in love, and while Gamila keeps their relationship a secret from her parents, Raouf is quick to introduce Gamila to his mother; an Italian woman who has lost the ability to speak because of a brain tumour. Although surgery could make her speak again, the grief she still feels over her husband's death makes such an operation, in her eyes, pointless.

Claiming to have a mother who kissed his father upon falling in love with him, Raouf is impatient for them to consummate their love in the little hut near the Fayoum Falls, where they are celebrating Raouf's birthday.[1] Gamila, however, wants to marry first; but being in a totally isolated place, without witnesses, Raouf wonders how they can marry straight away. 'Let's marry like our ancestors. I propose to you and you accept, and then we'll announce our marriage,' he suggests; Gamila agrees. To be on the safe side, they also write down on a piece of paper that they both consent to the marriage.

Soon after, Raouf and his mother optimistically leave for Italy. Being very happy with her son's new relationship, she has finally agreed to have the operation in Italy that will give back her ability to speak, and to ask Gamila's family for their daughter's hand.

In Cairo, however, things take a bad turn after Gamila's jealous admirer, Haitham, releases to her headmistress a tape on which he had filmed Gamila and Raouf's night at the Fayoum Falls. When Gamila's mother hears the news of the tape and the secret love affair, she accuses her daughter of being a whore who has tarnished the honour of her family. Gamila protests that she and Raouf are married, but in the absence of witnesses, and with only a sheet of paper to prove the marriage, her mother does not consider it valid. Aware of the suffering she is causing her parents, Gamila feels she has no choice but to commit suicide, as did Cleopatra.

Gamila survives the suicide attempt, only to learn from the doctors in the hospital of an unborn child, who has also survived. The news of the pregnancy infuriates her mother even more, and it is Gamila's paternal aunt who stops her from physically attacking her daughter in hospital. Gamila explains to her aunt and mother that she is determined to keep the baby, and that Raouf will be delighted at the news. And her father, was he not the one who sacrificed his heart to marry his cousin (Gamila's mother) instead of the love of his life? He surely would not want his daughter to suffer the same fate. Accordingly, when Raouf and his mother ask for Gamila's hand, he will be happy to accept.

Yet there is no happy ending. Grieving over his mother, who had died during the operation in Italy, Raouf is alone when he asks for Gamila's hand. Gamila's father accepts, but angrily and feeling he has no other choice. In his eyes Gamila has brought them shame, and when Gamila reminds him of his own love affair, he responds that a man's love is never a crime – he does not get pregnant – but Gamila's love has brought them shame and turned her into a whore.

In the end, Haitham rapes Gamila, causing her to lose the baby. Despite Raouf's reassurance that they will have other babies, Gamila tells him that her romanticism has vanished; she is all bitter cruelty. No longer able to love, she asks Raouf to leave her.

'Semi-Secret' Marriages

Memoirs of a Teenage Girl[2] was broadcast in 2001, a year after a new Personal Status Law created a furore in Egyptian society. The points of controversy included the right of women to travel without the consent of their husband, to divorce unilaterally through a procedure called *khul'*,[3] and for those in informal marriages, to ask for a divorce as long as the marriage could be proven by some form of written evidence. One of the main points of criticism was that women were irrational and emotional beings who needed to be guided by their husbands. Hence it was thought that giving them the freedom to travel, divorce and even marry secretly would lead to chaos and to the breakdown of Egyptian family life.[4]

During the debate, many people had fiercely rejected the legalising of divorces from informal marriages, marriages which were called *'urfi*. Referring to practices that to a great extent matched that in *Memoirs of a Teenage Girl*, it was claimed that the law would legalise marriages which young people had concluded secretly, without the knowledge of their parents, and many feared the number of such marriages would skyrocket. Whereas many young people saw *'urfi* as a way of giving their relationships a degree of religious legitimacy, in the debates *'urfi* was represented as a disguise for prostitution, which would tarnish the reputation of the girl.⁵ No doubt, for many the release of the film confirmed all their worst fears.

Based on ethnographic fieldwork conducted in Egypt, particularly Cairo, during the period May 2003 and September 2005, this chapter will show that the extant representation of informal marriages tells only one part of the story, concealing a reality in which such unions also take the form of a secret *second* marriage. Interestingly, in many a secret second marriage it is the woman who makes a greater financial contribution, and sometimes even marries a man who is her junior. In a country where ideal notions of men and women's roles in marriage, and by extension in society, are still determined by the notion of *kafa'a* and what can be described as the maintenance-obedience relationship, these characteristics of informal marriages demonstrate an inversal of gender roles.

Being a condition for a marriage contract to become binding, the conception of *kafa'a* – as developed by Hanafi jurists – assesses the groom's suitability in such matters as Islamic religion, lineage and financial situation.⁶ More recently, this notion has come to emphasise the groom's ability to provide a dower and to shoulder the financial responsibilities of marital life.⁷ These responsibilities are further established in the legal rights and duties of husbands and wives, as defined succinctly in the maintenance-obedience relationship: in Egypt, the law assigns husbands the legal duty to support their wife and children, and in return wives have a legal duty to be obedient to their husband (Article 1 of Personal Status Law 25 of 1920; Article 11 *bis* 2 of Personal Status Law 100 of 1985). Women who are 'disobedient' lose their right to maintenance. During my fieldwork it became clear that ideas concerning maintenance and obedience play an important role in Egyptian society, not only on a legal but also on a social level. Ideal roles for men and for women in marriage are still determined by this notion, structural changes such as women's inclusion in the workforce and high unemployment rates among men notwithstanding. In this chapter I will show that the reversal of gender roles in informal marriages exemplifies husbands' failure to bear the financial consequences of marital life. This not only challenges husbands' authority (*qiwama*) in the household, it also brings into question wives' duty to remain obedient to their husband.

The reversal of gender roles also characterises many formal marriages, showing that the differences between formal and informal marriages are not as profound as public opinion in Egypt would have us believe – all the more so, since the secrecy for which informal marriages are condemned requires rethinking: while in polygamous marriages, the second marriage often remains 'secret' to the first wife, it simultaneously serves to give the second wife the respectable status of a married woman.[8] With its public face being of paramount importance, this characteristic of informal marriages makes clear that marriage remains the prime means of acquiring a social position, and women have to become obedient, at least symbolically. Given that in some situations it is desirable to make the marriage public, while in others it is not, we could better speak of 'semi-secret' marriages. By elaborating on the notion of secrecy, this paper will examine why the public makes such a rigid distinction between two categories of marriages that often look the same in practice.

Formal and Informal Marriages Distinguished

From a legal point of view it is easy to make a distinction between formal and informal marriages. The former are marriages that are officially registered with the state authorities, while the latter are not. This distinction is probably a relatively new one, since traditionally all marriages were informal in Egypt. Being unions that met Sharia requirements on marriage, they were not registered with the central authorities simply because there was no obligation to do so.[9] It was only at the end of the nineteenth century that registration requirements were issued within the Ottoman Empire.[10] In Egypt, a procedural Personal Status Law, issued in 1931, does not make the registration of marriage compulsory, but nevertheless states that courts are prohibited from hearing a claim concerning a marriage when its existence is denied, unless the marriage is established by virtue of an official marriage document. It seems likely that from that moment onwards unregistered marriages became denoted with the term *'urfi* (customary).

Interestingly, present-day *'urfi* marriages in Egypt have also come to include marriage liaisons that are 'novel' rather than 'customary', and that often do not meet Sharia requirements. In the film described above, for example, Gamila and Raouf's marriage was referred to as an *'urfi* marriage, although there were no witnesses when they proclaimed themselves husband and wife, and Raouf did not pay Gamila a dower. In the same vein, the so-called *misyar* marriages are also frequently put on a par with *'urfi* marriages. *Misyar* marriages are not registered with the relevant authorities, at least not in Egypt.[11] In a *misyar* marriage, husband and wife consent not to live together, and for the husband not to bear any financial responsibility.[12] According to some Egyptian scholars, these novel liaisons are illegitimate or secret *'urfi* marriages, and while a legitimate *'urfi* marriage is not officially documented either, it does fulfil the religious conditions of legitimate matrimony. Other scholars oppose referring to secret marriages as *'urfi* at all; according to them the public should make a distinction between *'urfi* marriages, i.e. those that lack registration with the state authorities but fulfil all the presumed religious conditions, and secret marriages that lack both.[13] Yet, Article 17 of Personal Status Law 1 of 2000, seems to recognise divorces from all these different forms of informal marriages, as it only requires them to be established by *any* written evidence.[14]

Although the difference between formal and informal marriages seems clear from a legal point of view, the practice of marital registration in Egypt is fraught with loopholes, with the result that what looks like an informal marriage can legally speaking be a formal marriage. The fact that an interviewed *ma'dhun*, the civil registrar responsible for registering marriages and divorces, claimed to have put up a billboard saying that he does not register *'urfi* marriages, makes it clear that there are *ma'dhun*s who do register marriages of which the couple's parents and family are oblivious. In other cases, *ma'dhun*s are bribed or fooled into registering polygamous marriages of which the first wife has no knowledge.[15]

In this chapter, I do not intend to establish whether a marriage that looks informal is in legal effect formal. Instead, I examine why the public makes a rigid distinction between these two types of marital unions which in effect often look the same. In the public debate, for example, informal marriages are not only presented as concealed from state authorities but also from parents and family. Their secrecy is associated with images of men's and especially women's excessive and uncontrolled emotions and feelings of lust, and hence of spouses not fulfilling their marital obligations. In the public's eye, formal marriages are the opposite of informal marriages in all respects. They are thought to be open and public; not only are they officially registered with the relevant authorities, but their registration is also thought to go hand in hand with a large wedding party, through which the individual relationship is made public to family, friends and neighbours.[16]

In relation to the alleged publicity of these marriages are notions on wedding preparations, reflecting a strong and persistent perception in Egyptian society that the groom (and his family) must bear the primary burden for the costs of such preparations.[17] Together they make clear that the new relationship will be marked by general assumptions concerning the proper role of men and women in marriage. These, as mentioned earlier, concern a husband's duty to provide maintenance for his wife (and future children) and a wife's duty to work in the house her husband has provided her with. Sonbol also argues that in Jordan at the heart of marriage are a number of assumptions, the most important of which is the responsibility of a husband to support his wife financially.[18]

Why Conclude an Informal Marriage: The Costs of Establishing Marital Life

The controversy surrounding *'urfi* marriages raises the question of who resorts to them. Is the practice of *'urfi* confined to youngsters such as Gamila and Raouf, who are in love and looking for a minimal Islamic standard for premarital sex, and to film stars such as Ahmad al-Fishawi, whose secret *'urfi* marriage with Hind al-Hinnawi brought the issue of *'urfi* marriages to the forefront of public discourse in 2004 and 2005?[19] Or do other social categories also make use of *'urfi*?

My fieldwork in Egypt made it clear that the practice of *'urfi* marriages was not confined to youngsters or film-stars alone. *'Urfi* has been and still is used by women who wish to remarry but who do not want to lose the state pension of their deceased husbands or their fathers.[20]

Divorced women who want to remarry but who are afraid that they will thereby lose custody of their children sometimes remarry through *'urfi* as well. Temporary marriages are also practised in Egypt. In the Red Sea resorts, both married and unmarried Egyptian men wed foreign women. Being in need of money, these men prostitute themselves to women who come to the Red Sea for two or three weeks' holiday. Since Egyptian law forbids Egyptians to share a hotel room with someone they are not married to, these men and their 'brides' conduct temporary *'urfi* marriages.[21] During the summer months, when rich men from the Arab Gulf come to Cairo for a holiday, stories abound of them marrying young girls from the villages surrounding Cairo. By paying a certain amount of *mahr* (dower), these men are said to marry temporarily for the period of the summer, after which they return to their countries leaving the sometimes pregnant girls behind. These marriages are rarely registered by the Egyptian authorities.[22]

Nevertheless, in an article on perceptions of *'urfi* marriages in the Egyptian press, Abaza shows that there was moral condemnation of especially young people and women's loose sexual norms.[23] This assumption was reinforced in 2004 when costume designer Hind al-Hinnawi won a high-profile paternity case against the famous Egyptian actor Ahmad al-Fishawi, after the latter had refused to recognise the baby born of their secret *'urfi* marriage.[24] Her court case is connected with a related point of criticism in the Egyptian debate, namely that informal marriages would not serve to raise a family. For example, the former president of the Maglis al-Dawla (the State Council, an administrative court) believes that: 'In most cases [...] youths resort to such a marriage to fulfil a sexual desire, but not to form a family – which should be the main target of marriage.'[25]

Interestingly, he added that: 'The husband resorts to this type of marriage because he cannot fulfil the financial obligations of traditional matrimony. According to Sharia, however, the man should be financially capable of getting married [...].'[26] His statement seems to imply that *'urfi* should not only be seen in relationship to fulfilling a psychical need, but also as an option open to men who want to marry and raise a family, but who do not have the financial means to bear the high costs of the wedding and the subsequent establishment of marital life.²⁷ This ability of men – or their inability – is captured in the notion of *kafa'a* mentioned above, i.e. the equality and suitability of the groom. Although under Egyptian law the prevalent opinion of Abu Hanifa (i.e. the Hanafi school of law) must be applied when the issue of *kafa'a* is brought before the court,²⁸ in other Arab states, such as Jordan, the notion of suitability is reduced to financial terms: it now 'only' requires a groom to pay the prompt dower (*muqaddam al-sadaq*) and maintenance (*nafaqa*).²⁹ This is a condition many Egyptian men fail to meet, in large part due to a combination of the high costs of marriage preparations and high unemployment rates among young people.³⁰

In the media and among themselves, Egyptians often express their worries about the financial expense which marriage (of their children) entails.³¹ Apart from organising a large and expensive wedding party, it is claimed that much money must be invested in the *shabka* (engagement presents, often consisting of gold), a marital home and furniture. Singerman and Ibrahim estimate that the total cost of marriage in Egypt was four and a half times higher than annual GNP per capita in 1998.³² During my fieldwork, I noticed that when talking about marriage, Egyptians often point an accusatory finger at the future wife and her family, who are said to overcharge the future groom and his family, or worse, abuse a husband's financial investment in the marriage for years on end. This also transpired in the debate on *khul'* where it was claimed that women would divorce their husbands and use the latter's investment in the marriage to marry other men.³³ One informant even suggested introducing the so-called *zawag al-frind* ('friend marriage') in Egypt. In 2003, Shaykh Zindani issued a *fatwa* suggesting the idea of a *zawag al-frind* for Muslims living in the West. In order to prevent illicit relationships, the Sheikh had suggested that youngsters should be able to marry each other while continuing to live with their parents until they were financially capable of buying or renting a flat and establishing real marital life. Although the Sheikh had addressed a Muslim audience in the West, my informant believed that he was also surreptitiously trying to change marital customs in the Middle East by encouraging the family of the bride to lower their financial demands towards the groom.³⁴ In a study on *'urfi* and *misyar* marriages in Egypt and the United Arab Emirates, Hasso also pays attention to the problems many young men, especially those from the middle classes, encounter in dealing with the high costs of traditional marriage and how it leads them to marry through *'urfi* or *misyar*.[35] Arabi claims that *misyar* marriages in Saudi Arabia are conducted by young men. Desiring to marry, but unable to meet the financial expectations of traditional marriage, a *misyar* marriage becomes a viable option.[36]

What seems to be in contradistinction to the notion of men's huge financial investments in marriage preparations is the increasing contribution of the bride (and her family) to the marriage costs. My fieldwork in Egypt made it clear that putting the emphasis on husbands' contribution to marriage preparations concealed women's increasing financial involvement in this matter.[37] In this light, Singerman states that:

> [...] the per cent of women reporting equal sharing of costs increased from only four per cent in the 1960's marriage cohort to 25 per cent in the 1990–1995 cohort. Even more revealing, because of the role reversal it implies, 15 per cent of marriages contracted in the 1990s involved a *lower* contribution from the groom's side (compared to only 6 per cent reporting a lower groom's contribution in the 1960s.[38]

This raises the question of why women would enter marriages in which the additional financial burden of marriage preparations is imposed on them, and most likely that of marital life itself too. According to Singerman and Ibrahim, this development results from the fact that especially younger women have entered the workforce.[39] Women I met in the field often had another explanation, claiming that women's increasing financial contribution was a result of (marriageable-age) females outnumbering males in Egyptian society by a ratio of 3:2. They claimed that men could choose whomever they wished to marry; and unless women wanted to end up in a polygamous marriage they had better not set their marital demands too high. In a study on the dowry and the position of single women in Bangladesh, Rozario shows that, as in Egypt, people tend to think that there is a surplus of unmarried women. This leads parents who are eager to marry off their daughters to refrain from asking for a dower, and rather to pay large dowries to the groom (and his family) instead.[40]

According to Fargues, this perception of a surplus of marriageable Egyptian women is accurate, but not because females outnumber males in Egyptian society.[41] According to the Central Agency for Public Mobilisation and Statistics, there were 33,542,913 females and 35,105,576 males in Egypt in 2004.[42] Instead, it is the frequency of marriage and an important age difference between the two spouses that explains the surplus of marriageable women.[43] Some women, moreover, were of the opinion that the perceived surplus in Egypt was leading to an increasing number of marriages in which the groom is not only younger than the bride, but also from a lower class. Statistics confirm that these phenomena, which defy the notion of *kafa'a* and which are frowned upon in Egyptian society, are now growing in number. In the 1990s, in three age groups, more than a quarter of the official marriage contracts were between an older wife and a younger husband.[44] In the 1960s, by contrast, such marriages represented only 2 per cent of all (formal) marriage contracts.[45] Within such marriages, husbands are often from lower-class backgrounds compared to their wives, and these men marry older women on condition that the latter will not burden them financially.[46] Providing women with a way out of their unmarried status, these marriages make clear that any marriage is seen as better than being single or alone, or, as the well-known Egyptian proverb goes: 'The shadow of a man is better than the shadow of a wall.' By also providing young men with an opportunity to marry, the proverb is equally applicable the other way round.

While the numbers presented above refer to formal marriages, during the fieldwork I also came across informal marriages concluded between a man and a woman from different class backgrounds who both benefited from the marriage in ways similar to those of the formal marriages mentioned above: where the man was exempted from bearing the costs of the wedding and of marital life, the woman escaped the status of spinsterhood or that of a divorcee. These informal and formal marriages shared many similar features, and the differences between them were not as profound as the Egyptian public and the Egyptian press believed them to be. Interestingly, some of these marriages took the form of a second marriage. The story of a divorced Cairene woman from the lower-middle classes will serve as an example. This woman, to whom I have given the fictitious name Nura, willingly entered into a polygamous union, not because she was looking for a provider, but because she believed a polygamous marriage was a way to safeguard her freedom to work and to remain independent.

Presenting: Nura's Polygamous Marriage

I first met Nura in 2004 in the Cairene court where she had filed for a *khul'* divorce. Being a mother of three young children, this woman, in her early thirties and from the lower-middle class, had several reasons for divorcing her husband. He regularly mistreated her, both physically and verbally; also, they often fought because he did not want to work, and at a certain point he was not even able to do so as he had to serve a three-year sentence for fraud. Just before his imprisonment, he married a second wife, a divorcee who, like Nura, came to live in the house of her new mother-in-law. In addition, Nura's husband also had a habit of divorcing Nura by pronouncing *talaq* every time emotions were running high. This, Nura emphasised, had caused her much anxiety and after he married his second wife, she decided to file for a *khul'* divorce. The divorce came at a high cost, as she was forced to leave her three children in her mother-in-law's house. Although she had started working again, her salary was too small to allow her to provide for her children. In addition, the tiny house of Nura's old and handicapped mother in a poor Cairene neighbourhood – which lacked running water – could not accommodate three children and their mother.

During and after the *khul'* procedure, Nura often claimed that she never wanted to marry again. Marital life had disappointed her and instead of becoming the new wife of a husband who might forbid her to work again, she sought to find a second job in order to be able to rent a flat and take her three children back into her care. But a year after her divorce she expressed a desire to remarry: societal pressure had become too great and she was no longer able to endure the way her colleagues were gossiping about her single status.

The first man who came to ask for her hand was the son of her mother's neighbour. Although he was already married with children, Nura claimed that from the time they were little he had been in love with her. His family, however, had wanted him to marry a woman from their own family. But now, after many years, he proposed to marry Nura and take her as his second wife. Since he did not wish his wife and children to know, he wanted to marry Nura through *'urfi*. Nura wanted to accept his offer, but because his family took care of her handicapped mother, she was afraid that they would find out and stop caring for her mother, who was living on her own after the death of Nura's father, more than five years previously.

Other men came to ask for Nura's hand but since they were all widowers she refused to marry them. She was afraid they would want her to give up her new job and take care of their household and children instead, in much the same way her first husband had demanded of her. Nura, who was struggling to get her three children back, did not want to become dependent on a man again, and to take care of children who were not even hers. Nura decided to start looking for a husband herself, and found a man who, again, was married with children. He was looking for a second wife because, so she told me, his first wife was no longer a real *zawga* (wife) to him. Like Nura's old neighbour, he did not want his first wife and children to find out.

Whereas in the public debate on *khul'* opponents had frequently claimed that women in a *khul'* procedure would want to divorce to marry more handsome or wealthier men, the husband of Nura's choice was not rich, as he had to work in two jobs to eke out a living. They agreed that he would pay for the rent of the flat and visit her at least once a week, while Nura would furnish the apartment. They concluded the marriage in the presence of a small group of people, including Nura's sister, but excluding Nura's mother, who only heard of it a few weeks after it had been concluded. Some months into the marriage, Nura started complaining that her husband often did not pay the rent; even worse, when he visited her she herself had to pay for his cigarettes and for the food she cooked him. Moreover, since it was important to Nura that the neighbours knew her to be married, she felt rather uncomfortable when he started visiting her only once a week. At a later phase in their marriage she would even stop complaining about the fact that he hardly contributed to the rent of the flat, but the occasional nature of his visits remained a great worry to her.

Where in the public debate informal marriages are thought of as concluded secretly by young people who are in love, and formal marriages as involving a public ceremony and including specific marital rights and duties, Nura's marriage does not fit either one of these categories. During my fieldwork it became clear that polygamous marriages are an option used by divorced, and to a lesser extent, widowed women. Under societal pressure to remarry, but with protocols which dictate that a woman who herself is no longer a virgin cannot marry a man who has never been married before, divorced women lack options. They are able to marry a younger man in the way described above, a widower, a divorced man or an already married man, and I found that the last of these options was not at all uncommon. In some cases, the woman felt that she had no choice and that 'the shadow of a man was better than the shadow of a wall.' Other divorced women, however, saw marriage to an already married father as a means of achieving a situation that would give them the maximum possible amount of freedom and independence. While the second marriage would give them the status of being married, it would simultaneously provide them with an opportunity to continue working, as married fathers who already had a family to maintain would rarely object to their having a job or a career.

Now one could object and claim that Nura's is an exceptional case, since statistics show that only a small percentage of husbands marry more than one wife. Cuno notes that the proportion of Muslim men in polygamous marriages is declining, from 2.5 per cent of married Muslim men in 1976 to 1.9 per cent in 1986.[47] Although Fargues is of the opinion that polygyny has never been common practice among Arab Muslims, he nevertheless notes a rise in polygamy during the last quarter of the twentieth century.[48] Statistics by the National Centre for Sociological and Criminological Research (NCSCR) support this: they show that during the first three years of marriage 25 per cent of

Egyptian husbands marry another wife. Some 70 per cent of these second marriages end up in divorce.[49] I was unable to access the statistics myself and find out how the research centre had arrived at such a high number of polygyny cases, and whether the number included informal marriages. However, I have decided to include them at this point since the NCSCR's findings are in line with the reality which I observed in Egypt, where a significant number of husbands leave the marital home for another woman without divorcing their first wife. Even when such marriages are registered with the *ma'dhun*, in most cases the second marriage is kept a secret from the first wife. This makes it clear that we should take into consideration the possibility that polygynous marriages might occur more frequently than statistics suggest,[50] and perhaps more importantly, that characteristics ascribed only to informal marriages often pertain to both categories of marriage.

Becoming a Second Wife by Choice?

> I was relieved when he wanted to marry this other woman. I did not want to have sex with him anymore and I wanted him to be occupied with someone else. We all lived in the same house. When he died, I was happy and felt strong and that my life was again in my own hands... No one can talk about me for I am a good woman and, to tell you the truth, I do not care. I know myself and I am happy without a man (Umm Sherif, a 50-year-old-widow from a lower-class area in Cairo, the mother of five children).[51]

Taking into account the alleged attributes of informal marriages, there are several reasons to believe that the public would categorise Nura's marriage as informal. Obviously, the fact that the two men whom Nura considered marrying wanted to marry her in secret is a strong indicator of an illegitimate *'urfi* marriage. As married fathers, both men hoped that their second marriage would offer them something which their first marriage could not. According to Nura, they both wished to marry her for sexual fulfillment, and, in line of this, for the freedom they would have with her.[52] They did not want to raise a new family, and Nura and her new husband even took great care to prevent a pregnancy. What also strongly points in the direction of an informal marriage is the fact that Nura's husband did not provide maintenance and housing. Even though he had promised to pay the rent of her flat before they married, Nura often complained that he was not living up to this promise, worse even, that his visits were a financial burden for her. He had not even given her a *dibla* (wedding ring) at the time of their marriage, a fact which she tried to hide from her colleagues by telling them that he had given her a refrigerator instead. All this deviates from the features of formal marriage in Egypt as defined in social perceptions that see men as investing the revenues of years of hard labour in expensive wedding celebrations and in the establishment of marital life.

In discussions about polygamy, the woman is generally seen as a victim, a person who submits to a man's sexual desires in return for protection, maintenance and housing. At the beginning of the twentieth century Egyptian men and women from the upper classes revolted against the institution of polygyny. Qasim Amin and Muhammad Abduh, for example, were famous opponents of it, and the Egyptian Feminist Union fought hard to abolish it from the Personal Status Law.[53] Yet, where Turkey and Tunisia have abolished polygamy, Egypt is among those countries where the legislature has made only token attempts to curtail husbands' rights to it. In Egypt, the husband needs to notify his first wife of the second marriage and include in the marriage contract the names and addresses of all his wives. The wife also has the right to request a divorce on the basis of polygyny. To this day, advocates of women's rights are still trying to abolish the practice.

Where advocates of women's rights view polygamy as detrimental to women, Umm Sherif, quoted at the beginning of this section, was relieved when her husband married a second wife. Nura too preferred a polygamous to a monogamous marriage, even if this meant that she would have no right to housing and maintenance. Social pressure played an important part in her decision to remarry: she was tired of being 'outside the social structure' and of living in a society in which a woman's position is defined by her relation to a man. My fieldwork made it very clear that unmarried women are considered a threat to married women, and are under a great deal of pressure to remarry. It was not so much Nura's wish to remarry but rather her taking the initiative to look for a new husband and deciding whom she wanted to marry that amounted to going against the grain of socio-religious Egyptian customs. Women are not supposed to take an active role in the search for a marriage partner, although legal requirements with regard to the marital proposal (*ijab*) and acceptance (*qubul*) state that the proposal and acceptance can be expressed by either party.[54] Nura defied such notions, because she did not want to give up the small measure of freedom she had gained after her divorce, and for that reason she was prepared to enter into a polygamous marriage, and in doing so to give up her right to maintenance (*nafaqa*) and housing. These were the rights she was entitled to during her first marriage, but was unable to secure; she hoped to attain them through her own labour, and she did not consider giving up her new job, however meagre its salary.

The picture of a woman preferring a polygamous marriage to a monogamous one for very pragmatic reasons contrasts significantly with the image of the young and self-proclaimed 'romantic and overemotional' Gamila, who in the film was looking for real love. Nura had been married before, and had reached the conclusion that marital life was disappointing, but unavoidable in a society which sees unmarried and especially divorced women as a threat. Her marriage to a married man neither served to raise another family nor secured her any financial rights: it functioned only in response to a social protocol: being, albeit only nominally, under the guidance and obedience of a husband. In fact, to a large extent Nura's marital situation resembled that of a controversial *misyar* marriage.

Misyar Marriages and the Issue of Husbands' *Qiwama*

In 1996, the Grand Mufti of Saudi Arabia, 'Abd al-Aziz Ibn Baz, issued a landmark fatwa that paved the way for the legalisation of *misyar* marriages.[55] In Saudi Arabia, fatwas issued by the Grand Mufti automatically take on the status of law, and hence he was according legal permission for a type of marital union that had been spreading in Saudi Arabia for the previous decade and a half. According to local opinion in Egypt, the *fatwa* was subsequently brought to Egypt by Egyptian men working as migrant workers in Saudi Arabia.

In a *misyar* marriage husband and wife agree contractually not to live together, and the husband is not expected to bear any financial responsibility for his wife with regard to housing and maintenance (*nafaqa*). The couple also agree that he visits her only occasionally, and that the marriage remains on such a basis.[56] Instead of living in her husband's marital home, the wife will remain with her family.[57] Generally, the woman also accepts a condition that the marriage is not made public.[58]

Misyar marriages in Saudi Arabia are also related to polygamy. As a marriage agent claimed in an interview: 'Married men are more numerous than bachelors in contracting this marriage which is without commitment [...] This marriage is popular with already married men since their [previous] wife and children are unaware of their [new] marriage'.[59] Secrecy *vis-à-vis* the first wife, in particular, excited much controversy in Saudi Arabia, as did the fact that husbands in *misyar* marriages do not provide for their wives and any children that may result from the marriage. In his well-known and controversial 1998 television declaration on al-Jazeera, Yusuf al-Qaradawi also related *misyar* to polygamy, saying that in most cases a *misyar* marriage constitutes a second or third marriage, and that he had not come across cases in which a husband's first marriage was a *misyar* marriage.[60] *Misyar* marriages are often kept secret from the first wife,[61] even though Saudi law requires that they be made public. That is to say, their public face requires more than the presence of two witnesses and the *wali* (male guardian) of the bride at the time of its formal registration.[62]

In a way, however, it would be wrong to label *misyar* marriages as 'secret', as it is of paramount importance to the second wife to announce her marital status to the outside world. This raises the question as to why women would agree to enter a marriage that is often denigrated as prostitution and in which they have to renounce their financial rights in return for the status of a married woman. According to Arabi, the education of an increasing number of women plays an important role in this development. Pursuing their education, women postpone marriage until they are in their late twenties. With women's average age at marriage still being in the late teens, these women will almost literally study themselves out of the marriage market, but through a *misyar* marriage they can marry and at the same time safeguard their independence and autonomy.

Although Yusuf al-Qaradawi did not mean to encourage people to conclude *misyar* marriages, he nevertheless claimed that they were permissible (*halal*), and typically practised by professional and financially independent women: 'If a woman is rich and a professional, she does not need financial support. It is a way for rich women to separate sexuality from obligations.'[63] This is well exemplified by the newspaper story of a 46-year-old Egyptian professional woman who became the second wife of a married man. She says: 'The concierge, the grocer and the neighbours show more respect towards me now than when I was single.' This woman sees her husband three or four times a week: 'It suits me fine. I have to travel a lot because of my work, and not having a husband at home means I'm not tied down and can move when the job calls.' Entitled 'Part Time Marriage: The Rage in Egypt', the newspaper article argues that this kind of convenience is appealing to more and more Egyptians, of both sexes.[64] In another case, a 42-year-old female Egyptian journalist claims that her work keeps her so busy that she feels that her husband needs a second wife. Although her husband refused, she has started a campaign in favour of polygyny, and even helped to form an association, Al-Tayseer, which promotes the idea.[65]

During the fieldwork, I found that women have different ways of dealing with their unmarried status, and that their contrasting approaches cannot solely be explained by their class differences. During her first marriage, Nura's co-wife was a divorcee who, according to Nura, was willing to marry a married father with a prison sentence because she felt that, as a divorcee, she had little choice. Nura's second and polygamous marriage was a deliberate choice. Whereas some professional and financially independent women would rather live alone than in bad company, others preferred polygamous unions, precisely because they were professional women who felt that their work did not allow them to marry in the conventional way.

It remains to be seen to what extent *misyar* marriages increase women's freedom and independence in Saudi Arabia. Where Arabi sees such marriages as a sign of Saudi women's empowerment, he simultaneously questions whether they will give a wife greater autonomy and freedom, as her parents will take over her husband's responsibilities.[66] In Egypt, however, the authority of the husband is not replaced by that of the wife's family, at least not in the fieldwork cases I came across. They show that *misyar*-resembling marriages in Egypt enable the wife to leave the parental home and to start living on her own. It undoubtedly leads to the establishment of different marital relationships: how can a husband in such cases demand that his wife remain obedient to him while she has her own domicile and sources of income? Although an issue explicitly raised by the questioner, 'The fatwa [of the late Mufti of Saudi Arabia, Ibn Baaz] remained silent on the basic structure of maintenance (*nafaqa*), of which the provision of marital domicile and sustenance by the husband was the corner stone'.[67]

In his al-Jazeera interview on *misyar* marriages, Yusuf al-Qaradawi was also asked several times how the non-provision of sustenance would affect husbands' *qiwama* (authority). He responded by saying that even when husbands in such cases do not provide maintenance (*nafaqa*) and housing – because the wife is more affluent, or because the husband already has a family and children – they still have authority in the marriage. After all, he added, when in a 'normal' marriage the wife provides for her husband, this also does not render the marriage void, nor does it affect his *qiwama*. Moreover, in responding to a question on whether *misyar* marriages would open the door to poor men depriving rich women of their capital, al-Qaradawi again drew a parallel between the practice of formal and informal marriages, saying that he was continually receiving telephone calls and letters from formally married working women whose husbands tried to appropriate the money they were earning.

By comparing practices in *misyar* marriages to those in some formal marriages, al-Qaradawi, whether intentionally or not, was making a number of points about changes taking place in formal Muslim marriage practices. Most important was his pointing out that working women in formal marriages bring in a source of income that sometimes exceeds that of their husbands, and that he did not expect practices in informal marriages to be any different. The fact that his remarks encountered stiff resistance, from both the host of the show and the viewers, reflected unease about a growing number of women generating sources of income of their own, undermining husbands' *qiwama* in the process. The host and the viewers clearly felt that this was the main factor justifying a husband's authority over his wife. Al-Qaradawi's remarks made it abundantly clear that it was not only husbands in informal marriages but also husbands in many a formal marriage who failed to live up to their marital duties, and it was perhaps this that was most unsettling. With formal and informal marriages sharing many characteristics, there is not only a need to rethink the difference between these two types of marriage, but also the approach to the study of marriage in Egypt and in the Arab world as a whole.

Rethinking the Difference Between Formal and Informal Marriages

Hasso describes *'urfi* and *misyar* as a challenge to 'traditional' marriages, suggesting that in the latter it is the man who bears most of the financial costs, and who provides for his wife throughout the marriage.[68] According to Abaza, these marriages are governed by the Muslim Personal Status Laws as first codified in the 1920s, while '[m]ost, if not all, of the [*'urfi*] marriages covered in the press today are not registered under this law'.[69] In this chapter, however, I have tried to make it clear that while the registration requirement allows for a distinct legal separation between formal and informal marriages, in social practice it is actually not easy to classify a marriage as either one or the other. For instance, it was unclear to me whether Nura's marriage was formal or informal. Although she had admitted that she was prepared to marry through *'urfi* during the period in which she was looking for a new husband, and notwithstanding the fact that her polygamous marriage to a great extent resembled a *misyar* marriage, after her marriage she always evaded questions about her status.

The purpose of this chapter is not to assess whether Nura married formally or informally, but to examine why formal and informal marriages are being contrasted so strongly in the public debate, while in reality it is not at all easy to differentiate between them. Such an analysis signals the need for a different approach to the study of marriage in Egypt and the Arab world. According to Drieskens:

> Demographers have drawn our attention to the increase of celibacy, the reduction of the age difference between the partners and the fluctuations in divorce rates in the contemporary Middle East. Nevertheless, few anthropologists have focused on these changes and on the implications of these changes on social relationships and on marriage in particular.[70]
>
> While the patterns and processes of marriage have changed at accelerated levels, our social understanding of them has remained slow in its pace and classical in its outlook.[71]

The mere fact that there are women who marry husbands with no intention of establishing a household or of raising a family, and who express a desire to become financially independent, is an indication that the norms of Egyptian marriage and the family unit have changed. Contrary to both legal and social perceptions, some husbands do not provide for their wives at all. Although this is seen as a characteristic of informal marriages, it should not conceal the fact that it applies to many formally registered marriages too.

When the reality of marital life defies the notion of *kafa'a* as well as the maintenance-obedience relationship, women no longer have an obligation, at least in theory, to remain obedient to their husbands. In practice, however, the issue of non-maintenance by the husband attracted little attention in the public debate, or, as in the case of al-Qaradawi, was presented as not affecting the authority *(qiwama)* of the husband. Yet the unease with which his words were met, and the vigour of the public debate on informal marriages, point out that when masculinity is defined as the capacity to provide for the family through a salary, this condemns men who, for whatever reason, are unable to work, 'to perceive economic problems as castration threats'; '[...] a woman who earns a [larger] salary will be perceived as either masculine or castrating. If the privileges of men become more easily accessible to women, then men will be perceived as becoming more feminine.'[72] Hence Arabi's statement that while the introduction of new structures of marriage did not change the authority of the husband on a symbolic level, in practice *misyar* marriages have changed the dictum that in return for their husbands' maintenance wives must pledge obedience to them.[73]

In Egypt, the notion of women's mobility – the right to travel – serves best to illustrate the ambivalent legal position on women's role in marriage. During the Nasser era, women were given the same constitutional rights as men. Mobility, however, remained a notion for which women still required the permission of their husbands or other male guardians. As long as the husband was providing for his wife, she was still legally obliged to remain obedient to him. If she rebelled, by leaving the premises of the house without his permission, the husband could bring a *ta'a* claim in court, and if he won the judge would declare the wife *nashiz* (recalcitrant) and deprive her of the right to be maintained by her husband. In the first year of the twenty-first century, a ruling of the High Constitutional Court seemed to give recognition to the fact that women's place in society was not confined to the home by giving them the right to travel without their husband's permission. According to Personal Status Law 100 of 1985, however, women still need their husbands' permission, not only to travel abroad but also to leave the house in the first place. Just as in the Nasser era, a husband can still bring a disobedience claim in the courts if his wife leaves the marital home without his permission. With a woman's duty to obey her husband remaining unchanged, she was exposed to what Yüksel would call 'half-baked' reforms, which contained conflicting messages about her role in marriage and society.[74] Such reforms make clear that notions of men and women's proper roles in marriage have such strong roots in society that it renders the legal abolishment of men's authority and women's obedience very difficult.

When legal and social perceptions concerning the roles of men and women in marriage deviate from the reality of marital life in Egypt, it forces a number of women – most particularly those who have been married before, and who have experience of maintenance and housing being difficult to secure through a 'traditional' marriage – to look for a solution where they will attain the best of both worlds: acquiring the respectable status of a married woman, while at the same time enjoying a measure of freedom and financial independence. Their semi-secret polygamous marriages are the tip of the pyramid, brief glimpses of something largely hidden.

Conclusion

Although very controversial, the practice of informal *'urfi* marriages in Egypt, especially that of polygamous marriages, has shown that the differences between formal and informal marriages are neither as many nor as profound as the Egyptian public debate seemed to assume. Two features were mentioned in that debate to denote the difference with formal marriages. First, and most controversial, was the secrecy allegedly surrounding informal marriages. Not only are they kept a secret from the state but also from parents and family, with the latter case being regarded as more problematic. In this study it was shown that informal marriages are often only partially secret. In fact, the publicity of the marriage *vis-à-vis* the outside world is of paramount importance to the informally married wife, and her main reason for concluding such a marriage in the first place. This feature of informal marriages blurs the distinction between the two categories of marriages.

The second feature, though not mentioned as frequently as the first, concerned the husband's financial input into the marriage. The Egyptian legislation dictates that a husband's ability to pay a dower and to provide maintenance (*nafaqa*) is a requirement for the contract to be binding (*kafa'a*). Informal marriages subvert this obligation by allowing a man to marry without having any responsibility to provide sustenance for his wife. But according to Egypt's Personal Status Law, even when a woman is wealthy or has her own sources of income, it is still the husband's duty to provide financially and materially for his wife (Article 1 of Personal Status Law 25 of 1920). Husbands' failure to meet their financial requirements, however, was an issue which did not receive due attention in Egypt. Instead, the press and popular culture made it look as if informal *'urfi* marriages were only a means for young people and film stars to have premarital sex without the knowledge of their parents.

My research revealed that the practice of informal marriages, however, is not confined to youngsters and film stars, but also takes the form of relationships in which women who are divorced or widowed, or who have passed the socially-expected age for marriage, marry men who lack the financial means to bear the huge costs of the wedding preparations and to establish traditional marital life. Most interestingly, informal marriages also take the form of polygamy. While this might not be a novelty, contemporary polygamous marriages are concluded by women who provide for their husbands, instead of the other way around, and who use the marriage institution to obtain the socially-acceptable status of a wife. These polygamous marriages are the tip of the iceberg; only a glimpse of something largely hidden, namely, husbands' difficulties in providing maintenance, and women's growing contribution to the household economy.

The question of how women's financial input affects the maintenance-obedience equation is a question which did not gain much public exposure, making clear that inability on the part of a husband to provide maintenance for his wife was a contributing factor to the public's preoccupation with what is regarded as secret and informal marriages. By contrasting formal marriages with some types of informal marriages – the secret and sexually-motivated love marriages of young people – the picture of the strong and authoritative man was kept alive.

From a legal perspective it is difficult to say whether the number of unregistered marriages is increasing, and the aim of this chapter was not to answer that question. By working with the notion of 'semi-secret' marriages, it was made explicit that from a social perspective the distinction between formal and *'urfi* marriages is unclear and in need of rethinking. Seen in this way, the latter are indeed increasing, but not because so-called emotional women and young people were given the freedom to marry and divorce of their own free will – rather because many pragmatic women, like Nura, were forced to come face to face with reality: a reality which promotes a model of marriage in which the husband provides and the wife obeys, and the everyday reality which proved the necessity for women to stand on their own feet.

Notes

* The author wishes to thank the Leiden University Centre for the Study of Islam and Society (LUCIS) for generously funding the writing of this article.

1. The Fayoum Waterfalls are located in al-Fayoum oasis, an hour's drive from Cairo.
2. Directed by al-Daghaydi.
3. Before the implementation of *khul'* in 2000, Egyptian women could only divorce with the consent of their husband. When a husband did not consent, the wife had no other choice but to file for a judicial divorce in court, where she had to prove her just reasons for divorce before a judge. Such court cases can easily take up to several years, and do not guarantee finalisation of a divorce.
4. *Al-sha'b*, 18 January 2000: 3; *al-jumhuriya*, 20 January 2000; *al-wafd*, 26 January 2000: 1; 28 January 2000: 3; *Cairo Times*, 20–6 January 2000; *al-'arabi*, 30 January 2000.
5. Cf. *al-wafd*, 30 September 1999; 1 October 1999; *al-ahram*, 3 January 2000; 17 January 2000; 29 January 2000; 2 February 2000. See also Abaza 2001: 20–1; Zubaida 2003: 180–1.
6. El Alami 1992: 69–70.
7. Welchman 2000: 99.
8. In this chapter, I use the terms 'polygamy' and 'polygyny' interchangeably.
9. In classical Islamic law, a marriage does not need to be registered in order to become valid. Instead of registration, it must meet other requirements, such as the consent of both parties to the marriage – and in most schools of Islamic law the consent of the *wali* (marriage guardian) is also a condition for a previously unmarried girl to marry; the presence of witnesses – which means that the marriage has been announced and made public; the payment of a dower; and *kafa'a* – compatibility between the bride and groom in terms of their social status; see El Alami 1992: 65, 68–74, 107–8.
10. Cuno 2008: 198–200; Welchman 2007: 53.
11. In Saudi Arabia, *misyar* marriages were legalised in 1996, after a landmark fatwa by the Grand Mufti. It is sometimes claimed that such marriages can be registered with the state authorities in the United Arab Emirates; cf. al-Jazeera, 3 May 1998; Hasso: 2007: 63. Welchman, however, claims that while there were reports that one purpose of the 2003 draft law was to recognise *misyar* marriages, the Explanatory Memorandum to the law, as promulgated in 2005, makes it clear that stipulations waiving a husband's responsibility to pay his wife maintenance are void (2007: 54–5, 103).
12. Cf. Arabi 2001: 147–68; Welchman 2007: 102–5.
13. *Al-ahram*, 17 January 2000; 2 February 2000.
14. Article 17 of Law no. 1/2000, section 2, states: 'In cases of negation/denial, the actions arising from marriage contracts shall not be accepted in respect of the facts subsequent to August 1, 1931 – unless the marriage is established

by virtue of an official document. However, actions for forced divorce (*tatliq*), or for dissolution (*faskh*) exclusively shall be accepted to each case, if the marriage is established by any written evidence.'

15 The first wife has a legal right to be notified of her husband's second marriage. Although it is the legal duty of the *ma'dhun* to make sure she is so notified, my fieldwork in Egypt made it clear that sometimes the *ma'dhun* is bribed not to let the first wife know, while in other cases husbands give the *ma'dhun* a false address.

16 Welchman also claims that formal registration, rather than unofficial documentation, is sometimes claimed to help to fulfil the Sharia requirement of publicity for the marriage (2007: 54).

17 Cf. Singerman 2008: 40; Sonneveld: 2009.

18 Sonbol 2003: 32.

19 *Al-Ahram Weekly*, 29 December 2005–4 January 2006.

20 See also Abaza 2002.

21 See also Abdalla 2007.

22 Mikhail 2002: 43–9.

23 In the case of Turkey, Yilmaz also argues that young people, usually university students, increasingly contract (religious) marriages in secret, without informing their parents (the *gizli* – hidden – marriages referred to above). In this way they hope to avoid the stigma of pre-marital intercourse, although the real intention might not be to conclude an official marriage in the future. Apart from the fact that religious marriages are not recognised by the state, parents similarly do not acknowledge these secret marriages (2003: 39). In a study of informal marriages in a Damascus court, the prevalence of the practice is not related to youngsters and university students; according to judges and lawyers working there, conscripted soldiers form the largest group of men entering into such contracts. After completion of their military service, they often officially register the marriage; see Carlisle 2008: 11–14.

24 Abaza 2002.

25 *Al-Ahram Weekly*, 18–24 February 1999; see also *Middle East Times*, 7 April 2000.

26 Ibid.

27 In Iran and Lebanon, young people from Shia communities also conclude temporary *mutʿa* marriages, because they do not have the financial means to marry and establish a family; see Mervin 2008.

28 According to Article 280 of Draft Ordinance 78 of 1931; see El Alami 1992: 70.

29 Welchman 2000: 99.

30 Singerman 2008.

31 For an analysis of the perceived Egyptian marriage crisis in the early twentieth century, see Kholoussy 2010.

32 Singerman and Ibrahim 2003: 92.

33 Sonneveld 2009.

34 According to al-Jazeera, the fatwa sparked much public debate among scholars of Islamic *fiqh* and the authorities (*awliya' al-umur*). It was also discussed in an episode of al-Jazeera's *li-l-nisa' faqat*, 18 August 2003.
35 Hasso 2007; see also Singerman 2010.
36 Arabi 2001: 155.
37 Sonneveld 2009. In an anthropological study of the lives of low-income families in Cairo, Hoodfar also notes that the family of the bride is increasingly expected to contribute more to marriage preparations (1997: 66).
38 Singerman 2010: 40.
39 Singerman and Ibrahim 2003: 98.
40 Rozario 1998.
41 Fargues 2001.
42 Central Agency for Public Mobilisation and Statistics 2004:6.
43 Fargues 2001.
44 The three age groups in question are: the wife's age is 25–9 and the husband's 20–4; the wife's age is 30–4 and the husband's 20–4; the wife's age is 30–4 and the husband's 25–9; see Osman and Shahd 2003: 54.
45 Osman and Shahd.
46 Ibid: 58.
47 Cuno 2008: 206.
48 Fargues 2001: 254.
49 *Al-Ahram Weekly*, 26 February–3 March 2004.
50 See also Hill 1979: 89.
51 Bibars 2001: 64–5.
52 Haeri claims that the main reason for concluding a temporary marriage in Shia Iran (*mut'a* marriage) is sexual pleasure (1989). In a study of HIV and men's extramarital relationships in Mexico, Nigeria, Uganda, Vietnam and Papua New Guinea, Hirsch et al (2009) claim that the failure of men to fulfil their marital obligations and to be good breadwinners leads them to engage in sexual relationships outside marriage that are free of these expectations.
53 Badran 1995.
54 El Alami 1992: 20–1.
55 Arabi 2001: 147.
56 Cf. Arabi 2001; Welchman 2000: 102–5.
57 Arabi 2001.
58 Welchman 2000: 103. A Lebanese Shia cleric has claimed that Sunni *misyar* marriages to a great extent resemble Shia *mut'a* marriages, in his eyes proving the success of the institution of temporary marriages; see Mervin 2008: 21.
59 Arabi 2001: 154.
60 Al-Jazeera, 3 May 1998.
61 Ibid; Arabi 2001; Welchman 2000: 104.
62 Arabi 2001: 165–7.
63 Al-Jazeera, 3 May 1998; see also Abaza 2001: 20.

64 *Straits Times*, 12 October 1998.
65 *Desert News*, 4 September 2005. For Indonesia, see at <http://news.bbc.co.uk/1/hi/8412496.stm>, accessed 21 January 2010.
66 Arabi 2001: 160.
67 Ibid: 165.
68 Hasso 2007: 61–3.
69 Abaza 2001: 20.
70 Drieskens 2008: 1.
71 Omar, cited in ibid: 2; see also Sonneveld 2009.
72 Mernissi 1987: 171.
73 Arabi 2001: 167.
74 Yüksel 2007.

References

Books and Journal Articles

Abaza, Mona, 'Perceptions of 'urfi marriage in the Egyptian press'. *ISIM Newsletter*, 7 (2001), pp. 20–21, at <http://www.isim.nl/newsletter/7/regional/9.html>, accessed 29 March 2002.

Abdalla, Mustafa, *Beach Politics: Gender and Sexuality in Dahab* (Cairo, 2007).

Arabi, Oussama, 'The itinerary of a fatwa: ambulant marriage (*al-zawaj al-misyar*), or grass roots law-making in Saudi Arabia of the 1990s'. In Arabi, O. (ed.), *Studies in Modern Islamic Law and Jurisprudence* (The Hague, 2001).

Badran, Margot, *Feminists, Islam and Nation: Gender and the Making of Modern Egypt* (Cairo, 1995).

Bibars, Iman, *Victims and Heroines: Women, Welfare and the Egyptian State* (London, 2001).

Carlisle, Jessica, 'From behind the door: a Damascus court copes with an alleged out of court marriage'. In Drieskens, B. (ed.), *Les métamorphoses du mariage au moyen-orient* (Beirut, 2008), at <http://ifpo.revues.org/454>, accessed 8 February 2010.

Central Agency for Public Mobilisation and Statistics, *The Statistical Year Book 1995–2003* (Cairo, June 2004).

Cuno, Kenneth, 'Divorce and the fate of the family in modern Egypt'. In Yount, K.M. and H. Rashad (eds.), *Family in the Middle East: Ideational Change in Egypt, Iran, and Tunisia* (London and New York, 2008), pp. 111–135.

Drieskens, Barbara, 'Changing perceptions of marriage in contemporary Beirut'. In Drieskens, B. (ed.), *Les métamorphoses du mariage au moyen-orient* (Beirut, 2008), at < http://ifpo.revues.org/454>, accessed 8 February 2010.

El-Alami, Dawoud Sudqi, *The Marriage Contract in Islamic Law: In the Shari'ah and Personal Status Laws of Egypt and Morocco* (London, 1992).

Fargues, Philippe, 'Terminating marriage'. In Hopkins, N.S. (ed.), *The New Arab Family* (Cairo, 2001), pp. 247–273.

Haeri, Shahla, *Law of Desire: Contemporary Marriage in Iran* (London, 1989).
Hasso, Frances S. 'Comparing Emirati and Egyptian narratives on marriage, sexuality, and the body'. In Elliott, E., J. Payne and P. Ploesch (eds.), *Global Migration, Social Change, and Cultural Transformation* (New York, 2007).
Hill, Enid, *Mahkama! Studies in the Egyptian Legal System: Courts and Crimes, Law and Society* (London, 1979).
Hirsch, Jennifer S., Holly Wardlow, Daniel Jordan Smith, Harriet M. Phinney, Shanti Parikh and Constance A. Nathanson, *The Secret: Love, Marriage, and HIV* (Nashville, TN, 2009).
Hoodfar, Homa, *Between Marriage and the Market: Intimate Politics and Survival in Cairo* (Berkeley, CA, 1997).
Kholoussy, Hanan, *For Better, for Worse: The Marriage Crisis that Made Modern Egypt* (Stanford, CA, 2010).
Mernissi, Fatima, *Beyond the Veil: Male-Female Dynamics in Modern Muslim Society* (Bloomington, IN, 1987).
Mervin, Sabrina, 'Normes religieuses et loi du silence: le mariage temporaire chez les Chiites du Liban'. In Drieskens, B. (ed.), *Les métamorphoses du mariage au moyen-orient* (Beirut, 2008), at < http://ifpo.revues.org/454>, accessed 8 February 2010.
Mikhail, Susanne Louis B, 'Child marriage and child prostitution: two forms of sexual exploitation'. In Masika, R. (ed.), *Gender, Trafficking and Slavery* (Oxford, 2002), pp. 43–49.
Osman, Magued I. and Laila S. Shahd, 'Age-discrepant marriages in Eygpt'. In Hopkins (ed.), *The New Arab Family* (Cairo, 2003), pp. 51–61.
Rozario, Santi, 'Disjunctions and continuities: dowry and the position of single women in Bangladesh'. In Risseeuw, C. and G. Kanesh (eds.), *Negotiation and Social Place: A Gendered Analysis of Changing Kin and Security Networks in South Asia and Sub-Saharan Africa* (New Delhi, 1998), pp. 259–275.
Sholkamy, Hania, 'Why kin marriages? Rationales in Rural Upper Egypt'. In K. M. Yount and H. Rashad (eds.) *Family in the Middle East* (London and New York, 2008), pp. 139–150.
Singerman, Diane, 'Marriage and divorce in Egypt: financial costs and political struggles'. In Drieskens, B. (ed.), *Les métamorphoses du mariage au moyen-orient* (Beirut, 2008), at <http://ifpo.revues.org/454>, accessed 8 February 2010.
—— and Barbara Ibrahim, 'The costs of marriage in Egypt: a hidden dimension in the new Arab demography'. In Hopkins (ed.), *The New Arab Family* (Cairo, 2003), pp. 80–116.
Sonbol, Amira El-Azhary, *Women of Jordan: Islam, Labor and the Law* (Syracuse, NY, 2003).
Sonneveld, Nadia, *Khul' Divorce in Egypt: Public Debates, Judicial Practices, and Everyday Life*. Unpublished PhD thesis, University of Amsterdam, 2009.
Welchman, Lynn, *Beyond the Code: Muslim Family Law and the Shar'i Judiciary in the Palestinian West Bank* (The Hague, 2000).

Welchman, Lynn, *Women and Muslim Family Laws in Arab States: A Comparative Overview of Textual Development and Advocacy* (Amsterdam, 2007).
Yilmaz, Ihsan, 'Non-recognition of post-modern Turkish socio-legal reality and the predicament of women', *British Journal of Middle Eastern Studies* 30/1 (2003), pp. 25–41.
Yüksel, S., *The State's Response to Legal Pluralism: The Case of Religious Courts Law and Courts in Israel, Egypt and India*. Unpublished PhD thesis, University of Washington, Seattle, WA, 2007.
Zubaida, Sami, *Law and Power in the Islamic World* (London, 2003).

Articles in Newspapers and Magazines

Al-ahram, 3 January 2000; 17 January 2000; 29 January 2000; 2 February 2000.
Al-'arabi, 30 January 2000.
Al-Ahram Weekly, 18–24 February 1999: Gihan Shahine, 'Illegitimate, illegal or just ill-advised?', at <http://weekly.ahram.org.eg/1999/417/li1.htm>, accessed 31 January 2007; 26 February–3 March 2004: Reem Leila, 'Polygamous duplicity', p. 25; 29 December–4 January 2006: Amany Abdel-Moneim, 'Stunning revelation', at <http://weekly.ahram.org.eg/2005/775/eg93.htm>, accessed 15 January 2010.
Al-Jazeera, 3 May 1998, 'Zawag al-misyar', at <http://www.aljazeera.net/news/archive/archive?ArchiveId=90777>, accessed 1 March 2007; 18 August 2003, 'L-al-nisa' faqat', at <http://www.aljazeera.net/Channel/archive/archive?ArchiveId=92223#L1>, accessed 27 February 2008.
Al-jumhuriya, 20 January 2000.
Al-sha'b, 18 January 2000, p. 1.
Al-wafd, 30 September 1999; 1 October 1999; 26 January 2000; 28 January 2000.
BBC News, 17 December 2009, 'Club promotes polygamy in Indonesia', at <http://news.bbc.co.uk/1/hi/8412496.stm>, accessed 21 January 2010.
Cairo Times, 20–6 January 2000.
Desert News (Salt Lake City, UT), 4 September 2005, Mariam Fam (Associated Press), 'Egyptian wife promotes polygamy', at <http://findarticles.com/p/articles/mi_qn4188/is_20050904/ai_n15330673>, accessed 14 February 2007.
Middle East Times, 18 February 2000: Abeer Allam, 'Urfi delivers the goods, at half the price', at <http://www.metimes.com//2000/02/18/urfi_delivers_the_goods_at_half_the_price/5260/>, accessed 6 February 2007; 7 April 2000, Kamel, Yomna and Rasha Mehyar, 'Yet another marriage without strings', at <http://www.metimes.com/storyview.php?StoryID=20000407-042210-7478r>, accessed 6 February 2007.
Straits Times, 12 October 1998, 'Part time marriage the rage in Egypt'.

DISCOURSES OF THE LAW

5

WAITING TO WIN: FAMILY DISPUTES, COURT REFORM, AND THE ETHNOGRAPHY OF DELAY*

Christine Hegel-Cantarella

Section I

Introduction

One afternoon in 2005, I stood outside the courthouse in Port Said, Egypt, making conversation with a man I knew from a local print shop, where I often bought office supplies and made photocopies. We had run into each other by accident and, since we were standing in front of the courts and I had just been observing a session, we ended up talking about the legal system. He pointed out that he had never personally been involved in litigation and dismissed the possibility of obtaining speedy justice through the Egyptian civil courts, declaring sarcastically, 'The donkey will die!' He and another man standing near us, who overheard the comment, broke into laughter. Noting my confusion, he explained that 'the donkey will die' is a shorthand reference to a parable of Goha:

> Goha says he will teach a donkey to speak and give it to the king as a gift. But, the people asked, how is such a thing possible? It would take forever to teach a donkey to speak! Goha replies 'It will take me forty years. By that time, the donkey will be dead, I will be dead, and the king will be dead!'

Justice, in short, is slow. Cases can linger in the courts for years and by the time the judge issues a decision either all the parties will have died or so many years will have passed that the decision will have little or no consequence. As with other routine inconveniences and injustices, court delay is so widely acknowledged as an annoying feature of the Egyptian legal system that it makes perfect fodder for jokes and is the subject of parables.

My interlocutor's observation highlights two interrelated phenomena: the civil courts do not consistently provide expeditious legal resolution, and because civil litigation is slow the public's faith in the legal system is weak. Recent development initiatives in Egypt have focused on court reform to address these issues. In addition to projects related to the rule of law, political participation and the growth of civil society institutions, four multi-million-dollar projects have been initiated since the late 1990s, each designed to streamline the administration of the courts and improve access to justice in Egypt.

This essay is an analysis of delay as a particular object of concern in court-reform initiatives in Egypt. Reform projects in the civil, criminal and family courts focus on the remedying of institutional causes of court delay, including outdated administrative procedures, a shortage of well-trained clerks and judges and a backlog of cases, and are premised on the argument that court delay has significant economic and social costs. Yet even where court reform has succeeded in eradicating a backlog, streamlining case management through the use of technology, and in expanding the capacity of the courts through staffing and training, strategic uses of procedural law and other voluntary forms of delay persist. This suggests that delay is also a productive temporal space through which litigants and their lawyers manoeuvre to achieve specific aims.

Formalist assessments of institutional weaknesses have been useful for delineating how court delay discourages meritorious litigation, disadvantages plaintiffs, weakens confidence in state institutions, and thereby inhibits capitalist investment and trade. Yet this approach overlooks facets of delay that may counteract the benefits of even the most successful court reform. Alternatively, an ethnographic approach reveals the situated experience of delay and enables closer examination of its social and economic costs. I posit that delay causes inconvenience, distress, and even suffering, yet it also constitutes legal subjects as they accrue legal knowledge and agency, and provokes potentially therapeutic interactions through which relationality may be reworked.

Positioning court delay as situated experience marks a critical shift toward an understanding of delay as both temporally and spatially constituted. Delay is often configured as a failure to progress and an inert temporal space in which something is *not* happening. I posit that it is productive to see the ways in which delay draws litigants, often repeatedly or for extended periods of time, into peripheral and focal legal spaces that beget specific types of interaction and enable participant-observation in/of the work of law.

I begin with a discussion of contemporary court-reform projects in Egypt to pinpoint the way court delay is framed as a problematic, and examine some of the causes of delay. I then consider forms of voluntary delay and the role that litigants, lawyers, clerks and judges play based on their ability to manipulate documents, hearing dates and procedural actions. The analysis of causes of delay is then juxtaposed to situated experiences of court delay among litigants in Port Said, through which I examine the ways in which delay is generative. I consider two types of spaces that litigants frequent throughout extended litigation: lawyers' offices and the Office of the Experts, an office under the administration of the Ministry of Justice that provides technical expertise to judges on evidentiary matters. In these offices, litigants wait, observe and participate in activities related to their own and others' cases. Although the litigants I focus on are involved in disputes related to family matters, including divorce and post-divorce alimony, inheritance and property, the disputes are not solely litigated in the family courts but in the civil and criminal courts as well. As such, the ethnography further illustrates how litigants shift family disputes into other jurisdictions in order to ensure outcomes that would not be obtainable in the Family Courts.[1]

Re-conceiving Delay

A situated analysis of court delay in contemporary Egypt is to an extent uncharted territory. There is a vast literature by US legal scholars that interrogates the causes of court delay, and a particular emphasis in the area of law and economics that addresses the roots of delays caused by litigation rather than settlement.[2] These generally quantitative studies focus on the inventory and measurement of, among other causes of delay: case backlog, court time spent on the disposition of suits for jury and non-jury trials, time to disposition based on type of case, time to disposition in cases referred to experts, settlement ratios, number of lost trial days, and the like.[3] Moreover, many of these studies are pragmatically focused on the identification of remedies for removing delay as well as on assessments of the potential outcomes of implementing various remedies.[4] Although this type of research can be productively applied to the administration of justice, it only accounts for bureaucratic or institutional causes of delay. Further, although such scholarship is premised on the argument that court delay has significant social costs,[5] the specificity of these costs is not interrogated. As Zeisel et al note:

> Delay in the courts is unqualifiedly bad. It is bad because it deprives citizens of a basic public service; it is bad because the lapse of time frequently causes deterioration of evidence and makes it less likely that justice be done when the case is finally tried; it is bad because delay may case severe hardship to some parties and may in general affect litigants differentially; and it is bad because it brings to the entire court system a loss of public confidence, respect, and pride.[6]

The assertion that delay is an unqualified harm provokes a number of questions that may enable us to qualify the harms associated with it: what do citizens do when they are deprived of the basic public service of legal recourse, or when evidence deteriorates because of lengthy court delay? What specific hardships might delay cause, and upon what bases does it differentially affect litigants? Less easily answered through rigorous statistical analysis, these questions suggest a point of entry for a qualitative approach.

The findings of institutionally-focused and quantitative studies can be contrasted with those that diagnose court delay as rooted in cultural forms. Legal scholar and anthropologist David Zammit notes that research on courts in the Mediterranean area tends to view court delay as a window onto other cultural phenomena, pointing out that such studies typically neglect to examine legal practice itself.[7] For instance, sociologist David Nelkin suggests that Italian criminal trials are renowned for their undue length, because of both the internal legal culture of Italy, which includes multiple procedural safeguards and an overly complex organisational structure, and the external legal culture – the pace of Italian social life and the contested nature of the state.[8] Anthropologist Michael Herzfeld, in respect of Greece, sees the routine use of aggressive and accusatory rhetoric – by both litigants and legal professionals – and judicial capriciousness as rooted in an expressions of the broader cultural context.[9] Lawrence Rosen's study of *qadi* courts in Morocco likewise suggests that judicial practices reflect and rely on local and normative concepts.[10] Given the relative dearth of studies of courts in the Mediterranean area and the Middle East, these studies add critical regional specificity to debates about how cultural context might shape legal practice. At the same time, law and society scholars have pressed for an increasingly nuanced approach to analysing the impact of cultural frameworks on the nature of legal proceedings, and further emphasise that legal institutions are sites of contestation over meaning, and not merely reflective of social realities.[11] As such, a socio-legal analysis of courts, and of court delay, must be rooted in an understanding of law and society as mutually constitutive.

In order to re-conceptualise delay as generative rather than merely indicative of administrative failure or cultural character, I draw on insights from theories of time reckoning, temporalisation, and time perception. The anthropology of time, in conjunction with an analysis of its relationship to space, provides a framework for separating delay as an institutional problem from delay as practice and lived experience.

First, in arguing that court delay is an unqualified harm to be remedied, quantitative legal analyses, like court-reform initiatives, espouse a conception of delay as an aberrant duration. To conceptualise it thus requires time measurement, an undertaking that, according to Heidegger, 'derives from the more fundamental imperative of "reckoning with time", or "taking [it] ... into account"', which in turn derives from our existing in the time taken up by everyday activities.[12] Moreover, telling the time, or measuring it, presupposes that 'there is a [right and wrong] *time to do* this ... Without some sort of presupposition like this, time-telling or measuring would hardly take place.'[13] This presupposition must also be extended to that of a right *amount* of time in which to accomplish something. Delay, in the court-reform framework, is an indication that litigation is not proceeding according to an expected or desired pace, rhythm or duration. Often, duration or pace is slowed through repetition – repeat visits to the same or multiple offices, re-filing actions, multiple appearances before the judge and the like – which makes the experience of time circular rather than linear and progressive. As David Engel points out, 'Linear time provides a yardstick for change and development rather than an understanding that the future will return people to old and familiar contexts. Thus, the linear time model has great significance for social reformers as well as capitalists.'[14]

Secondly, time-reckoning in the juridical framework in particular must be understood as the imposition of 'world time' inexorably related to modernity and the changing sources of power that regulate and reckon activity in the post-colonial world.[15] Anthropologists have noted that the imposition of world time through colonial and missionary efforts manifests itself in many ways. This includes the conversion to Gregorian calendrical time, which creates a quantitatively segmented continuum without qualitative differentiation,[16] and in defined standards of timing that create disjunctures between 'body time' of everyday activities and external markers.[17] These efforts enroll societies in a wider universe of power. They also operate according to the logic of capitalist modernity, whereby time is commodified: time is money and should not be wasted. As such, concerns about efficiency and delay in the courts are not fundamentally rooted in ideas about access to justice, but reflect capitalist imperatives.[18] Links between the imposition of world time and the notion of efficiency are integral to modernisation projects unrelated to the administration of justice, including mechanisation, industrialisation and digitalisation. Therefore, the interpretation of court delay as an indication of a failure fully to modernize and rationalise the courts is rooted in a more general post-colonial discourse.

Finally, reckoning with court delay as a temporal phenomenon requires taking into account its spatiality as well. As Nancy Munn points out, understandings of temporality 'hinge on the way we conceptualize its connections to space, action, and actor'.[19] Examining the connection between time and space and the body's relationship to space, which points to Bourdieu's notion of *habitus*, is a means to consider how court delay may generate particular forms of consociality, subjectivity and agency.[20] In Bourdieu's rendering, the place in which actions are performed organises and symbolises their enactment in particular ways. Moreover, he posits that one's relationship to time emerges through engagement in the rhythm of activities, and emphasises that practices are simultaneously part of the spaces in which they are enacted.[21] Court reform project descriptions tacitly suggest that delay is an inert space in which something is *not* happening. If we instead apply Bourdieu's concept of activity rhythm to court delay, as a process that repeatedly brings litigants into legal and semi-legal spaces such as the courts and lawyers' and experts' offices, where they wait, strategise, testify, listen and participate in putting various documents together, delay may be understood as a temporal as well as a bodily activity constituted through the space of its enactment.

Section II

The court-reform initiatives in Egypt mentioned above merit further consideration in relation to the claims they make regarding delay and inefficiency. Project proposals and reports issued by governmental and non-governmental bodies inevitably abbreviate the complexity of the task at hand. Yet they also provide insights into the way issues are perceived, prioritised and addressed. Moreover, the court-reform projects under examination focus on institutional-level changes to improve the administration of – and in turn, access to – justice. It is also critical to delineate sources of delay that are not directly related to institutional shortcomings but derive from legitimate procedural avenues for extending the length of disposition; litigants' experiences in Port Said encompass delays derived from both these sources.

Court Reform, Justice and Expediency

In December 2006, the Egyptian Ministry of Justice, along with the National Council for Childhood and Motherhood (NCCM), began implementing the Family Justice Project.[22] This project is a five-year initiative funded by the US Agency for International Development (USAID) to support recent legislative initiatives, and in particular Law 10 of 2004, which established the Family Courts as a separate civil-law jurisdiction and mandated mediation in divorce, maintenance and custody cases. The Family Justice Project has two main components, the first of which is the improvement of the capacities of mediation offices by training mediation specialists and by standardising mediation procedures and practices. It also introduces training for family-court judges, which, like that for mediation specialists, is being implemented by the National Center for Judicial Studies in Cairo and includes workshops on legal, sociological and psychological issues that families may face. The second component includes raising awareness of Family Court procedures and services, of positive parenting and of reconciliation techniques; establishing counselling services through NGOs; providing child-protection services, and a further cluster of services that include micro-loans, capacity-building, legal assistance and child care.[23]

Jurisdictional changes stipulated in Law 10/2004, and implemented through the Family Justice Project, were intended to improve efficiency.

Unlike the former family court system, cases are no longer separated into those dealt with in 'summary' and those in 'first instance' courts, but are all seen in the latter. All disputes in one family under judicial review are included in one court file, and a special public prosecutor is assigned to deal solely with family-law cases. Mediation lasting 15 days or a month is mandatory, although following a failed mediation parties can file a lawsuit within a week.

Within the first year of implementation of the Family Justice Project, researchers at the American University in Cairo Social Research Council initiated a 12-month ethnographic study to assess the strengths and weaknesses of the new family courts in relation to their capacity to meet the legal needs of female litigants. The researchers found that, along with problems with implementing mediation agreements, poorly trained mediation experts, a lack of adequate facilities to ensure privacy for disputants, and judges' resistance to making use of mediation reports as a resource for legal determination, one of the primary goals of the new family courts – to make family-law procedures more expeditious – was not being fulfilled. In fact, mediation processes, which were most often ineffective, tended to delay cases further. This suggests that in addition to other structural factors that create delays – such as the shortage of judges and a focus in legal proceedings on the submission of myriad documents rather than on interacting directly with litigants to assess the problems to be resolved – mandatory mediation may be another structural impediment to expeditiousness.

One area of family law in which prioritising expeditiousness has been the subject of intense debate concerns Law 1 of 2000, also known as the *khul'* law. Law 1/2000 enables women to seek a no-fault divorce but requires that they give up their rights to maintenance and deferred dowry, and that they return promptly the dowry and gifts they received from the husband. The rationale for Law 1, and the basis upon which many women legal activists supported it, was that it provided women with a quick way to exit an unhappy or abusive marriage and thus to avoid the long legal process involved in obtaining a judicial divorce on the basis of harm. Others have argued that it places poor women post-divorce in an especially vulnerable economic position, and therefore is only a feasible option for middle- and upper-class women who have a support system or personal source of income.

The debate over Law 1/2000 highlights the relative lack of public debate over prioritising expeditiousness among law-reform goals more generally. In the case of *khul'*, the sacrifice women make for the sake of a speedy divorce is explicit, and there has been much heated discussion about whether *khul'* divorce sacrifices long-term security for a somewhat quicker divorce proceeding. But plans to streamline other aspects of the family and civil courts through the introduction of new technology or the re-organisation of administrative procedures have not provoked much consternation among Egyptian activists and observers.[24]

There are a number of parallels between the Family Justice Project and the Administration of Justice Support I (AOJS I, 1996–2002) and the Administration of Justice Support Project II (AOJS II, 2004–09), which were also funded by USAID and implemented by the Egyptian Ministry of Justice, America-Mideast Educational and Training Services (AMIDEAST) the National Center for Judicial Studies and various NGOs.[25] The Administration of Justice projects focused on the civil/commercial courts, which until 2004 still adjudicated family-law cases, and included improving judicial training, introducing new technology to centralise and organise record-keeping, public-awareness efforts, and other reforms to improve the functioning of the civil courts and thus the public's access to justice.

The overarching aim of the AOJS projects was to ensure that the Egyptian judicial system would become more transparent, functional and equitable by addressing legal administrative issues, which acknowledges disparities between law on the books and law on the books and law in practice.[26] The first AOJS project was focused on streamlining case management and introduced a number of changes in the process by which litigants initiate cases in the civil/commercial courts. The project was initially implemented in the Cairo Civil Courts and included centralised case-filing, automated case-tracking, and a public information desk. These measures were aimed at alleviating confusion caused by the previous system in which litigants had to visit multiple offices; in relation to this, the measures were intended to alleviate multiple requests for unofficial payments. As noted in the summary report issued upon conclusion of AOJS I:

> USAID designed AOJS in response to a nationwide concern about systematic delays in case management. Among the many consequences of those delays were weaknesses in the overall administration of justice and the lack of public confidence in the court system as a whole. Most telling was the negative impact on the business community and the local economic environment. This was evidenced by reduced investor and business confidence in the legal system.[27]

Reduced investor and business confidence are pinpointed as indicators of a lack of public confidence in the court system more generally. This points to the way in which expeditiousness, capitalist enterprise and confidence in the courts are linked and their joint improvement is prioritised in reform projects.

The second phase of the project built on the first by implementing similar measures in more courts across Egypt and by expanding the goals of the project to gender inclusion. According to the project summary by one of the lead implementing organisations, AMIDEAST:

> The AOJS II strategic approach is guided by the team's vision, which includes an Egyptian judicial system with strong, inclusive, strategic oversight by the Ministry of Justice (MOJ), courts that are more efficient and transparent, a constituency for court reform both within and outside of the MOJ, more women in senior positions, and greater public confidence in the courts.[28]

In project descriptions for AOJS I and AOJS II, bureaucratic inefficiency is linked to a shortage of judges and poor training and technical skills among judges. Prior to the infusion of funding to support hiring and training new judges, there existed a vast discrepancy between the small number of judges and courts and the extraordinarily high number of cases being processed. According to the Ministry of Justice's yearly Legal Statistics Report, there were 1,462,897 civil and commercial cases and 124,208 criminal cases under review in 2002.[29] This massive number of cases was presented before approximately 224 summary and primary courts.[30] Moreover, some pending cases dated back more than 30 years, in part because of the case backlog resulting from a perpetual shortage of judges.

AOJS II initiated a project to resolve pending cases in order to enable judges to focus on new cases entering the system and to alleviate further backlog. This may have greater long-term consequences; for the present there remains a shortage of judges in Egypt's relatively high-volume court system. A lawyer who had been practising law for over 20 years in Port Said pointed out some of the implications of this disparity:

> Well, you find that in one session (*galsa*) there are about a hundred civil cases discussed. The judge will listen to a few words in each case and take any papers related to each one. After the session and before the next one, the judge reviews the papers in an attempt to understand everything about each case and then he gives his decision. In this way, no case is given the proper attention.

The courts are unable to give adequate time for review of all the new cases opened each year; as a result – cases from one judicial year roll over onto the case roster for the following judicial year, and the backlog thus continues to grow.

As Chodosh et al note, backlog and delay are critical issues that must be addressed.[31] Not only are there widespread problems in many legal contexts:

> If left unattended, the backlog and delay problem discourages meritorious litigation, provides defendants with undue advantages, and forces plaintiffs to bear alleged losses or seek alternative measures of retribution. Access is only valuable if it includes the prospect of a timely legal determination of the issues at hand. Defendants generally benefit from backlog and delay, forcing plaintiffs to suffer alleged losses and incur litigation costs for several years. Thus, the failure to achieve timely remedies

increases the cost of doing business. To the extent settlement is pursued, knowledge of the defendant's economic advantage, enhanced by delay, reduces both the interrelated value of and incentive for civil claim settlement.[32]

This assessment, like development-project reports, focuses on the increased costs of 'doing business'. However, the problems and undue advantages caused by delay and backlog are similarly present in non-commercial cases. Importantly, Chodosh et al echo the language of ministerial and development-agency reports that articulate explicit connections between inefficiency, court delay and inhibited access to justice. Project-justification reports for both the Family Justice Project and the AOJS projects identify delay as a leading reason why the courts fail citizens, and have invested millions of dollars in finding ways to restoring confidence in the courts. Yet administrative shortcomings as a source of delay are only part of the story, and projects that address these shortcomings do not necessarily attend to the ways in which litigants and lawyers use legitimate and fraudulent strategies to create advantageous delays. These 'voluntary' forms of delay suggest that legal actions sometimes serve particular purposes not served by efficient and straightforward litigation.

Voluntary Delay

Family law and Family Court reform-initiatives generally focus on the ways in which court delay has particularly harmful consequences for women, yet there are also forms of court delay initiated by women or their families that are strategically useful and economically fruitful. Rosen addresses delay strategies among Moroccan litigants, pointing out that women use delays to bolster their position and better their financial allotment in divorce and maintenance cases. For instance, women sometimes postpone actions in divorce suits to 'keep the clock running' on support payments.[33] Ziba Mir-Hosseini makes a similar observation among Iranian litigants:

> A woman's strategy in such a case is to delay a divorce as long as possible, and meanwhile to take as much as she can. She

makes one petition for *nafaqa* (marital support), and another for *mahr* (payment of her dower), and makes their waiver contingent upon getting custody of the children, a share of the marital home and a set maintenance payment for the children.[34]

Therefore, delay can play a role in rational economic strategising in the context of divorce cases, and as Rosen notes, 'These are tactics born to a considerable degree out of both statutory inequality and possibilities inherent in the legal arrangements themselves.'[35] When women use delay strategies to claim rights they do so to reorganise the allocation of advantage within the framework of laws that grant men and women differential status. These adaptations run parallel, or perhaps even counter, to efforts by legal reformers in the Middle East who advocate, on behalf of women, more sweeping changes in substantive and procedural law.

Voluntary court delay in the civil/commercial courts similarly arises through legitimate procedural postponements, referrals and stop actions, as well as through practices that take advantage of bureaucratic failure. In addition to litigants and lawyers, clerks and judges also play a significant role in aiding these forms of strategic delay. Egyptian economist Bahaa Ali El-Dean finds that, according to an Egyptian Ministry of Justice report on the causes of backlog and delay, the average civil litigation requires between 30 and 40 appearances before the trial judges, stretching over three years or more. This is in part due to the way these various actors introduce forms of postponement, facilitated by the procedural laws governing litigation that permit extensions.[36]

Judges therefore use postponements to expedite their workload. Because their daily dockets can include between 70 and 200 cases per sitting in the civil courts and between 150 and 200 cases per sitting in the family courts, they are prone to grant postponements, including stop actions or appeals (*ta'n*) and injunctions (*musta'jil*), that lawyers or litigants request.[37] The motivation for requesting extensions or postponements may vary, but extensions typically benefit the defendant to the disadvantage of the plaintiff by buying time the better to prepare a case, devise a new legal strategy or pressure the plaintiff to drop the case. Judges also initiate postponements by referring cases to the Expertise Office of the Ministry of Justice for technical review. El-Dean notes that sometimes judges refer matters to experts that do not actually raise serious technical questions, and in so doing simultaneously remove cases from the docket in the present and create further backlog in the future.[38]

Whether it serves the purpose of clearing the docket or because there is actually a need for technical review or verification, judges may refuse to admit documentary evidence and may file a request for expert review or for verification of its authenticity or validity by an employee from the office which issued the document. Following this, the matter is forwarded to the clerks' department, where a requisition must be submitted for the expert or employee to attend before the judge to conduct the investigation, or to initiate the review process out of court and submit a report.

Court clerks also play a role in creating delay. The processing of case-related documents, the assessment and receipt of fees and the verification of case status undertaken by clerks may be more prone to error and involve more time to complete than when these processes are automated. Although for some processes the codes of procedure designate time limits, clerks are not generally required to observe them. Beyond this, litigants may collude with poorly-paid court clerks; Nathan Brown reports that the positions of *amin al-sirr* and *muhdir* (bailiff and process-server) are perceived as the most corruptible amongst court employees. They are charged with 'losing key documents, delivering papers to the wrong address, forging signatures to indicate that papers were served that actually were not, and failing to find a valid address – often in return for a bribe from one of the litigants'.[39] Furthermore, employees in the Office of the Experts can sometimes be induced with a bribe to write a report unduly advantageous to one party, or to delay submitting their report to the court.[40] Because incidents involving 'lost' (discarded or hidden) documents and misdirected court notifications occur with some regularity, as Nathan Brown points out, judges are often willing to delay cases if a needed document is not in the file or a party fails to appear.[41]

Litigants and their lawyers contribute perhaps most significantly to deliberate delay through the use of procedural law to introduce postponements and stop actions. These (legitimate) actions are common legal strategies to move a case toward a desired outcome. For instance, they may buy time for the lawyer (in most cases, the defence lawyer) to gather evidence that may aid the client's defence, induce the plaintiff to participate in informal negotiations or mediation that will produce a favourable settlement, or put pressure on the plaintiff to drop the case entirely.

Some lawyers in Port Said are particularly known for their clever use of delay to advantage their clients. Hesham, a client of one such lawyer, noted that he had specifically hired his lawyer because of his reputation for successfully using delay tactics in civil litigation. Hesham was aware that he had a very weak case regarding a lease agreement, and expected to lose at both the primary and appeals levels. He felt that his only option was to delay the case as long as possible until family members who could help mediate the contractual dispute in his favour visited from overseas. His lawyer was happy to comply, particularly because Hesham did not expect him actually to win the case, but simply to create propitious conditions for reaching a favourable settlement.

Other litigants insist that the lawyer find a way to postpone a hearing out of a sense of spite or revenge, or to buy time to collect money they owe to the plaintiff. As an example of the latter, a lawyer named Abdullah was representing a mother and daughter who were being sued for breach of trust (*khiyanat al-amana*); they had purchased goods on credit from a small store and then found themselves unable to pay the instalments. The shop owner filed an action and a hearing date was set. Abdullah planned not to attend the session, and had advised his clients not to attend either. If the judge passed a sentence against the mother and daughter, Abdullah would raise an appeal to reject the sentence based on the fact that they had not been present for sentencing. The case would take a couple of months to reach the appeals court, after which it would take several more months for the case to move back to the primary court to receive a date for reinstatement of the original judgment and its validation. This would give the women time to save the money they owed so that they could repay it and settle the case without further litigation.

Legal scholars and court reformers have identified areas of weakness in legal institutions that can be strengthened in order to streamline justice. At the same time, some of these initiatives have had a reverse effect by increasing delay and making litigation more arduous. Even where such initiatives fail it is still the case that, at present, Egyptians rely heavily on voluntary delay as a legal strategy. As delay persists, and as litigants take steps to protect their interests and achieve a favourable outcome of the dispute, whether it pertains to alimony, inheritance, custody or other matters, how does being a litigant and the experience of endless delays in litigation alter the relationship between the parties? Moreover, how might delay, as experienced in peripherally legal spaces of lawyers' offices and the Office of the Experts, shape legal subjectivity and agency? If court delay, through temporal and literal spaces, generates particular interactions and subject-formation processes, what are the implications for eradicating non-voluntary forms of delay? In taking up these questions, my broader aim is to qualify the seemingly unqualified good of court reform, in order to examine the complexities of the assumptions it relies upon and to consider whether it actually serves its stated aims.

Section III

Situated Delay: Lawyers' Offices

When involved in litigation, people still go about their ordinary lives and work, visit, cook, shop, care for children and the like. Yet this everyday routine may be interrupted or otherwise affected by activities made necessary by the lawsuit. Although some litigants may rely heavily on their lawyer to attend to lawsuits to which they are a party, many are likely to spend time in the lawyer's office, discussing their case, signing documents, checking in on dates set for hearings, or simply waiting to be seen. This situates litigants in spaces that engender particular practices and modes of discourse. Moreover, solo and small-firm lawyers in Port Said work in very small offices, typically comprising a reception area adjacent to the lawyer's desk and bookshelves, in some cases without a wall or door separating the two spaces. So a lawyer may advise one client while other clients wait, listening and observing. Daily, weekly or monthly visits to the lawyer results in time taken from important work, educational, religious or social duties. Yet these visits also enable litigants to become participant-observers in their own and others' legal cases.

The amount of time clients may spend meeting, or waiting to meet, their lawyer is due in part to economic factors and to modes of social networking. The vast majority of lawyers in Port Said are solo and small-firm lawyers. Although there are a handful of large law firms that in some cases have multiple branches in other cities in Egypt, these latter firms primarily specialise in maritime law and international commercial law, and do not take on small claims, routine family law, or 'garbage' cases.[42] There are over a thousand lawyers listed in the local directory issued by the Port Said branch of the National Lawyer's Syndicate, which suggests a ratio of approximately one lawyer per 500 residents. Competition for clients is high, and is reflected in lawyers' fees: with the exception of those who have earned a reputation for superb legal ability or by virtue of their longevity in the field, solo and small-firm lawyers tend to keep their fees competitive so that they can attract new clients. Clients who do not pay much for legal services use frequent visits to their lawyer to keep their case a priority. Additionally, compensation for legal representation may take other forms besides monetary fees: clients barter and put their social networks to use in exchange for services. Clients use 'face time' with their lawyer to cultivate a good relationship, and to discern the kinds of goods and services they might fruitfully exchange.

This was true for Amina, an elderly woman who was involved in two cases with her husband. After he took a second wife the marriage became unbearable for Amina, and she sought a judicial divorce on the basis of harm (*darar*), and although she won her case was forced to return to the courts to petition for the maintenance and 'enjoyment' (*muta'*) money the court had awarded her. While this case was moving through the courts she received notification that she was being prosecuted for criminal breach of trust for non-delivery of LE 500,000

(Egyptian pounds), allegedly entrusted to her according to two trust receipts (*isalat amana*) in her name for LE 250,000 each. As such, she was a plaintiff in a case against her husband to obtain monies she was owed, and a defendant in a misdemeanour case alleging she owed money to the agent designated on the commercial document.

Although Amina's ex-husband had a good job working for the Suez Canal Company, she had married him against the will of her family and did not have a strong economic support-system outside her marriage, or marketable skills. As such, she was barely able to meet her basic needs and could ill afford to pay for legal representation. Although the state is legally required to provide such representation for indigent defendants in criminal cases, this does not apply when the charge is a misdemeanour. Therefore, when she originally sought out Salma to represent her they came to an arrangement that Amina would help Salma in the office and at home in exchange for her legal services.

Bartering for legal services placed Amina in consistently close proximity to her lawyer. Salma had a baby that she often brought with her to her office, and Amina cared for the boy while she worked; she also served as a gatekeeper between the reception area and Salma's office, ushering in clients when Salma was ready. Moving constantly between the reception area where she sat to greet clients as they arrived, and Salma's office where she would mind the baby near his mother, Amina overheard the intimate details of many clients' cases.

It became clear what an important form of informal legal education this was for her when she began talking to me about her own cases one evening. Salma had previously told me that Amina was basically illiterate, so I was surprised when she described to me not only the background to the divorce case, in intimate detail, and her theory about her ex-husband's involvement in the criminal misdemeanour charges, but also the legal criteria upon which her judicial divorce was based, and the relationship between a judicial determination of harm and her right to alimony. Amina discussed letters she had sent to the Minister of Justice, the Minister of Internal Affairs and the Head of State Security in Port Said to contest the judgment against her for non-delivery regarding the two trust receipts; she included in these letters what she determined to be important evidence for official consideration in her case.

Although Salma was working hard on her behalf to press for her rights to alimony and to contest the breach of trust case on the basis of forgery, Amina had amassed enough legal knowledge during the three years that had passed since she first filed for divorce to keep abreast of her own cases, and even to pursue avenues for petition independent of her lawyer. In Salma's estimation, Amina had began her ordeal heartbroken and overwhelmed but had gradually taken control of the situation, developing a better understanding of her rights as a divorcee as well as the myriad steps involved in claiming them.

Moreover, by bartering office work for legal representation, Amina, a housewife, spent an increased amount of time in a public space where she was required to interact with strangers. As a gatekeeper, she held a small degree of authority in asking clients to wait and in conveying to them estimates about how long it might be until Salma could see them. Sometimes clients talked to her about their cases, and although typically she did not try to dispense legal advice, her opinion was sought and she engaged in discussions, largely with female clients, about the complications of married life, motherhood and money.

Even clients who had no need to barter for legal representation like Amina did kept abreast of their cases through frequent short visits to their lawyer's office. I encountered many of the same clients numerous times when meeting with lawyers, including Michael, a client I encountered on each of the eight occasions I visited his lawyer's office. Michael, a Coptic Christian, had been involved in over 40 cases involving his ex-wife. Some of these were still pending, and he came several nights a week to sit with the lawyer and discuss strategies. Most of his cases lingered in the courts for months or years, primarily through the use of deliberate postponement strategies. As in Amina's misdemeanour case, many of Michael's cases involved commercial receipts, cheques or contracts over which he was accused, or he was accusing his ex-wife, of breaching. Among other delay strategies, Michael and his lawyer relied on stop actions on the basis of suspected forgery; further hearings would have to be postponed until the forgery expert in the

Office of Experts in Ismiliyya reviewed the document, took handwriting samples and issued a report.

One afternoon in early 2006 he arrived at the court to submit some documents when a lawyer greeted him and asked why he had not attended a session earlier that day. Unbeknownst to Michael, a case in which he was a defendant regarding a trust receipt on which he claimed his signature to be forged, had gone before the judge. In his absence, he had been found liable and received a three-year prison sentence. He estimated that a clerk had been bribed so that he would fail to receive notice to appear in court, and he and his lawyer would therefore miss the opportunity to submit an objection (*muʿarada*) regarding the forged signature. He explained:

> The trick is as follows: I have several places where I can stay [apartments that he owns or rents], and I still have them. One of these flats is on the beach and I go to stay there just in the summer every year. I don't go there a lot because it's on a high floor and there's no elevator. Yet it's written in my name [rented or owned by him]. When they went to inform me, they went to this flat. Of course they didn't find me, or anyone, there and that was it. At the court, I was informed [by a clerk in the notification office] that this was my address. So the notification is correct. But I don't go there [regularly] so I didn't know.

He later discovered the notice waiting for him at this address. His interpretation of how it came to be delivered there rather than to his primary residence is based on his experience with the courts over the years. Having suffered (and perpetrated, he indicated with a mock innocent gesture) a similar deceit in the past, Michael assumed that his ex-wife's lawyer had bribed someone in the notification department to send the notice to the vacation home. The clerk could not be accused of wrongdoing because the address was correct, but the strategy assured that Michael would not receive it on time.

Another case against Michael involved a forged trust receipt to the value of LE 70,500. The man who had married Michael's ex-wife was a lawyer, and had been granted proxy for an Egyptian man who lived in

Australia. The lawyer used his absence to forge a commercial receipt in his name and to raise a fraudulent case on his behalf against Michael, claiming that Michael had borrowed this sum of money from his client and accusing him of failing to pay it back when it came due. As the civil case against him proceeded, Michael's small building- and construction-supplies company was 'waxed' (temporarily closed by order of the court; historically, the closure notice was affixed to the door with wax) for two years while the court assessed the value of his assets in preparation for seizing them to repay the loan. During these years, Michael lost a significant amount in unearned profits, and ultimately took matters into his own hands.

Michael traveled to the *mugamma*, the main government administration-building in central Cairo, and obtained information related to the plaintiff. He managed to get documents from the passport department that he personally submitted to the court to prove that it was impossible for him to have signed the loan agreement because it would have occurred when this man was already in Australia. He further presented documents proving that the man had left Egypt because there were cases pending against him for debts, and that he had worked as a barber in Port Said; Michael even tracked down documents showing how much this man had paid in taxes on his barber's shop. How, Michael asked the judge, could this man – a mere barber! – have had LE 70,500 to lend him? Not only that, Michael recalled arguing before the judge, he was a barber who was two years behind on his tax payments, which only amounted to only LE 7 per month! Michael not only did extensive research to determine which types of documents would provide compelling evidence in his defence, he located and then presented these documents in court, and won his own case.

These examples highlight the way that court delay may bring litigants into prolonged contact with lawyers, as well as other legal personnel; moreover this contact is situated in focal and peripheral legal spaces (the courts, lawyers' offices).[43] In both of these examples, the litigants had clearly suffered from their prolonged legal problems. Although Amina defiantly pointed out that she would not allow her ex-husband to pressure her into giving up her rights, quoting the proverb

'Oh mountain, the wind cannot shake you' (*ya gebel, ma yahzak rih*) she just as often expressed a sense of deep despair over her situation. Moreover, her labours garnered her legal representation rather than income to put towards her long-term and household expenses, and although Salma treated her kindly, as if she were Amina's niece, the terms of their informal arrangement were largely dictated by Salma. During the period of roughly two years she had thus far spent as a litigant, her legal woes were embodied in her bartered labour.

Likewise, Michael took pride in having prevailed in many of the cases against him, yet admitted to being psychologically and financially worn down by all the years of litigation. Because he spent so much time in his lawyer's office and the courts he inevitably neglected other activities and people in his life. Late nights are usually a time when Port Saidians visit, shop and eat together; like most lawyers, Michael's lawyer saw clients between approximately nine in the evening and midnight, precluding Michael's regular participation in these social activities.

At the same time, enduring long delays must also be seen as generating the possibility and the circumstances for these litigants to gain knowledge of legal procedure and doctrine. Waiting entailed countless hours of observing, listening and discussing legal matters; in other words, processes by which information was shared and absorbed, between (for instance) Amina, her lawyer, and other clients. In contrast to efficient litigation, where representation remains primarily the domain of the lawyer and a client need not interact with him/her except sporadically, waiting made law visible to these litigants. Over the years Amina, Michael and others in similar situations, acquired legal knowledge to such an extent that despite having lawyers they also took on some tasks themselves (writing letters to influential persons, raising formal objections (*muʿaradat*), seeking out and befriending court clerks to get useful information on their cases, collecting evidence and the like). They even became sources of information and strategy for their representatives. Their informal education as frequent observers in a lawyer's office and at the courts inevitably played a significant role in their development as legal subjects. As Amina intimated and Michael articulated, they came to see themselves as knowledgeable about not only their own cases and their legal rights and responsibilities but also about the law and legal procedure more generally.

The months and years of waiting, in frequent proximity to their lawyers, for their cases to be resolved, created a temporal experience conducive to action.[44] Waiting enabled both absorptive and productive practices, and provoked action through frustration, increasing confidence and awareness. As such, the waiting involved in slow litigation, as experienced in the particular setting of lawyers' offices, may be conducive to the development of legal knowledge and agency.

Situated Delay: Office of the Experts

The Office of Experts (*maktab khubara'*) in Port Said, under the administration of the Egyptian Ministry of Justice, is not housed in or even near the main courthouse in the central Arab District. Rather, it is located in an outlying district of the city and disaggregated into several small offices in mixed-use concrete buildings. One office for several of the Agricultural Experts is in an area known colloquially as *masakin il-lunch* adjacent to the old Sweet Water canal that in the nineteenth century brought in potable water from a Nile tributary. I accompanied five members of the el-Sayyid family and their lawyer there one June afternoon, and on four subsequent occasions in the months following.

Eighteen members of the extended family, including the children, nieces and nephews of a small-landowner and farmer named Mohammed el-Sayyid, were involved in multiple lawsuits with another of his sons, Ramadan. Although the history of this complex family dispute and related lawsuits cannot be thoroughly examined here, all of the cases stem from Ramadan's claim to the entire estate of 22 *feddans* (1 Egyptian *feddan* is equivalent to 1.038 acres) that his father left on his death in 1983. The inheritors, each of whom was granted shares of the property to be held in common, designated Ramadan manager of the property in the early 1990s to oversee the maintenance of the land, buildings and equipment, and the cultivation, harvesting and sale of the crops. This decision was based in large part on the fact that Ramadan did not obtain a university degree like his siblings and remained in the village while the other inheritors moved away to Port Said and Cairo and entered professions there. According to an agreement composed and signed by the inheritors, Ramadan was to draw compensation for his work as manager from the profits, and each shareholder would also receive some of the yearly profits proportional to their designated shares. But Ramadan had refused for over ten years to grant the other inheritors their part of the profits. He argued that because he had stayed on the land he had earned a right to it by 'placing his hand' (*wad' yad*) upon it.[45]

After many years of trying and failing to resolve the dispute through mediation, the inheritors finally filed a legal case in 2003 against Ramadan to claim compensation for unpaid profits from the plots they each owned. In addition, they filed a second suit contesting an allegedly forged contract of sale, and a third for breach of contract (Ramadan purchased land from a family member, claimed it, but did not pay in full). The lawsuit brought by the family members against Ramadan for compensation required a land survey to ascertain the precise boundaries of the agricultural plots as well as the value of the crops harvested from them. The judge thus postponed the hearing and referred the case to the Agricultural Expert; between December 2003 and June 2005 the parties had appeared before the Agricultural Expert seven times, and in the following six months at least five more times to give evidence, present witnesses and provide information for the expert's report, which would eventually be submitted to the judge with a summary recommendation on compensation. These reports carry a great deal of weight, and judges rule according to the expert's recommendation in the majority of cases. Ramadan and his lawyer, as well as several family members from the plaintiff's side of the case, were present at each of these meetings.

At the first meeting I attended with the plaintiffs, in June of 2005, we stood in an anteroom as the expert concluded a meeting with another group of litigants and while waiting encountered a female agricultural expert. The plaintiffs' lawyer, Mustapha, greeted her effusively and in introducing us repeatedly complimented her by pointing out how she excelled in her work and was known for being extraordinarily smart and quick. 'This amazing woman,' said Mustapha, holding her by the arm affectionately, 'finished a case in only two months. Two months! She's so efficient!' The expert smiled and nodded, concurring with confidence that she was indeed very efficient in her investigations and in submitting reports to the court. Mustapha later told me that she was a distant relative of the el-Sayyids and was 'working' with him to help move their case forward; his flattery was both a mode of networking and a commentary on the leisurely pace of litigation that marks efficiency as rare or notable. Earlier, when first introduced to two of Mustapha's clients in the case, they eagerly shook my hand and joked that perhaps I could bring *baraka* (good fortune) to the case, and that my presence at the meeting would surely get things moving again after being stalled for so long.

We were then called in to meet with the expert, one Mr. Rady, with whom everyone was well acquainted from prior meetings, referring to him respectfully as '*bash mohandas*' ('pasha-engineer'). Our group of six litigants, two lawyers, and a researcher filled Mr. Rady's small office, and he opened a new page in his ledger to take notes by hand. As he reviewed some documents the lawyers gave him the plaintiffs joked with one another and even with Ramadan, the defendant, and his lawyer, asking after the health of various people in the village. Although some of the joking was barbed, this casual repartee was genial compared with the disparaging language Mustapha and his clients used when privately discussing Ramadan and his lawyer.

Mr. Rady, mild-mannered and dressed in a short-sleeved shirt, spread out a survey map of the land. Initially, everyone gathered around to look at it and although the tone in the room became more serious, the meeting retained an informal quality: the lawyers took calls on their cell phones, one plaintiff stepped out to pray, two of the plaintiffs sat on a couch in the room and conversed together quietly. Mr. Rady began carefully pointing to each agricultural plot, requesting specific dates for when parcels had been bought and sold and the names of the contracting parties, which gave rise to animated debate between them. Mustapha disputed the accuracy of some of Ramadan's statements, and in turn Ramadan's lawyer argued that information being given by the plaintiffs was not correct, while the expert pressed forward with his questions, continuously making notes.

Throughout the meeting, which lasted half an hour, there were multiple flare-ups. Mr. Rady asked about specific plots, the respondent answered slowly and clearly so that the expert could write down his exact words, and the lawyers and other family members interrupted to contradict or confirm statements, speaking loudly over one another in an effort to be heard. The parties accused one another of lying, chided one another with mild insults, and generally attempted to pick apart the veracity of each statement through counter-statements and accusations intended to malign the other's character. The expert often let them argue, but when things began to get out of hand he would lift his hand in a calming motion, saying simply *mashy, mashy* ('okay, okay'). Finally, he folded the map, closed the ledger, and told everyone to return the following week and to bring witnesses from the village to give statements about the boundaries of the land, the crops being grown, and their current market value.

Each of the litigants and the lawyers thanked the expert and shook his hand. However, an argument continued between Ramadan and one of the plaintiffs, Dr. Zaki, Ramadan's eldest brother, as we all filed out and down the open-air stairwell. Upon reaching the street there was suddenly a shout; the two were facing one another with raised voices and arms, gesticulating and arguing. Ramadan called his brother a dog, to which he responded with a threat to 'finish him' and lunged. Ramadan's lawyer grasped his client and Mustapha did the same, holding Dr. Zaki back in a strong bear-hug to keep him from striking Ramadan. Mustapha spoke in a soothing tone and repeatedly kissed the top of the man's head. The two men, restrained, continued to shout insults at one another until they could be wrestled into their respective cars. As soon as we were all in the car, the doctor immediately composed himself and began laughing, quoting the insults and threats he had just directed at Ramadan.

This mixture of geniality and acrimony was common during and after most meetings at the Office of the Experts. Whereas normally the plaintiffs and the defendant in this dispute avoided one another, using intermediaries to convey information, these meetings provided a context in which they were required to encounter one another. The Office of the Experts was both a legal milieu and a space unbound by the formal constraints of the courtroom. Although lawyers have the right to request that the opposing party take an oath before responding to questions by the expert, this is rarely done. As Mustapha explained, statements under oath must be taken as sworn truth and the process required to refute or disprove them is more arduous. Instead, the parties sparred verbally over the particulars of plot boundaries and market value, each side trying to appear more honest than the other and to influence the expert in his evaluation. Unlike the courthouse, there are no security officers or police at the Office of the Experts; without this security presence, parties perhaps feel less constrained in their interactions, even going so far, in the case above, to attempt a physical attack on one another.

In the process of getting their side of the story on the record, i.e. in the expert's ledger, the parties to this dispute were both revitalising ties as relatives through humour and gossip, and expressing the strong feelings of anger and bitterness they felt about the unresolved dispute. After multiple attempts at mediation through the years, they had arranged a meeting in 2004 with one of their representatives to the People's Council who, in his capacity as an important local politician and a family friend, attempted to help them resolve the issue. This effort failed, and although Mustapha had supported his clients' desire to settle the matter out of court, after this event he decided that it was no longer feasible. He dissuaded them from engaging in further mediation, which had the effect of turning the meetings at the Office of the Experts into their only opportunity to debate the issue and to appeal to one another to compromise on the basis of relationality and honour.

Both institutional shortcomings and procedural strategising generated delays in this case and the others in which they were named parties. In Mustapha's view, Ramadan was being very clever in his use of postponement strategies; according to Mustapha: 'Each *feddan* is worth LE 2,000–3,000 a year, so the more time the case takes the more money he gains'. The lawsuit against him limited the amount of damages that could be paid to the plaintiffs to the equivalent of only five years of their designated portion of income from the crops. Even if Ramadan eventually lost the case, he would still have earned money from the land that would not be counted in with the damages awarded. This infuriated Mustapha's clients, but they were helpless to do much about it, and their frustration emerged during the shouting matches at the Office of the Experts. At the same time, the eldest brother admitted to me that his aggressiveness during these meetings was intended to show Ramadan that they would not give up their lawsuit.

Conclusion

In the preceding, I have sought to use anthropological and ethnographic perspectives on delay, both generally and in the specific context of litigation in contemporary Egypt, to reconceive delay as a situated experience rather than a temporal aberration or suspended progression. As court delay disrupts a particular flow or pace of events, it instigates alternate events. In the cases discussed, court delay provoked litigants to respond to suits and charges by developing a deeper understanding of substantive and procedural law, or enabled the accrual of such knowledge through passive activities like waiting and listening in semi-legal spaces. Moreover, parties with previous litigation experience or access to good legal advice are better positioned to take advantage of legal loopholes to pursue their aims and to stymie the claims of the opposing party. In addition, delay inadvertently created spaces for attending to the deeply interpersonal and relational aspects of litigation between family members in particular, for whom a judicial response may fall short of their broader aims in pursuing litigation.

My intention was to qualify the social and economic harms that court reform efforts in the country aim to address. In light of these ethnographic detours into lawyers' and experts' offices, one might be inclined to concur with the assessment of court delay as an unqualified harm. These litigants bore the intense frustration and economic burden of lengthy litigation with little relief in sight. Yet delay also created spaces – both figurative and literal – in which litigants participated in developing rights consciousness and through which they emerged as particular legal subjects. If we consider that litigation is a process by which citizens frame their problems as having legal solutions, respond to lawsuits through legal channels, and act as bearers of rights, then litigation that is extended through repeated delays magnifies and reinforces these processes. Further, it generates the possibility for more consequential interactions through and with law.

Analysis of court delay as experienced by litigants in particular institutional spaces reveals how states and subjects are mutually constituted and how people experience multiple and overlapping subjectivities.[46] In her study of women's divorce claims in Iranian family courts, Arzoo Osanloo points out that 'legal spaces are imbued with multiple ideologies [...] that [...] contextually frame the multifaceted subjectivities their agents possess. Subjectivities are not singular or total but are contingent, dynamic, and shifting.'[47] This has particular implications for litigants involved in disputes with family members in that legal relations come to bear in new ways on social relations. Legal and peripherally legal spaces like lawyers' offices and the Offices of the Experts shape how parties interact in the context of family disputes, and the norms and rules of these spaces enable parties to shift between legal and familial subjectivities.

These findings certainly don't upend the call for court reform; law reform plays an important role in streamlining judicial procedures in order to facilitate meritorious litigation. At the same time, an ethnography of delay complicates the anticipated outcomes and achievements articulated by reformers. There are limitations on the potentials of litigation and citizenship that court reform alone cannot overcome. As Tamir Moustafa notes, judicial institutions are constrained by a 'profoundly illiberal political system'.[48] Citizens' access to legal institutions and information is limited by the broader political culture, which shapes civics education, access to political power, and other processes by which a rights bearing legal subjectivity may be constituted in relation to the state. AOJS projects have indeed sought to improve the public's access to information about legal rights, filing claims, required fees, and litigation procedures. Unfortunately, information counters in the courts designed to answer litigants' queries are unequipped to profoundly empower citizens or to create a fundamental shift in rights consciousness even where they successfully facilitate access to justice in particular instances. Acknowledging the interconnections between the political system, citizenship rights, and the realities of litigation allow us to shift the perception of court delay as neither culturally embedded nor even strictly the result of inefficiencies in case management, but rather derived from particular institutional constraints within an illiberal political system.

Notes

* Ethnographic data for this chapter was collected as part of a research project supported by Fulbright, the Social Science Research Council, and the National Science Foundation. I wrote this essay while an affiliated scholar in the Department of Anthropology and the Institute for Money, Technology, and Financial Inclusion at the University of California, Irvine, for which affiliation and support I am indebted to Bill Maurer and Karen Leonard.

1. I conducted research on contracting and dispute-processing strategies in Port Said, Egypt, throughout 2005 and in 2007, and the material introduced here focuses on cases of pending and unresolved litigation. Primary research sites included the Port Said courts, lawyers' offices, the Office of the Experts, and neighbourhood administrative centres. I was present during the meetings discussed in this chapter, and include as 'primary experiences' discussions of past and possible future events which occurred during the meetings, as well as practices and actions. I also include background data related to the litigants or their cases where relevant.
2. See Kessler 1996.
3. In addition to Kessler, see also Heise 1999–2000; Kakalik et al 1996; Nimmer 1971); Zeisel et al 1978.
4. See for example Zeisel et al 1978: xxvi on causes of delay and potential remedies in the Supreme Court of New York County (Manhattan).
5. Kessler 1996, p. 432.
6. Zeisel et al 1978: xxii
7. Zammit, 2009.
8. Ibid, p. 3.
9. Herzfeld 1991, pp. 174–5.
10. Lawrence, *The Anthropology of Justice: Law as Culture in Islamic Society*, (Cambridge, 1989).
11. See for example Engel 1984; Greenhouse 1986; Merry 1990.

12 Heidegger 1982: 258, cited in Munn, Nancy D., 'The cultural anthropology of time: a critical essay', *Annual Review of Anthropology*, 21 (1992), p. 105.
13 Riceour 1981: 169, cited in Munn 1992: 105.
14 Engel 1987: 611.
15 Munn 1992: 110.
16 See for instance Burman 1981.
17 Munn 1992: 104.
18 Giddens states: 'As time becomes acknowledged as a distinguishable phenomenon in its own right, and as inherently quantifiable, it also of course becomes regarded as a scarce and an exploitable resource. Marx rightly pinpointed this as a distinctive feature of the formation of modern capitalism. What makes possible the transmutation of labour-power into a commodity is its quantification in terms of labour-time, and the creation of the clearly defined "working day"' (1979: 201).
19 Munn 1992: 116.
20 Bourdieu 1977: 89–91.
21 Bourdieu 1990: 76.
22 The governorates of Port Said, Giza and Minya were designated as pilot sites for the Family Justice Project, and based on the outcomes in these courts the project is slated for nationwide replication in all governorates in Egypt in the years to come.
23 See Al-Sharmani 2010.
24 On the other hand, scholars studying US courts have expressed concern about the potential of legal expediency to inhibit justice for segments of the population. As Collier notes: 'The legal system ... acts to reinforce the class structure by subjecting the poor to summary justice. Spradley's data (133) shows that some Seattle tramps are sentenced to jail after hearings lasting less than 2 minutes; Mileski (104) observed a lower criminal court where 72 per cent of the cases were handled in a minute or less; Moulton (109) claims that trials involving the poor in California small claims courts last from 5 to 15 minutes; and Forer (56) argues that the poor receive quick trials and long sentences' (1975: 137).
25 The precursor to the Family Law and AOJS projects was the Administration of Criminal Justice (AOCJ) project, also funded by USAID, which included automation of the Prosecutor General's Offices to reduce delay and improve efficiency.
26 It is important to note that the same issues being addressed in contemporary court-reform projects, including delay, were present in early debates about the Mixed Courts, on which the national courts were closely modelled. For instance, in 1900, Raymond West (British Procureur-General/ Public Prosecutor in Egypt in 1884) pointed out: 'The object of executive arrangements affecting civil Courts is to make them adjudicate speedily and well, and the judges of higher rank know best how this is to be effected' (1990: 496). Likewise, historian Byron Cannon discusses frustration over

the dual court system in his analysis of a plan published in 1884 by an appeals court judge in Alexandria: 'He [the judge] admitted that most parties agreed that the cumbersome mixed charter and the disparate jurisdictions in Egypt demanded rational reform. Already deficiencies in the native courts were causing delays and a high rate of appeals which augured chaos for the average peasant litigant' (1972: 60). On Sanhuri's concerns about delay in the new National Courts and proposals for reform, see Asad 2003.
27 Quoted from an internal USAID report obtained from USAID Egypt, Democracy and Governance Program.
28 *Administration of Justice Support, Project II Report*. At http://www.amideast.org/ programs_services/institutional_dev/democracy_governance/default.htm, accessed 2 July 2010.
29 From the Egyptian Ministry of Justice Yearly Statistics, 2002–03.
30 Bernard-Maugiron and Dupret: 2002.
31 Chodosh et al 1996: 871.
32 Ibid: 874.
33 Rosen 2002: 138–44.
34 Ibid: 14ff, 14, 197.
35 Ibid: 141.
36 El-Dean 2002: 225.
37 Al-Sharmani n.d.: 11. She notes that the figure for the family courts applies to Cairo and to some other urban contexts; numbers are far lower for rural courts.
38 El-Dean 2002: 225.
39 Brown 1997: 193.
40 El-Dean 2002: 225.
41 Brown 1997: 193.
42 Yngvesson 1993. She describes 'garbage' cases as disputes between neighbours, acquaintances or family members, which are often perceived by court clerks as better resolved through private channels and as a waste of the court's time.
43 They also illustrate that disputes related to prompt and deferred dowry, maintenance and alimony can be played out in the civil/commercial courts in lieu of, or in addition to, litigation in the family courts, which I discuss elsewhere; see Hegel-Cantarella, (forthcoming). For more on uses of trust receipts as forms of guarantee, see also Zulficar 2008; Brown 1997: 200.
44 Guyer 2007.
45 The relationship between *wad' yad* and use rights is derived from claims by nomadic Bedouin Egyptians (like the Awlad 'Ali) to land-use rights based on continuous occupation or use of certain territories. As Altorki and Cole (1998: 202) note, use rights from 'placing a hand' on land are not formally recognised in law and are more akin to squatter's rights. However, there is informal recognition of *wad' yad*, and Anwar Sadat instituted processes

by which Bedouin could be compensated for selling such lands in state-approved sales.
46 See for example Messick, 1993 and 1998.
47 Osanloo 2006: 193.
48 Moustafa, 2008.

References

Al-Sharmani, Mulki, 'Recent reforms in personal status laws and women's empowerment family courts in Egypt: executive summary'. Report for Pathways of Women's Empowerment, Social Research Council, American University in Cairo (Cairo, n.d.). At <www.pathwaysofempowerment.org/Familycourts.pdf>, accessed 2 July 2010.

Altorki, Soraya and David Powell Cole, *Bedouin, Settlers, and Holiday Makers: Egypt's Changing Northwest Coast* (Cairo, 1998).

Asad, Talal, *Formations of the Secular: Christianity, Islam, Modernity (Cultural Memory in the present)* (Stanford, CA, 2003).

Bernard-Maugiron, Nathalie and Baudouin Dupret, *Egypt and Its Laws* (The Hague, 2002).

Bourdieu, Pierre, *Outline of a Theory of Practice* (Cambridge, 1977).

—— *The Logic of Practice* (Cambridge, 1990).

Brown, Nathan, *The Rule of Law in the Arab World* (Cambridge, 1997).

Burman, R., 'Time and socioeconomic change on Simbo, Solomon Islands', *Man* 16/2 (1981), pp. 251–68.

Cannon, Byron. 'A reassessment of judicial reform in Egypt, 1876–1891', *International Journal of African Historical Studies*, 5/1 (1972), pp. 51–74.

Chodosh, Hiram E., Stephen A. Mayo, Fathi Naguib and Ali El Sadek, 'Egyptian civil justice process modernization: a functional and systematic approach', *Michigan Journal of International Law*, 17 (summer 1996), pp. 865–9167.

Collier, Jane, 'Legal processes', *Annual Review of Anthropology*, 4 (1975), pp. 121–144.

El-Dean, Bahaa Ali, *Privatisation and the Creation of a Market-Based Legal System: The Case of Egypt* (Leiden, 2002).

Engel, David M., 'The oven-bird's song: insiders, outsiders, and personal injuries in an American community', *Law and Society Review*, 18 (1984), pp. 551–582.

Giddens, Anthony, *Central Problems in Social Theory: Action, Structure and Contradiction in Social Analysis* (Berkeley, CA, 1979).

Greenhouse, Carol J., *Praying for Justice: Faith, Order and Community in an American Town* (Ithaca, NY, 1986).

Guyer, Jane I., 'Prophecy and the near future: thoughts on macroeconomic, evangelical, and punctuated time', *American Ethnologist*, 34/3 (2007), pp. 409–421.

Hegel-Cantarella, Christine, 'Family-to-be: betrothal, legal documents, and reconfiguring relational obligations in Egypt', *Law, Culture & Humanities* (winter 2010).
Heidegger, M., *The Basic Problems of Phenomenology* (Bloomington, IN, 1982).
Heise, Michael, 'Justice delayed: an empirical analysis of civil case disposition time', *Case Western Reserve Law Review*, 50/813 (1999–2000).
Herzfeld, Michael, *A Place in History* (Princeton, NJ, 1991).
Kakalik, James S., Terence Dunworth, Laural A. Hill, Daniel F. McCaffrey, Marian Oshiro, Nicholas M. Pace and Mary E. Vaiana, *Just, Speedy, and Inexpensive? An Evaluation of Judicial Case Management under the Civil Justice Reform Act* (Santa Monica, CA, 1996).
Kessler, Daniel, 'Institutional causes of delay in the settlement of legal disputes', *Journal of Law, Economics, and Organization*, 12/2 (October 1996), pp. 432–60.
Merry, Sally, *Getting Justice and Getting Even: Legal Consciousness among Working-Class Americans* (Chicago, IL, 1990).
Messick, Brinkley, *The Calligraphic State* (Berkeley, CA, 1993)
—— 'Written identities: legal subjects in an Islamic state', *History of Religions*, 38/1 (1998), pp. 25–51.
Moustafa, Tamir, 'Law and Resistance in Authoritarian States: The Judicialization of Politics in Egypt', in Ginzburg, Tom and Tamir Moustafa (eds.), *Rule by Law: The Politics of Courts in Authoritarian Regimes*, (Cambridge, 2008), pp. 132–155.
Munn, Nancy D., 'The cultural anthropology of time: a critical essay', *Annual Review of Anthropology*, 21 (1992), pp. 93–123.
Nimmer, Raymond T., *The Omnibus Hearing: An Experiment in Relieving Inefficiency, Unfairness, and Judicial Delay* (Chicago, IL, 1971).
Osanloo, Arzoo, 'Islamico-civil "rights talk": women, subjectivity, and law in Iranian family court', *American Ethnologist*, 33/2 (2006), pp. 191–209.
Riceour, Paul, 'Narrative time'. In Mitchell, W.J.T. (ed.), *On Narrative* (Chicago, IL, 1981), pp. 165–186.
Rosen, Lawrence, *The Anthropology of Justice: Law as Culture in Islamic Society* (Cambridge, 1989).
—— *The Culture of Islam* (Chicago, IL, 2002).
West, Raymond, 'Recent changes in Egypt', *Journal of the Society of Comparative Legislation*, 2/3 (1900).
Yngvesson, Barbara, *Virtuous Citizens, Disruptive Subjects: Order and Complaint in a New England Court* (New York, 1993).
Zammit, David, *Court Delays and the Social Relations of Maltese Legal Practice*. Paper presented at the Tenth Mediterranean Research Meeting, Florence and Montecatini Terme 25–28 March 2009, organised by the Mediterranean Programme of the Robert Schuman Centre for Advanced Studies at the European University Institute.

Zeisel, Hans, Harry Kalven Jr. and Bernard Buchholz, *Delay in the Court* (Westport, CT, 1978).

Zulficar, Mona, 'The Islamic marriage contract in Egypt'. In Quraishi, Asifa and Frank E. Vogel (eds.), *The Islamic Marriage Contract: Case Studies in Islamic Family Law* (Cambridge, MA, 2008), pp. 231–274.

6

DIVORCE PRACTICES IN MUSLIM AND CHRISTIAN COURTS IN SYRIA

*Esther van Eijk**

Introduction

Syria is a multi-religious and multi-ethnic country, with a Muslim majority and several religious minorities.[1] The various religious communities have long since enjoyed the right to regulate and administer their family relations according to their respective religious laws. The main law in Syria that regulates family relations, the 1953 Syrian Law of Personal Status (hereafter SLPS), is predominately based on Islamic legal sources, most notably Hanafi *fiqh* (Islamic jurisprudence).[2] The SLPS is the general law and applies to all Syrians, but the Druze, Jewish and Christian communities have limited legislative and judicial autonomy in certain personal status matters, such as marriage and divorce. Catholics, however, are in an exceptional position: they were granted full jurisdiction over all personal status issues when the Syrian government enacted a new Catholic family law in 2006.

Both the SLPS and the Catholic family law prescribe that in divorce cases judges should try to reconcile the disputing parties. During my fieldwork, I noticed that if reconciliation fails, judges seemed to prefer to reach an amicable divorce settlement, in an effort to preserve relations for the future; this is deemed generally desirable, especially when there are children involved. However, upon closer inspection, a clear difference appears in the way judges in the Muslim personal status courts and those in the Catholic equivalent perform their reconciliation duties. This chapter examines divorce practices in a Catholic and an Islamic personal status court in Damascus, in relation to the themes of reconciliation and the restoration of social harmony.

1. Personal Status Laws in Syria

The 1953 Syrian Law of Personal Status

In Syria various personal status laws can be found, the major law regulating family relations being the 1953 Syrian Law of Personal Status (*qanun al-ahwal al-shakhsiyya*). The SLPS 'enjoys the status of *primus inter pares* by being the general law';[3] Berger uses these words to describe the position of the personal status law of Egypt, but the same applies to the SLPS. It is the general law and only excludes the Druze, Christian and Jewish communities on certain specified matters.[4]

The SLPS was enacted in 1953.[5] At the time, it was considered to be the most comprehensive and progressive code in the Middle East,[6] including innovations that had not been incorporated into any other code in the Arab world.[7] According to Anderson, the Syrian reformers of the mid-twentieth century, like their Egyptian counterparts, sought to combine the demands of modern life with the wish to ground their legal interpretations in religious authority.[8]

The SLPS consists of 308 articles, dealing with marriage, its dissolution, paternity, nursing, legal guardianship, custodianship (*wisaya*), bequests and inheritance. Article 305 states that in respect of matters left unspecified in the Code, resort should be had to the most authoritative doctrine of the Hanafi school. For the practical application of this provision judges and lawyers today still consult the code (based on Hanafi *fiqh*) compiled by the Egyptian jurist Muhammad Qadri Pasha in 1875. The copy of the SLPS issued by the Syrian Bar Association, for example, consists of two parts: first the law itself, then the complete text of the Qadri Pasha code. In this way, the Hanafi doctrine remains not only the point of departure, but also the final resort.

Amendments to the SLPS and Recent Developments

The last major amendments to the 1953 Personal Status Code were made in 1975 (Law no. 34), with the intention of improving the position of women. The annotation to the 1975 Law says that the state has a constitutional obligation to 'lift the bonds that restrain the development of women' and 'their participation in the development of society'.[9] The amendments concerned various SLPS provisions related to, for example, polygamy,[10] the dower, maintenance, divorce, nursing, legal guardianship and custodianship.[11]

It took until 2003 before any further changes in the SLPS were implemented, and this time they amounted merely to a minor amendment. Following Syria's ratification of CEDAW[12] in March 2003, both the government and civil-society groups drafted proposals for amendments to the family law,[13] which were fervently debated in Parliament and wider society.[14] Some religious conservatives accused activists for women's rights of seeking to tarnish the Quran and religious laws by calling for equality between men and women, which they considered an imitation of the West.[15] The women activists claimed that the current law was a male law, not necessarily Islamic, and questioned the patriarchal interpretation of the existing laws.[16] In the end, only one amendment (Law no. 18) – in adjusted form – was promulgated by the President, Bashar Al-Assad.[17] Article 146 was modified and now gives a divorced mother the right to nurse (*hadana*) her children until the age of 15 for girls and 13 for boys, an increase of two years respectively. The original proposal intended to abolish the age distinction between boys and girls, and leave them both in the *hadana* care of their mother until the age of 15.[18]

In May 2009, various lawyers, judges, representatives of churches and of civil-society organisations and others were taken by surprise when they received a copy of a draft for a new family law.[19] Apparently, a committee of anonymous Islamic legal scholars appointed by the Council of Ministers had been working on a new draft for two years, in secret.[20] The draft was heavily criticised by members of parliament, religious figures, lawyers and intellectuals, in national newspapers and on the internet – the latter including media forums such as Facebook (even though this is officially banned in Syria).[21] Opponents accused the committee of imposing extremist Islamic views 'similar to those of the Taliban';[22] in their view, the proposal was regressive. One controversial issue, amongst many, was the proposal to create a body that could divorce a couple without their consent if one of them was deemed to be an apostate (*murtadd*; someone who had renounced his/her faith, i.e. Islam).[23] In early July, the draft law was withdrawn by the President; a few months later, a revised draft was published. Although less controversial than the first, this second draft also never made it past the concept stage. In September 2010, however, an amendment was made to article 308 SLPS, expanding the jurisdiction of all the Christian and Jewish communities to include matters of inheritance and bequests.

Application and Jurisdiction of the SLPS

Article 306 SLPS provides that: 'The provisions of this law apply to all Syrians except for what is stated in the following two articles.' Article 307 provides that the Druze community is explicitly exempted from those provisions that run counter to their beliefs, such as polygamy.[24] Article 308 provides that Christians and Jews apply their own religious regulations in matters of betrothal, conditions of marriage, marriage conclusion, wife's obedience, wife's and children's maintenance, annulment and dissolution of marriage, and nursing and, inheritance and bequests. Although these communities may draft and change their legislation internally, official government approval is required by law.[25] In 2006, the situation changed for the Catholic community when they obtained a new family law and thereby placed themselves outside the scope of the SLPS (see below).

The courts implementing the SLPS are called Sharia courts[26] and are part of the civil law system; the judges are state employees, trained in secular law faculties.[27] Nevertheless, this does not exclude the fact that most Sharia judges appeared, in my observation, to be faithful Muslims.[28] Cardinal writes that 'piety and circumspect behaviour are qualities demanded of a Sharia court judge' in Syria.[29] For example, just like Cardinal's experience in the Sharia courts, the judges I met in the Damascus courts would not shake my hand in greeting.

The provisions of the SLPS apply to all Syrians, which implies that the Sharia courts have general jurisdiction in all matters of personal status.[30] But this general jurisdiction is restricted by Articles 307 and 308, which grants the Druze, Jewish and Christian communities not only legislative but also judicial autonomy. In other words, these communities, including the Evangelicals (Protestants, of various persuasions) have their own personal status courts, where clerical judges apply their family laws.

The Sharia courts have full jurisdiction over all personal status cases involving Muslims, with no distinction made between Sunni, Shia, Ismaili, Jaafari or Alawi Muslims. In some specific cases, Jews and Christians also have to refer to a Sharia court, for example in cases concerning paternity (*nasab*), matters of legal capacity and representation (e.g. *wilaya* and *wisaya*).[31] This legal maze can create complex situations, not only for the parties involved but also for the lawyers who represent them. In addition, lawyers often lack knowledge about the other (non-SLPS) personal status laws. This is because law students are only trained in the SLPS – the other laws are not part of the university law curricula.[32]

Christian Personal Status Laws

The various Christian denominations are divided into the Orthodox Christians, the Protestants or Evangelicals, and the Catholic sects. The largest group of Christians belongs to the Orthodox denomination, with the Greek Orthodox (*rum urthudhuks*) being the largest,[33] followed by Syriac Orthodox and Armenian Orthodox. Each Orthodox group has its own recognised Orthodox law of personal status;[34] there is an Orthodox spiritual (*ruhiyya*) court in every diocese.

The second recognised Christian 'group' is made up of the Evangelical, Protestant communities.[35] The Evangelical churches include Baptists, Presbyterians, the Alliance Church, the Church of

Nazarene, and Reformed, Episcopal (i.e. Anglican)[36] and Armenian Evangelicals. The current Evangelical Law of Personal Status was drafted by the National Evangelical Synod of Syria and Lebanon, which has its headquarters in Beirut and dates back to 1949. The Syrian government accepted the Law in 1952 (amended in 1962).[37] The four Evangelical spiritual courts can hear cases of the following four denominations: Baptist, Presbyterian, Alliance Church and Church of Nazarene.

The family law position of Catholics is unique and different from the other Christian groups. In Syria there are six Catholic denominations[38] that recognise the judicial authority of the Pope. The legislation for the Catholic sects is predominantly based on canon law issued by the Mother Church in Rome. The Catholics have a court of first instance in every diocese; the Catholic court of appeal is situated in Damascus. In special circumstances, the Vatican 'Rota' court in Rome can hear appeals from decisions of the Catholic (appellate) courts.[39]

On 13 June 2006 the People's Assembly approved the new Personal Status Code for the Catholic community and on 18 June 2006 it was promulgated by presidential decree as Law no. 31. The new law declared Catholic canon laws, issued by the late Pope John Paul II, applicable to the Catholic communities in Syria.[40] The 2006 Catholic Code was comprehensive and covered all matters of personal status. Due to the new law, Catholic courts had full jurisdiction in all personal status matters. The law differed from the SLPS and other personal status laws to the extent, for example, that it guaranteed men and women equal inheritance rights, allowed Catholics to adopt a child, and gave fathers and mothers equal custody rights over their children in the event of divorce. The promulgation of the Catholic law happened quickly and quietly, and came as a great surprise to many.[41] During my fieldwork several Catholics told me that they were very pleased with their new law, while several Orthodox Christians admitted being slightly jealous of their Catholic brothers and sisters, and expressed a wish to have a similar law. The reason why the Catholics managed to be granted this special position *vis-à-vis* the other Christian groups remains a subject for further study.

2. Divorce Practices in Muslim and Catholic Court Rooms

There are a number of differences between the Sharia and the Catholic courts. A first difference one immediately notices when comparing a Catholic court with a Muslim one are the court premises. The six Sharia courts of Damascus proper are located in the city's main courthouse (*qasr al-'adli*), which is located right in the city centre, at a busy traffic junction, just off the entrance to the main shopping street, *suq al-hamadiyya*. Next to the six Sharia courts, *qasr al-'adli* houses numerous other courts, such as magistrates', criminal and civil courts. On weekday mornings, the building, both inside and out, is a crowded hive of activity. The Catholic first-instance court of Damascus is located on the premises of the *Zaytoun* church, near a city gate (*Bab Sharqi*) in the Christian quarter of the old city. The orderliness of the church premises outside is reflected in the inside of the court room. The tranquillity of the court is almost certainly the result of the considerably lower number of cases the Christian judges have to handle compared to their Muslim counterparts, if only because the number of Christians in Syria is much smaller (10 per cent of the total population, vs roughly 85 per cent Muslims).

In addition, there are other significant differences between the Sharia courts and the Catholic court. The most notable differences perhaps concern the judges themselves: in the Catholic court, the judge is a priest. Catholic judges receive their training in canon law at the Vatican colleges, as they are seen as representatives of the Mother Church in Rome. In the Catholic court where I was allowed to observe many divorce proceedings, the judges are dressed in a cassock (clerical robe), and the other court personnel usually wear a clerical collar. The Muslim judges I have come across usually wear a suit – with nothing to indicate their status except for the nameplate on the dais saying 'Judge (*al-qadi*)' followed by a name . Another significant difference I noticed concerns the way in which the judges prefer to be addressed in court. A Muslim judge would be addressed as *ustadh* (a polite form of address for an educated, respectable person), while a Catholic judge preferred *abuna* ('father'). In fact, litigants or lawyers would be corrected by the judges or the scribe if they used the word *ustadh* by mistake. The Damascus first-instance court consisted of two judges, a scribe, the *wakil al-'adl* ('church attorney') and the *al-muhami 'an al-withaq* or the *al-muhami 'an al-sirr al-zawaj fi-l-kanisa* ('defender of the marital bond'). As a rule, the *muhami* objects to a divorce request presented to the court, as it is his task to preserve and defend the marital bond.[42] The *wakil al-'adl*, on the other hand, has the authority to ask the court for nullification of a marriage if he thinks it is better for a couple to divorce.[43] To recapitulate, the Damascus first-instance Catholic court consist of five people. However, in the majority of the sessions I attended the court was seldom complete: usually only the two judges and the scribe would be present. By comparison, a judge in a Sharia court normally sits with his clerk in a rather small court room. During the court sessions I observed, judges regularly retired to their private offices next to the court room, while the clerk continued with the organisation and processing of the paperwork.

Apart from the outward appearances, court proceedings in a Catholic court differ from those in a Sharia court. Whereas the court sessions at a Catholic court were orderly, with cases processed one at the time, those at the Sharia courts in Damascus generally appeared slightly chaotic. During my visits to Damascus' main courthouse, the court rooms and the adjoining central hall were usually packed with court personnel, lawyers, litigants, witnesses and family members, including infants. Judges would go back and forward between the court rooms and their offices, with litigants, witnesses and family members patiently waiting their turn, sometimes for hours. The Catholic court, on the other hand, was a haven of peace. The judges were strict in their observance of the court's agenda; for example, lawyers were required to make appointments for future sessions before 10 a.m. If they appeared in court past 10 a.m. to make an appointment, they would be reprimanded by the judges.

Marriage and Divorce

Tucker argues that in seventeenth- and eighteenth-century Syria and Palestine marriage was considered 'a key to social harmony' and 'central to social relations', reinforcing social ties and promoting harmony and stability in the community.[44] Whilst it may be difficult to demonstrate that this still holds true for all geographical areas and social strata in Syria, the institution of marriage has seemingly not lost its significance, even though divorce rates have increased over recent years.

The SLPS describes marriage as a contract between a man and a woman, concluded in the presence of two witnesses.[45] Marriage is thus considered a contractual relationship, the aim of which is 'to establish a union for a shared life and procreation' (Article 1). According to the Catholic Code of Canons for the Eastern Churches, on the other hand, a Christian marriage is considered a sacrament (in Arabic: *sirr al-zawaj*): "By the marriage covenant, founded by the Creator and ordered by His laws, a man and woman by irrevocable personal consent establish between themselves a partnership of the whole of life; this covenant is by its very nature ordered to the good of the spouses and to the procreation and education of children.' (Can. 776 §1).[46]

In Syria, increasingly, many marriages end in divorce, among all religious groups.[47] Nowadays, couples filing for divorce are primarily young, which seems to be a widespread phenomenon in many personal status courts. While this observation cannot be supported by quantitative evidence, the trend has been observed by various legal practitioners with whom I interacted during my fieldwork in Damascus.

During divorce proceedings, in both Muslim and Christian personal status courts, the words *sulh* and *musalaha*, meaning 'peace', '(re)conciliation'[48] or 'amicable settlement', are often heard. Much is said about the concept of *sulh* in *fiqh* literature;[49] it has several meanings and connotations (religious, ethical, legal) and serves various purposes.[50] In the Syrian legal context, I would contend that the ideal of *sulh*, or the desired restoration and preservation of social harmony, is prominent during trials – in the Sharia court rooms mainly at the beginning of the proceedings, in the Christian court rooms from the start till the very end.

Divorce Practices in a Catholic Court in Damascus

The majority of the cases in the Catholic courts are, as in the Sharia courts, divorce cases, even though divorce in the former is difficult to obtain. A Christian marriage bond is deemed exclusive and permanent, for indeed what 'God hath joined together, let not man put asunder'.[51] The Catholic church even renounces the very word 'divorce' (*talaq*), and only acknowledges nullification of a marriage (*butlan al-zawaj*), meaning that the spouses have to prove that the marriage was unsound from the very beginning. To obtain a nullification of the marriage the parties have to deliver evidence to the court to support their claims, most importantly by witness statements. Divorce cases in the Christian court can take a long time before a settlement is reached, especially in the Catholic courts where the procedures are long, which might provide an additional discouragement for a couple looking to divorce. The nullification of a marriage first has to be pronounced by a court of first instance, subsequently this announcement (*'alan*) has to be confirmed, or rejected, in a ruling (*hukm*) by the appellate Catholic court in Damascus.[52] This explains why it takes at least a year and a half to conclude a *butlan al-zawaj* case.

In the Christian courts the clerical judges consider it their duty to seek a reconciliation between the spouses in order to avoid divorce. The focus on reconciliation in the Christian communities is a natural one, since marriage is considered a sacrament. According to the church, divorce contradicts the sacramental nature of marriage, and is correspondingly difficult to obtain. Before one or both spouses can file a claim for nullification of the marriage (*butlan al-zawaj*) in the Catholic court, the couple first has to turn to the local priest (*khuri*) to try to reconcile their differences. Only when no reconciliation (*musalaha*) can be reached are they able to refer to the court. At every stage of the case, the court will try to reach reconciliation between the spouses, or in the words of a Catholic judge: 'The door to reconciliation remains always open!' (*bab al-musalaha da'iman maftuh!*).[53] If a claim for *butlan* is submitted to the court the couple are usually given at least a month to try to reach reconciliation. A claim for *butlan* can only be filed if there is a lawful reason for nullification: the Code of Canons for the Eastern Churches lists the lawful reasons, such as deceit, duress, consanguinity or lack of understanding of the full implications of marriage.[54] When husbands file a case for *butlan*, they commonly present arguments such as: 'My wife left the marital home to stay with her family without informing me', or 'She does not fulfil her marital or household duties because she is always out of the house.' When a wife leaves the marital home without her husband's consent and this claim is accepted by the court, she will lose her right to maintenance (*nafaqa*). When women file cases to the court they often present arguments along the lines of: 'My husband does not support me financially', and/or 'My husband beats me.' The litigants are clearly instructed by their lawyers on what to say when they have to testify to the court.

The following case, pertaining to a request for nullification of the marriage by a young woman, in the Catholic court of first instance in Damascus, illustrates the constant emphasis on reconciliation as the ideal resolution.

A young couple enters the court room. The wife, who appears to be in her late twenties, has filed a case for nullification of the marriage (*butlan al-zawaj*). Since this is their first appearance in court the judge wishes to talk to the couple alone, without the lawyers present. The couple have been married for over a year, and used to live in France. The wife says that it has become impossible to live together because she has become aware that her husband only married her to take advantage of her, or more precisely of her French nationality. The husband is unemployed, and depends on her financially. The husband, on the other hand, claims that she does not wish to have children and that there is no marital life to speak of. The judge asks the wife whether this is true, whether she wants to have children or not. She replies that she does, but not by him. She refuses reconciliation (*musalaha*); she thinks that it is impossible to continue the marriage, and says that continuation would be unfair to both parties. This answer upsets the judge and he asks her angrily, 'Do you think marriage is a game? You married in a Catholic church, under God's eyes, in His house.'[55] The judge reminds her that there has to be an 'essential' reason for *butlan*, otherwise the court cannot and will not nullify the marriage. Therefore it is better for them to reconcile their differences and make the marriage work, 'invoke the Lord and reconcile!'.[56] The wife and husband, however, persist in their claim. The lawyers are summoned back to the court room, and the judge informs them that the court has tried to persuade the couple to drop their claim, but to no avail.

Four days later the couple are back for questioning by the court. Both husband and wife take an oath on the Bible, before the court starts with the actual questioning. The wife, being the plaintiff, is the first party to be interrogated. The judge asks her how they met and about their engagement. When the judge asks about the reason for the disagreement (*khilaf*) between them, she says that her husband is very jealous and a trouble-maker. She states that her husband hits her, calls her names, kicked her out of their house, and has asked her father to pay for several household goods, such as a washing machine and a refrigerator. She is afraid of her husband and says he always causes trouble: for example, he goes to her workplace and creates problems there with his jealous behaviour. At this point the wife indicates to the court that she would like to continue without any outsiders present in the courtroom, therefore a trainee lawyer and myself are asked to leave the courtroom. The session continues for about an hour.

Some four weeks later the couple are back in court, and the questioning of the wife and husband continues. The wife's main complaint is that her husband does not work and that he squanders her own and her father's money. She says that, in retrospect, they married too fast because she had to travel back to France, where she lived at the time. He joined her in France but never made a serious attempt to settle down there. After a month he went back to Syria. The husband, when questioned, says that they do not have a good marriage, partly because of the influence of his father-in-law. Indeed, a month later while being questioned as a witness, the wife's father acknowledges that he has been against the marriage from the very beginning, fearing that the husband was only interested in his daughter's French nationality and her (family's) money, and that the husband did not want to work. The husband, in fact, admits that the main reason why he married her was because of her French nationality and the fact that she had work in France. Both spouses declare that there is no hope of reconciliation between them. Although the court continues throughout each session to underline the importance of reconciliation, it appears in this case to have acknowledged that there was no more hope in saving this marriage. The judge warns the husband not to make the same mistake again, i.e. to get married for the wrong reasons.

During the various stages of this case,[57] like in all cases presented in the Damascus Catholic court, the court repeatedly emphasised the importance of preserving or restoring the marital bond, while at the same time continuing with the proceedings for nullification. The lengthy procedures keep this hope of reconciliation alive.

Divorce Practices in Syrian Sharia Courts

The Prophet (peace be upon him) said: If any woman asks her husband for divorce without some strong reason, the sweet odour of paradise will be forbidden to her.

This *hadith* (traditions of the prophet Muhammad) was pinned up on the wall of the Sharia courtroom in Damascus where I observed most cases. Apparently the *hadith* did not have the intended effect, as I came across numerous women who had come to the court to seek divorce. So-called *mukhalaʿa* divorce[58] (often called 'wife-initiated') in particular appeared to be a popular way to dissolve a marriage. But before looking into *mukhalaʿa*, I will first discuss the reconciliation obligations (by law) undertaken by the Sharia judges as part of SLPS divorce proceedings. We will see that the ideal of reconciliation is not as prominent as in the Catholic court rooms. The following case, however, provides a brief description of the reconciliation techniques used by a judge of one of the Sharia courts in Damascus.

An agitated man (a university teacher) and his wife (a doctor) burst into one of the Sharia courts in Damascus as a judge was midway through the dictation to his clerk of a witness statement he had just heard from another case. The judge tells them to stay quiet and wait until he has finished. Once the other couple and their witnesses have left the room, they are summoned to the dais by the judge who inquires into the reason for their disagreement. The husband says that his wife had left him a year ago and that she wants to get a divorce, but he does not agree. He claims that his wife would, in fact, like to return to him but her mother prevents her from returning to the marital home. The judge asks the woman whether this is true. She replies that she does not want to return to him because she does not want to upset her family. She claims that he has been very impolite to her mother: this is the only reason why she left him. The wife's brother concurs with this, adding that the husband treats their mother badly, for instance by raising his voice to her. The wife starts to cry and says that she does not know what to do. The judge tries to calm everyone down and proposes accompanying them to the mother's house once the court closes (i.e. after 2 p.m.). The judge urges the husband to apologise to the mother, after which they should try to find a solution to this situation; everyone agrees to act on the judge's advice. Before leaving the court, the husband tells the judge that they have a child and that his wife loves him and he loves her, but that pressure is placed upon his wife by her family. The judge reassures him that he will do his outmost to try and help them to resolve their differences.

However, such an approach is not necessarily common practice amongst the Sharia judges in Damascus. According to one of the lawyers I worked closely with, this judge was exceptional when it came to resolving social conflicts.[59] The lawyer told me that this judge was one of the few who personally visits litigants at home to try and resolve disputes between the parties by finding a solution acceptable to all. Other judges appeared to handle cases swiftly: sometimes a case would be concluded within a few minutes, for example the registration of a *mukhalaʿa* divorce (divorce by mutual consent). Despite the fact that the SLPS obliges a judge to try to bring about reconciliation in almost all divorce actions (see below), these reconciliation attempts were often conducted in an expeditious manner.

The SLPS recognises three types of divorce: first, a husband can divorce his wife by repudiation (*talaq*); secondly, a couple can file for divorce by mutual consent (*mukhalaʿa*); and thirdly, either spouse can file a petition for judicial divorce (*tafriq*). A considerable number of cases in the Sharia courts are *mukhalaʿa* cases,[60] meaning that the spouses sign a divorce contract in which the husband agrees to repudiate his wife in exchange for forgoing her financial rights. The wife relinquishes her right to any unpaid, outstanding dower (*mahr muʿajjal*) and her right to the maintenance (*nafaqa*) to which she is entitled during her waiting period (generally three menstrual cycles after the dissolution of the marriage).[61] This type of wife-initiated divorce requires the consent of both spouses. This is in contrast to Egypt where, according to article 20 of the Personal Status Law no. 1/2000, a woman has the right to initiate a *mukhalaʿa* divorce without her husband's consent.

The SLPS stipulates, in a way similar to the Egyptian law, that reconciliation attempts have to be made in divorce proceedings in Syria's Sharia courts. Article 88 (1) states that when an action for divorce (*talaq*) or divorce by mutual consent (*mukhalaʿa*) is brought to the court, the judge shall defer acting upon the case for one month in the hope of reconciliation between the spouses. Once that month has passed, both parties will be called to appear in court if either the husband persists in his action for divorce, or both spouses persist in their *mukhalaʿa* request. The judge will listen to their disagreement, and has a legal duty to try to resolve their differences. To this end the judge will involve the families of the spouses and any other person capable of resolving those differences (Article 88 (2) SLPS). If the reconciliation attempts fail, the judge will allow the registration of *talaq* or *mukhalaʿa* (Article 88 (3) SLPS).

The SLPS stipulates that if one of the spouses brings a judicial divorce petition to court on the grounds[62] of discord (*al-tafriq li-l-shiqaq bayna al-zawjayn*), claiming that the other is causing so much harm that it impossible to continue their marriage, the judge will first try to reconcile the couple (Article 112 (1) SLPS). If harm (*darar*) cannot be proven, then the judge will postpone the proceedings for at least a month in the hope of reconciliation. If the parties persist in their claim, and reconciliation cannot be achieved, the court will appoint two arbiters (Article 112 (3) SLPS),[63] who are assigned to try and reconcile the spouses. If they fail to reach reconciliation, they will determine the reason for the disagreement and advise the court how to dissolve the marriage. They will establish the level of culpability ascribed to the husband and the wife respectively, in order to determine if and how much of the remaining dower and possible alimony (*nafaqa*) has to be paid (Article 114 SLPS).

Whether the above procedures dictated by the law are always observed by the judges is questionable. According to my observations in the Sharia courts, and based on the information provided by lawyers I worked with, it is common practice for judges simply to register a *talaq* or *mukhala'a* request without undertaking a reconciliation attempt. On the other hand, it should be noted that the mandatory arbitration (*tahkim*) sessions in the case of a judicial divorce (*tafriq*) on the grounds of discord are in fact always conducted.[64] The reasons for the somewhat negligent attitude of judges towards their reconciliation duties are varied, but the main reason appears to be the massive workload and backlog of the Sharia courts.

Mukhala'a contracts are often negotiated by the parties with help of a lawyer, who on their behalf then submits the contract for registration by the court.[65] Nevertheless, the wife has to be present in court to register the divorce, and at this point, she is asked if this is what she really wants. If she accepts the terms of the contract, the divorce contract is registered by the court, without any attempt at reconciliation. This observation is in line with Sonneveld's findings in the Egyptian context: although Egyptian law requires marital arbitration before a divorce based on *mukhala'a* can be pronounced, she observed that most Egyptian judges regarded these compulsory arbitration sessions as a formality, 'something which they simply have to do'.[66]

As mentioned earlier, *mukhala'a* divorces make up a significant number of the cases handled by the Sharia courts. A possible reason is that a *mukhala'a* divorce is an expeditious alternative to the lengthy litigation of a judicial divorce, where the outcome cannot be guaranteed. Lawyers repeatedly told me that *mukhala'a* is the most efficient way of obtaining a divorce, especially since the amount of maintenance (during the waiting period) awarded in case of judicial divorce is often so low that it is hardly worth filing a petition for judicial divorce in the first place.[67] In contrast to a judicial divorce case, divorce by *mukhala'a* is not about determining fault or blame, and the wife is not required to establish grounds for divorce, though on the other hand it should be borne in mind that women might be pressured to contract a *mukhala'a* divorce. A *mukhala'a* divorce can be an easy and cheap way out for a husband; he can terminate the marriage and avoid the financial obligations of a 'regular' divorce.[68]

Divorce by mutual consent can thus be advised by lawyers because it is more efficient and expedient than a 'regular' divorce. Similarly, Carlisle observed that arbiters often advised the couple, during the mandatory arbitration sessions, to resolve their marital dispute by concluding a *mukhalaʿa* divorce, because it provided spouses with 'an opportunity to settle a case immediately and on known terms'.[69]

Even though the SLPS attaches importance to reconciliation in divorce cases, as also in cases of *mukhalaʿa*, in reality it appears that judges often skip or ignore these reconciliation obligations. Indeed, as observed by Carlisle during the mandatory arbitration sessions, the arbiters often proposed divorce by *mukhalaʿa* as a solution.[70] When they realised there was no chance of saving the marriage and reconciling the spouses, the arbiters offered them an expeditious alternative for dissolving their union.

Although the conclusion of a marital dispute by means of *mukhalaʿa* does not meet the 'ideal of reconciliation', since in the end the couple still divorce, nonetheless an agreement by mutual consent – at least on paper – is reached. This type of resolution can offer parties an opportunity to overcome their past differences and to try and restore their relations. According to one Damascus Sharia judge, this is especially desirable if a couple has children.[71]

3. Concluding Remarks

The personal status judges in the various courts deal mostly with marital disputes and divorce claims. In the event that marriage fails and continuation of marital life appears impossible, these judges ideally continue to try to restore the lines of communication and, better still, resolve the differences between the spouses so that the marriage will be preserved.

We have seen that both the Syrian Law of Personal Status (SLPS) and the Catholic personal status law oblige the judges to try to bring about reconciliation in a divorce case. However, it seems that a Catholic judge goes about his reconciliation duties more conscientiously than his Muslim colleague. Two reasons for this difference can be suggested: first, the 'ideal' of reconciliation for Christian judges seems to be obvious, due to the importance of a Christian marriage as a sacrament. Second, the number of personal status cases presented to the Sharia courts far exceeds the number of cases presented to the Christian courts, which leaves less time for reconciliation. Even though reconciliation actions are less obvious in the Sharia courts (except in the case of judicial divorce), judges there nevertheless try to persuade a disputing couple to settle their dispute by agreement. By proposing to resolve a divorce dispute by means of *mukhalaʿa*, an agreement by mutual consent, a judge (or an arbiter, or even a lawyer) tries to find an amicable way to end the conflict. Since there is no perfect outcome to a divorce dispute – apart from, if possible, reconciliation – the best (or least bad) solution is an amicable divorce settlement.

Notes

* The preliminary findings of this article are based on fieldwork undertaken in March–April 2008, and October 2008–July 2009. In some cases only the initials or first names of informants or interviewees are given in order to protect their privacy. The author wishes to thank Maaike Voorhoeve for her valuable comments and suggestions on earlier drafts of this chapter. Thanks are also due to Nadia Sonneveld and Mary Davies for their editorial comments.

1. There are no official statistics available on religion, but according to pre-conflict estimates about 74 per cent of all Syrians were Sunni Muslims, and around 16 per cent were non-Sunni Muslims, such as Druze, Shia and Alawi; about 10 per cent of the population belonged to various Christian denominations. In addition, a few Jewish and Yazidi families lived in Syria; see Central Intelligence Agency 2009; *International Religious Freedom Report* 2009.
2. Syria was part of the Ottoman Empire (1516–1918), and the official rite of the Ottoman Empire was the Hanafi school of law; as a result, the Hanafi *fiqh* remains notably important in Syria; this is particularly evident in the field of family law.
3. Berger 2005: 46.
4. For the sake of conciseness, in this chapter I will leave aside the regulations regarding matters of personal status in the Jewish and Druze communities.
5. The SLPS was promulgated as legislative decree no. 59 on 17 September 1953; it came into force on 1 November 1953, during the military rule of ʿAdib al-Shishakli. From the late 1940s until the mid-1950s Syria was subjected to

a string of military coups. In this period of successive military regimes, the most important legislation was promulgated, which – for the most part – is still in force today.
6   Anderson 1955: 34.
7   Ibid. For some scholars, the legal-religious foundations of some of the innovations in the law was rather narrow. According to Layish (1978: 270), drafters of statutory legislation in countries such as Egypt and Syria founded such innovations by referring to the principle of *maslaha* ('public interest'), to the extent that 'social need became a source of law in its own right'; see also 'Atari 2006: 10.
8   Anderson 1957: 31; 1955: 34–5.
9   'Atari 2006: 13.
10 Some amendments, for example Article 17, were drafted with the intention of restricting the traditional divorce rights of men. This article now stipulates that a man who wants to marry a new wife has not only to prove he is financially capable of providing for her, but also to provide a lawful justification (*musawwigh shar'i*) in order to obtain the judge's consent to such a marriage.
11 'Atari 2006: 13–19.
12 *Convention on the Elimination of All Forms of Discrimination Against Women* (CEDAW), adopted by the UN General Assembly on 18 December 1979 (GA Res. 34/180, UN Doc. A/34/46), entry into force 3 September 1981.
13 For example, Syrian women's organizations staged a petition for equal custody rights for divorced mothers. The petitioners collected 15,000 signatures, enough to induce the Syrian Parliament to study the proposed amendments. Amongst others, these projected changes included: girls being allowed to marry without the consent of their legal guardian; divorced mothers being enabled to stay in the marital home when they take care of the children; and the right of children of divorced parents to be given a choice at the age of 15 as to whether they want to continue to live with their father or mother (interview with former member of Parliament Hanaan Najmeh, Damascus, 2 April 2008).
14 Maktabi 2007: 14–15.
15 Ibid: 18–19.
16 Idem 2009: 18–19.
17 The amendment was not issued by Parliament but by presidential decree. The president 'intervened' by personally reforming the family law, in order to settle the debate between conservative clerics and civil-society groups; Rabo 2005: 85–6.
18 Interview with former Member of Parliament Hanaan Najmeh, Damascus, 2 April 2008.
19 They were given one week to study and comment on the draft, which, compared to the 308 articles of the current SLPS, comprised 665 articles.
20 Cardinal 2010: 208.

21 See for example Syrian Women Observatory, at <www.nesasy.org>, accessed 30 July 2010.
22 Ferguson and Muhanna 2009.
23 Ibid.
24 Article 307 para. b SLPS.
25 The recognised religious communities are defined by legislative decree no. 60/L.R., promulgated on 13 March 1936 by the French High Commissioner de Martel; see El-Hakim 1995: 148.
26 Article 33 of the Judicial Authority Law (Law no. 98/1961) states that there are three types of personal status courts, namely Sharia courts; a doctrinal court for the Druze sect (*al-mahkama al-madhhabiyya li-l-ta'ifa al-druziyya*); and spiritual (*ruhiyya*) courts (Article 33).
27 Botiveau 1993: 180–1.
28 The Judicial Authority Law is silent on this point, i.e. the religious background of judges. Except for the judge of the Druze doctrinal court, these judges have themselves to be Druze (Article 35).
29 Cardinal 2010: 206.
30 In addition to this, the Law also applies to non-Syrian Muslims who are subject to Islamic personal status laws in their home country; see Berger 1997:126.
31 Article 535 of the Law of Judicial Procedures; see Anderson 1957: 28.
32 Interview with 'Ali Mulhim, lawyer and member of the Board of the Syrian Bar Association, Damascus, 13 April 2009). Cardinal's assertion (2010: 205) should be noted here, that law-school students study the Muslim, Christian and Jewish personal status laws, but during the frequent interactions I had with various junior lawyers (as trainees) I noticed that their knowledge of Christian (and Druze) family law was very limited, and sometimes almost non-existent, which confirms the statement of the senior lawyer 'Ali Mulhim.
33 The Greek Orthodox Patriarchate of Antioch and All the East has its seat in Damascus.
34 Various sources have hinted that the Orthodox churches are drafting new laws, but as far as I know none of these drafts have been submitted to Parliament.
35 In Arabic commonly referred to as 'evangelical' (*'injii*).
36 A relatively new group in Syria, originally from Sudan; interview with Boutros Za'our, judge of the Damascus Evangelical spiritual court, Damascus, 26 March 2009.
37 It was hinted that a new draft law had been submitted to the government for approval, but I have no up-to-date information on the current status of this draft; interview with Boutros Za'our.
38 Roman Catholic, Maronite, Syriac Catholic, Armenian Catholic, Melkite Greek Catholic and Chaldean Catholic.
39 El-Hakim 1995: 149.
40 The 'Code of Canons of the Eastern Churches' (*Codex Canonum Ecclesiarum Orientalium*) was issued by the late Pope John Paul II in 1990. This Codex

applies to members of the Eastern Catholic churches, and can be considered as an adjustment of and supplement to the so-called 'Code of Canon Law' (or 'Latin Codex') of 1983. The 'Eastern Codex' comprises only those matters where the Latin and Eastern traditions diverge; interview with Fr. Antoun, involved in the drafting of the 2006 law and judge in the Damascus Catholic personal status courts, Damascus, 25 April 2008.

41 Rabo 2009: 7.
42 Interview with Fr. Antoun, judge in the Catholic first-instance and appeal courts, Damascus, 26 March 2009.
43 For example, when it is established that the husband and wife are in fact brother and sister. Fr. Antoun informed me (interview) that in the 15 years that he had been a judge in the Catholic courts, the *wakil al-'adl* had never filed a nullification request to the court interview.
44 Tucker 1998: 40–2.
45 Articles 1, 5, 12.
46 In addition, the sacrament of holy matrimony is a union of a baptised man and a baptised woman who voluntarily consent to marry before God (Code of Canons of the Eastern Churches, Cann. 776 §1, 817).
47 Unfortunately, there are no detailed statistics on divorce available. Syria's Central Bureau of Statistics only publishes the total number of marriages and divorces; it does not, for example, specify the form of divorce. In 2007, 237,592 marriages and 19,506 divorces were registered in the country (in Damascus, 26,135 marriages and 5,080 divorces); source: Central Bureau of Statistics, *Statistical Yearbook 2008*, issue 61).
48 Reconciliation or arbitration is recommended by the Quran: 'And if two factions among the believers should fight, then make settlement between the two' (*Sura* 49:9).
49 Generally, the concept *sulh* denotes the idea of peace and reconciliation. According to Khadduri (2010): 'The purpose of *sulh* is to end conflict and hostility among believers so that they may conduct their relationships in peace and amity.' Various Islamic jurists have maintained that application of *sulh* is especially desirable when the disputing parties are related to one another; Othman 2007: 77.
50 See for instance Othman 2007.
51 Matthew 19: 6, *King James Bible*, 1611.
52 Interview with Fr. Antoun.
53 Interview with Fr. Eliyas, judge in the Catholic first-instance, Damascus, 12 March 2009.
54 Code of Canons of the Eastern Churches, Can. 790 ff.
55 Catholic court observation, Damascus, 12 May 2009.
56 Ibid.
57 Since this case was still in its early stages and my fieldwork ended a month later, I could not follow up on this case.
58 Also referred to as *khul'* divorce; in this chapter I use the term *mukhala'a*.

59 Personal communication with A.H., Syrian lawyer, 26 February 2009.
60 For example, based on a personal count (January 2009) of the Damascus court's registry, 700 cases were taken to the six Sharia courts in the main courthouse in Damascus. The highest number (264) were *mukhala'a* cases, compared to, for instance, 186 *tafriq* (judicial divorce) cases. Also, the majority of the cases I observed in the Sharia courts were *mukhala'a* divorces.
61 Article 121.
62 The other grounds for a judicial divorce are the husband's inability to have sexual intercourse (Article 105.1); husband's insanity (Article 105.2); absence of the husband without justification for one year or more (Article 109); husband's imprisonment for more than three years (Article 109); and husband's failure to provide maintenance (Article 110).
63 According to Article 112, para. 3, these arbiters should be family members of the spouses or otherwise persons the judge considers capable of bringing about reconciliation. However, in actual practice the court appoints professional arbiters who are its employees. In the six Damascus Sharia courts 31 official arbiters are appointed, most of them trained lawyers (personal communication with U.M., Sharia judge, 21 May 2009).
64 For a detailed description of these arbitration sessions in the Damascus Sharia courts, see the unique, though unfortunately as yet unpublished PhD thesis of Carlisle (2007), who conducted extensive fieldwork in a Damascus court, in particular chapters 5–8.
65 See also Carlisle 2007a: 242.
66 Sonneveld 2009: 144–6.
67 Depending on the husband's financial situation, the Sharia judges will generally award a wife minimum monthly maintenance of 1000–1500 Syrian pounds (roughly US$20–32). The amount is based on an average Syrian monthly income, that is, for example, for a teacher without a university degree between 6,000–7,000 Syrian pounds (roughly US$130–150), and for a teacher with a university degree approximately 10,000 Syrian pounds (roughly US$215). A well-off husband has to pay more maintenance to his ex-wife than the minimum, but the wife will first have to prove his financial status – this is no easy task for most women (personal communication with A.H., Syrian lawyer, 15 February 2009).
68 See also Tucker 1998: 99; Sonneveld 2009: 176–8.
69 Carlisle 2007b: 189, 206; see also Carlisle 2007a: 251, 258.
70 Cf. n. 68 above.
71 Personal communication with U.M.

References

Anderson, J. Norman D., 'The Syrian law of personal status', *Bulletin of the School of Oriental and African Studies*, 17/1 (1955), pp. 34–49.

Anderson, J. Norman D., 'Law as a social force in Islamic culture and history', *Bulletin of the School of Oriental and African Studies*, 20/1 (1957), pp. 13–40.
'Atari, Mamduh (ed.), *qanun al-ahwal al-shakhsiyya* (Damascus, 2006).
Berger, Maurits S., *Sharia and public policy in Egyptian family law* (Groningen, 2005).
—— 'The legal system of family law in Syria', *Bulletin d'Études Orientales* (Damascus, 1997), pp. 115–27.
Botiveau, Bernard, *Loi islamique et droit dans les sociétés arabes. Mutations de systèmes juridiques du Moyen-Orient* (Paris, 1993).
Cardinal, Monique C., 'Why aren't women shari'a court judges? The case of Syria', *Islamic Law and Society*, 17 (2010), pp. 185–214.
Carlisle, Jessica, 'Asbab li-l-darb ktir basita: the legality of claims of violence during judicial divorce cases in Damascus', *Hawwa* 5 (2007a), pp. 239–61.
—— *Rules, Negotiation, Claims and Counter Claims: Judicial Discretion in a Damascus Shari'a Court*. Unpublished PhD thesis, University of London, 2007b.
Central Intelligence Agency, *The World Fact Book* (online edition, 2009), at <https://www.cia.gov/library/publications/the-world-factbook/geos/sy.html>, accessed 28 July 2010.
Canon Law Society of America, *Code of Canons of the Eastern Churches, Latin-English Edition, New English Translation* (Washington D.C., 2001).
El-Hakim, Jacques, 'Syria'. In *Yearbook of Islamic and Middle Eastern Law* 1 (Leiden: Brill, 1995), pp. 142–55.
Ferguson, Fay and Nadia Muhanna, 'Personal status matters'. In *Syria Today* (online edition), August 2009, at <http://www.syria-today.com/index.php/august-2009/377-society/2443-personal-status-matters>, accessed 30 July 2010.
International Religious Freedom Report 2009, at <http://www.state.gov/g/drl/rls/irf/2009/127358.htm>, accessed 28 July 2010.
Khadduri, Majid, 'Sulh'. In Bearman, P., Th. Bianquis, C.E. Bosworth, E. van Donzel and W.P. Heinrichs (eds.), *Encyclopaedia of Islam* (Leiden, 2nd ed. 2010).
Layish, Aharon, 'The contribution of the Modernists to the secularization of Islamic law', *Middle Eastern Studies*, 14/3 (1978), pp. 263–77.
Maktabi, Rania, 'State, law and religion – gendered debates on family law in Syria and Lebanon'. Paper presented at the 15th Norwegian Political Science Conference, Trondheim, January 2007.
—— 'Family law and gendered citizenship in the Middle East'. Paper presented at the World Bank/Yale University workshop on 'Societal Transformation and the Challenges of Governance in Africa and the Middle East', Yale University, 31 January–1 February 2009.
Othman, Aida, ' "And amicable settlement is best": sulh and dispute resolution in Islamic law', *Arab Law Quarterly* 21 (2007), pp. 64–90.

Rabo, Annika, 'Gender, state and civil society in Jordan and Syria'. In Hann, C. and E. Dunn (eds.), *Civil Society: Challenging Western Models* (London, 1996), pp. 155–77.
—— 'Family law in multicultural and multireligious Syria'. In Collste, G. (ed.), *Possibilities of Religious Pluralism* (Linköping, 2005), pp. 71–87.
—— 'To reform or not to reform? Elusive family law debates in Syria'. Paper presented at a conference on 'Re-imagining the Sharia: Theory, Practice and Muslim Pluralism at Play', Venice, 13–16 September 2009.
Sonneveld, Nadia, *Khul' divorce in Egypt: public debates, judicial practices, and everyday life*. Unpublished PhD thesis, University of Amsterdam, 2009.
Tucker, Judith E., In the House of the Law: Gender and Islamic Law in Ottoman Syria and Palestine (Berkeley, CA, 1998).

7

MAKTUB: AN ETHNOGRAPHY OF EVIDENCE IN A TUNISIAN DIVORCE COURT*

Sarah Vincent-Grosso

'In Tunisia, the judge rules with the papers (*al-maktub*). Only the papers' (Saida, during her divorce).

Saida (1)

When I first met Saida, a woman in her mid-30s, she was in the middle of not one but two divorce cases; both she and her husband had filed for divorce on different grounds in different courts. She brought me back to the small apartment where she shared a single room with her three-year-old son. Opening a cupboard, she brought out a thick file full of papers related to her divorce cases. In them rested her hopes of bringing over two years of painful divorce litigation to an end, of being released from an unhappy marriage and of being granted her rights. She told me that, in a recent meeting with the judge, she had held her tongue and allowed her husband to speak. Instead, she handed the judge some papers: her proof – the documents would speak for themselves.

By the time I met Saida, I had developed my own relationship with divorce files during months of ethnographic research in the court. As a result, my heart sank a little – I had read too many cases which had been forced to change track in the middle or had been rejected due to the difficulties of providing proof relating to such an intimate domain of life. Her anxiety was mixed with hope, based on her confidence that her evidence would hold up in court. I was not so sure.

Introduction: How to Make Evidence Ripe for Use[1]

Documents have been described as 'the most boring of ethnographic artefacts'.[2] Many of my informants, however, find them far from boring. For lawyers, expert weavers of legal texts, both their livelihood and their ability to gain justice for their client are at stake. For the judge, the documents map out his[3] scope of intervention and the kind of judgement which may be produced. For litigants like Saida, her divorce settlement, or as she put it, her 'fate', lies in these assembled pages. In her words, at the risk of using a pun lost on some of my Tunisian informants but which highlights the uncertainties at play, the *maktub* ('that which is written by God', thus 'predestined', 'fate') may literally lie in the *maktub* (that which is written, proof).

This chapter aims to respond to pleas made by scholars such as Latour and Riles to take documents seriously by exploring a particular kind of legal document: the evidence provided in cases of divorce for harm. Whilst documents can be read in many ways,[4] when it comes to the law, they are frequently read for what they can prove.[5] In the present case, not only does evidence structure the kind of divorce available to a litigant, but it also serves as the basis for the divorce settlement, including any compensation payments.

Taking documents seriously means acknowledging the degree of agency inherent in the documents themselves, and refusing to subordinate them to the human actors which vie for our attention. In this spirit, Riles has written that 'documents anticipate and enable certain actions by others' and this leads her to consider the broader question of 'how diverse types of agency are produced, stretched or abbreviated through the *medium* of the documents'.[6]

The core argument in this chapter – that in legal practice making evidence ripe for use engenders considerable anxiety and uncertainty for divorce litigants – hinges on the word 'medium'. Documents appear as liminal spaces; they are 'mediations, their writers mediators between the ... text of (the) law and the particular events of the world';[7] in short they are 'fallible'.[8]

Seeing documents as mediums, fallible bridges between the real and the ideal, inherently unstable or uncertain, has several implications of interest for the present exploration of evidence.[9] Taking documents seriously allows us to erase the artificial boundary perceived between the courthouse and its social surroundings; the documents are links in a chain extending from the court out to society as a whole. No sooner has this constructed boundary been demolished, however, than it must be rapidly rebuilt to enable the operation of the court; in Pottage's words, 'lawyers and judges work only with the world represented in the file' and a file can be seen as a 'map of the world'.[10] In order to cross between the 'map of the world' presented in the pages of the file and the social facts (or between the particular case in hand and the official texts of the legal code) the judge has no choice but to traverse the treacherous terrain constituted by the fallible documents and pieces of evidence provided in the file.

'Facts,' as Latour has suggested, and as Saida was slowly learning to her great dismay, 'do not speak for themselves.'[11] Only particular facts lend themselves to being woven into the 'map' of the divorce file: those which trigger the production of a particular kind of legal document – legally permissible evidence. Consequently, not all facts, or rather not all kinds of evidence, are equally convincing.

The devil lies in the procedures; if procedures condition the production of evidence, it is impossible to consider the life of these documents in isolation from them. Procedures set the rules of the game and constrain the moves made by the different players, whether litigants, lawyers or judges, whilst never actually determining the results (Kelly, Lynch and Boden). Particular spaces open up where there is room for manoeuvre *within* the law (Kelly 2006). Seeing evidence and procedures in this light – as framing but not fully constraining actions– helps to draw out the creativity of the actors involved, on the one hand. and the 'agency' of the documents themselves on the other.

Kelly, writing on the use of identity documents in an entirely different context (the second Palestinian intifada), found them to be 'an unpredictable and unstable technique of governance, producing considerable anxiety for all those concerned'.[12] Drawing our attention to the processes by which documents are created and the ways in which they are used and interpreted, he found that:

> It is in the spaces created by the gaps in the law, rather than the law itself, that distinctions between Israelis and Palestinians are produced in everyday life [and that] suspicions therefore fill the gap between legal documents and their application.[13]

Such suspicions are also at work in the divorce court. In spite of the good intentions underlying many of the legal procedures, they create space for 'diverse types of agency to be produced', and for litigants and their lawyers to follow varied strategies during the divorce case. Some unscrupulous litigants display considerable creativity in manipulating the law for their own ends; judges and other litigants are only too aware of this, and it has an impact on the ability of evidence to 'speak for itself'. The greater the space in the law for potential manipulation, the weaker the voice of the evidence produced.

In the kind of spaces to be located here, in addition to anxiety and uncertainty, distinctions are also created. These are gendered distinctions, which play against the 'gender equality' (if we are to read this at face value) purportedly promoted by the Personal Status Code (hereafter PSC) and highlighted in the Tunisian constitution.[14]

Categories of 'good' husbands and 'good' wives, who fulfil their marital duties according to the law, are created in contrast to 'bad' husbands and 'bad' wives. Being designated in either category has crucial – and highly concrete – consequences for the litigant. Their divorce settlement will be affected in a more or less favourable way, with considerable implications for their life in the future. Less tangibly, a sense of justice will be seen to have been fulfilled or not, which informs their emotional response to the divorce.

In order to suggest where these spaces in the gaps in the law are produced, and how they play out along gendered lines in the evidence, this chapter will follow both Saida's story and Latour (2010) in tracing the bridges built between two kinds of texts: the formal legal code and particular case files. The first task must be to introduce the legal framework within which these files and their evidence are produced. On which grounds can litigants file for divorce for harm? Which kinds of evidence carry authority and tie the judge to a particular decision?

Secondly, we will turn to the evidence itself. Contrasting a sample of files based on cases of divorce for harm filed by women with those filed by men, against the ethnographic backdrop of litigants' strategies, will reveal the gendered dynamics inherent in the use of evidence, based on marital duties differentiated by gender and upheld by the legal code.

Finally, two cases will be dissected to demonstrate how similar evidence can open up different strategic possibilities for different litigants and lead to strikingly different outcomes; this is in itself a testimony to the uncertainty and anxiety experienced by litigants like Saida.

Part 1
A brief Overview of Tunisian Divorce Law

Since 1956, divorce in Tunisia, defined as the 'dissolution of marriage',[15] has been organised under the Personal Status Code, one of the first laws to be promulgated after Tunisian independence, and a symbol of the new state's efforts to promote women's rights. Making divorce available to women on an equal basis with men was an integral part of this endeavour, alongside the elimination of polygamy. The Personal Status Code has persisted as evidence of the state's continued championing of 'equality between men and women'[16] and was reaffirmed by the current president as part of the National Pact, signed just after he came to power in 1987.

In the post-independence codified law, religious courts were abolished[17] and replaced by a unified state court system to which both women and men must apply if they seek a divorce.[18] The three types of divorce were opened up to men and women on equal grounds:[19]

1. by mutual consent (*bi-ttaradi*).
2. at the request of one spouse for harm suffered (*darar*; hereafter 'divorce for harm')
3. at the request of one spouse (*insha'an*; hereafter 'divorce without grounds')

In the latter two cases, one or both spouses may demand compensation for the 'moral and material' harm caused to them by the divorce. The wife's exclusive right to receive material damages is premised on the husband's duty to provide for her after the marriage has been consummated; husbands receive moral damages only. A reform to this law in 1981 added a new element of gender inequality,[20] specifying that a wife may receive these material damages in the form of monthly payments rather than a lump sum. These payments are to compensate for the loss of a breadwinner and enable her to maintain the 'standard of living she was accustomed to' (Article 31, PSC) during the marriage, until she remarries or her material circumstances change. Moral damages may be paid to either spouse, and their assessment is based on the judge's evaluation of the extent of the harm caused by the divorce.[21]

In Tunisia, therefore, 'harm' enters the files in two ways: as itself grounds for divorce, or as the basis for a demand for compensation where the divorce has been initiated unilaterally. Crucially, the damages do not always flow in the same direction; evidence acts as a weir directing this flow.

Litigants requesting divorce for harm must prove the harm caused to them, and can ask their spouse to pay for compensation for this if successful; the settlement will be in their favour. Litigants requesting divorce without grounds is not required to provide any justification or evidence for their request; they are, however, expected to pay compensation to their spouse, on whom they are effectively forcing an unwanted divorce, and the financial settlement will be in their spouse's favour. As we will see, if in practice litigants are unable to prove the harm suffered on the basis of legal evidence, they may be forced to ask for divorce without grounds. In this case, it is in the interest of litigants to attempt to persuade the court that their demand are in reality based on harm, in the hope of reducing the compensation they will have to pay the other party. Therefore, both spouses frequently attempt to provide evidence to show that they will suffer the greater harm from the divorce, in the hope of gaining a favourable settlement; this is central in structuring the acrimonious game of ping-pong that is played out between litigants in the files.

The files themselves provided a visual clue, signalling things to me about the case inside, as I selected them from the shelf. War-torn, bulging files, thick with pages of contradictory evidence and correspondence, fast becoming tattered and bursting out of their yellow jackets, reliably announced the months or years of pain and heartache depicted inside. A thick file generally referred to a long and complicated case, and was typically for harm or potentially divorce without grounds; in contrast, files for mutual consent contained only the few essential sheets of documentation required, and generally looked neat and new, having spent less time circulating between various court offices.

Saida (2)

I never saw Saida's file,[22] but was sure that it would have been one of the heavier and more bedraggled ones. The concerns described above had already had a significant impact on her experience of divorce.

When I met Saida, she had already been through two years of litigation and two failed divorce cases, both initiated by her husband. His first case, for harm, in which he accused her of being violent to his mother, was rejected by the court due to lack of evidence. The evidence he presented to the court was weak, as we will see further below. The second case, he filed for a divorce without grounds. This case was littered with accusations against her, including of adultery, as she had allegedly declared in public that he was not the father of their son. She strongly refuted this; and it does not seem logical that she would slander herself in this way in public. In return, she began claiming substantial material and moral damages, based on his generous income as the owner of his own business. Unwilling to pay her any money, he dropped the case, telling the court that he wanted to stay with his wife and son. In reality, neither spouse wished to remain in the marriage. The main impact of this second reconciliation was for Saida to lose the rent allowance that the court had allocated to her during the divorce proceedings; the reconciled couple were assumed to be resuming married life under the same roof. The rent allowance had been essential, since her family lived far from Tunis and it was not an option for her to live with them, as divorcing women typically do. They did not in fact resume marital life, and she was left living in highly precarious circumstances, with no fixed income to support herself and no help from her husband. In this predicament, she was compelled to file a case against him to force him into paying her maintenance, a procedure that will be examined in more detail below.

Evidence, or the absence of it, structures the kind of divorce a litigant can file for. The use of evidence in cases of divorce without grounds would seem to be a grey area, a portal to the kind of uncertainties produced by legal procedure and experienced by those like Saida. This chapter will, however, focus predominantly on divorce for harm, in which the entire case hangs upon the presence of legal evidence. The next section will examine the form that this evidence can take and the procedures required to produce evidence that is legally valid or, in other words, holds agency or authority in the eyes of the judge. The production of evidence will then be considered in the light of the different grounds on which it is possible to file for a divorce, with which these forms of evidence are intimately linked.

Part 2
Some Kinds of Evidence Are More Trustworthy than Others

What the wife said contains no truth. The husband does carry out his marital duties according to custom and habit. Whoever alleges harm, must provide evidence for it. The current file is devoid of any proof of harm, such as a penal case or final judgement (a husband's lawyer writing in defence of his client in a divorce file, after his wife filed for divorce for harm).

This lawyer's[23] defence of his client sums up the key problems facing a litigant trying to file for divorce for harm; although all forms of legal evidence are theoretically permitted in divorce cases, jurisprudence holds that only final judgments – those which are no longer subject to appeal – can justify divorce for harm. These are, therefore, the ones that speak loudest to the judge. Other forms of evidence, albeit with lesser powers of conviction, nonetheless find their way into divorce files and are worth brief consideration; this is designed to mention the forms of evidence most relevant to the present discussion, rather than to provide an exhaustive and complete account of all forms of legally permissible evidence.

Tunisian law is strongly focused on *maktub*, 'that which is written', as opposed to oral forms of evidence. Officially, the divorce judgement is exclusively based on the written divorce file. It was these files that I was able to examine in the court office. Although the litigants are summoned for a private interview with the judge to attempt to reconcile them, due to his heavy workload not all of these were held by the Family Judge in person. During most of my time in the court, these sessions were divided between the judge's colleagues. However, this was changing as I was leaving the field; the Family Judge felt a strong sense of responsibility towards his work, and did not wish to 'divorce' a couple he had never met. 'It is not the same as just seeing the papers,' he told me. 'It is *personal* status law. You need to see the *person*.' As a result, and in spite of the heavy workload implied, he decided to take all the reconciliation sessions himself, in an attempt to prevent couples from 'hiding the truth'.

Whilst this would appear to underline the interpretative (even personal) role of the judge, it does not negate the important role played by evidence. First, some types of evidence restrict this interpretative space, and tie the judge more than others. Second, it is the written file that will be passed on to the Court of Appeal and assessed by the judge's colleagues, should either spouse appeal his decision.

If authority lies in the author, it is possible to follow Messick in noting that alongside changes in the nature of the Tunisian polity, 'the weight of authority shifted from the notary to the state.'[24] When

I asked the Family Judge about 'harm' and the acceptable means of proof, he echoed jurisprudence, telling me that there must always be something 'final': a final judgement which was no longer subject to appeal and which was not delivered in the absence of the defendant (implying a longer appeal period). The evidence he trusts most is that which bears the seal of approval of a state court and the guarantee that a fellow judge will have followed the appropriate procedures to validate that judgement. In practice, then, authority lies both in the author and in the procedures.

The Family Judge continued by explaining that harm may be proven by 'all means of proof', all of which must be backed up in some way by the authority of the state. Declarations made in front of the judge and recorded (for instance, during the reconciliation sessions) are considered binding, although a majority of litigants appeared aware enough of this fact to avoid making incriminating statements in his presence.

Two or more witnesses may prepare a written statement in the court or in front of a notary. The Judge was aware, however, that it is difficult to find witnesses in personal status cases, and it was extremely rare to find this kind of evidence in the case files. Contemporary forms of sociality in the urban setting of Ben Arous do not lend themselves to witnesses being present during marital disputes. Whilst I knew that some neighbours in the area I studied would sometimes intervene to help resolve marital disputes, people seemed far more reluctant to become involved with a court case or issues involving the police. This form of evidence, therefore, was rarely forthcoming.

A far more prevalent form of evidence, prolific in the divorce files, was that authored by notaries. The trust placed in notaries (*'udul*, 'just men') as expert witnesses, long present in the Maliki school of jurisprudence prevalent in North Africa,[25] is now predicated on the authority of the state; notaries are public officials, whose honesty must not be challenged.[26] Without doubting the notary, this evidence nonetheless has considerable limitations as it is only able to say certain things; it can speak of social facts (the furniture in the room was broken), but not of the all-important authors or their intentions (the husband or wife who broke the furniture in a fit of rage).

Finally, medical certificates, another frequent inclusion in the divorce files, suffer from similar weaknesses to those of statements by notaries. They can attest to the physical damage suffered, but do not identify the author of the violence. In addition, greater trust is placed in certificates issued by public doctors, as opposed to private doctors paid by their clients. First, these certificates are not without suspicion, thanks to the 'creative' use of such evidence by some litigants. A lawyer told me about a woman who had suffered considerable injuries in a car accident. She took the opportunity to produce a medical certificate listing the bones broken and stitches needed and kept this safely tucked away in a drawer. Some months later, she had a serious dispute with her husband and used the certificate to try to file for a divorce for harm. In this case, her subterfuge was quickly unveiled, but abusive acts such as this do not help inspire judges' trust in this kind of evidence. Second, as we will see below, it is not the role of the Family Judge to rule on domestic violence cases, which fall under the jurisdiction of Penal law. We are returned once again to the logic of demanding a final judgement to prove divorce for harm.

Saida (3)

Saida's husband's first divorce case for harm was rejected, as the only evidence he had against her was a judgement for violence that was not final, as it had been ruled in her absence. She had been sentenced to one month in prison for hitting his mother, who had a medical certificate stating that she needed 45 days' rest as a result of her injuries. Saida vehemently denies this.

Saida did receive considerable moral and material support from various neighbours who had become friends. As they provided tea, sympathy, a break from caring for her boisterous toddler alone and the chance to earn some money doing odd jobs, they witnessed her poor living conditions and suffering. It was never suggested, however, that any of these people could be witnesses in her divorce case. To support her current divorce case for harm, she had obtained a judgement against her husband for domestic violence. He used to beat her, she told me. She would hold her baby in her arms to protect herself and so he beat her around the head; she claims to suffer from headaches to this day as a result. She believed that this was a final judgement. Her husband had been sentenced to prison for six months, yet he never went to prison; the sentence was commuted to a fine. Was this a 'final judgement' as required by the judge? By the time I left the field, the status of this evidence was still not clear, even though Saida questioned multiple lawyers about it, sometimes in my presence. She appeared convinced that her evidence would speak to the judge and her rights would be respected as a result.

As opposed to the theoretical legal rule that 'all means of proof' are accepted, a hierarchy of types of evidence emerges, which speak more or less persuasively to the judge. The next section will relate the procedures for producing convincing evidence as grounds for divorce for harm. Which grounds for divorce leave litigants in a stronger or a weaker position strategically, with greater or lesser uncertainty as to the outcome of their case? Which forms of harm can be backed up by the most authoritative final judgements? In other words, how is 'harm' defined in law?

Part 3
First, Do No Harm: Grounds for Divorce

It follows from these uncertainties surrounding evidence that judges do not like cases of divorce for harm, which all too often end in rejection by the court due to a failure to provide convincing evidence. Of the 51 divorce files for harm that I examined, only 16 were accepted by the court, whereas 20 were rejected.[27] By comparison, of the 81 cases of divorce without grounds, only four were rejected on procedural grounds. This section will explore which grounds underlie the successful and unsuccessful cases; in particular, it will highlight how these differ along gendered lines.

In the absence of a definition of 'harm' in the legal code, the natural reference point for understanding harm related to divorce would be a definition of marriage; here too the law is silent and does not try to define this complex, changing institution. As a lawyer suggested to me: 'The law could never define marital relations. The law could never enumerate all the details and all the actions between the couple.' Instead, divorce cases must be read against a backdrop of what the law does say about 'marital duties', The most explicit reference to marriage is found in Article 23 PSC, known in legal circles as the 'Constitution of the Family', which specifies that each spouse must treat the other well, avoid causing them harm and 'fulfil their marital duties according to custom and habit'. This article frequently enters the divorce files, whether cited explicitly or in an implicit reference to 'marital duties' or 'custom and habit', building a bridge between the harm done in the particular case and the legal code.

This reference to 'custom and habit' has several effects. First, it explicitly summons the social into the legal domain of the courthouse. Second, it introduces subjectivity and offers the judge, as interpreter, a degree of flexibility in dealing with the couples who come into the court. A postgraduate law student implied to me that this was a pragmatic way for the legislator to allow the judge to deal with social diversity and change: 'Can we say that the legislator organises rights and obligations when they are left to "custom and habit"? Their definition is allowed to change with society'.

With Article 23 potentially a source of tension in itself, in encouraging creative interpretation of the law and underlining the important role played by family judges in this,[28] the article's subjectivity does not lend itself to the production of legally valid evidence. It is not surprising, then, that the key 'marital duties' that tend to be cited in cases of divorce for harm are backed up by specific laws and procedures elsewhere in the legal code which allow for the production of evidence. The agency or authority attributed to the evidence produced in each case, the degree to which the judge is inclined to view that evidence with suspicion, is a consequence of the procedures used to generate it.

The two main reciprocal duties viewed in this light are fidelity and the absence of violence. Violence is legislated against in the penal code, which was amended to introduce a stronger sentence (two years in prison and a fine of 1,000 dinars) in cases of violence perpetrated by the victim's spouse.[29] Like Saida's husband, spouses may also file for divorce if the violence was directed against a member of their family.

Adultery is equally forbidden in penal law and subject to five years' imprisonment and a fine of 500 dinars (Article 236, Penal Code); since 1968, this law has applied equally to men and women.

Both adultery and domestic violence law share the feature that the perpetrator's spouse may drop the charges at any time, and the state will not continue the prosecution, implying a desire to encourage the couple to reconcile and to protect the 'continuity of the family', as one lawyer put it to me. The same lawyer explained that these are seen as crimes of the 'couple' rather than as a matter of 'public order' in which the state and its police must intervene regardless of the desires of the immediate victim, as in the case of burglary.

Neila, another lawyer who frequently worked on divorce cases, lamented that, other than catching the couple *in flagrante delicto*, adultery is particularly difficult to prove. The female body may end up providing this evidence in the form of pregnancy or childbirth; modern DNA testing used to prove paternity also opens men up to being exposed as adulterers by the birth of a child.

Both violence and adultery have the potential to produce authoritative forms of evidence, it remains to be seen whether litigants are able or willing to go through the procedures necessary to produce them. If successful in enabling the production of final judgements, these could be seen as the most definitive forms of harm. Spaces for litigants to exercise different strategies are nonetheless opened up, and may not lead to the results we might have expected.

Tarek

In the court, I was told about a man we shall call Tarek. He had been married for around 20 years and had three sons, when he discovered that he suffered from a chronic illness. During a visit to the doctor, he was informed that this illness meant that he had always been infertile. Surprised, he told the doctor that this was impossible as he had several children. The doctor regretfully informed him that he could not be their father. A DNA test confirmed the bad news, and could have provided evidence to prove his wife's infidelity and to justify a divorce for harm. Court staff witnessed an emotional, tearful scene in which the children told him that they loved him, as the only father they had ever known. The court clerks were impressed with Tarek's capacity for forgiveness, as he decided to reconcile with his wife for the sake of his family.

Making Bad Husbands: A Husband's Duty to Provide Maintenance

Whilst the above duties, to refrain from violence and infidelity, apply to both spouses, the following duties – of providing maintenance *(nafaqa)* and cohabitation explored below – are distinctly gendered, relating respectively and exclusively to the husband and the wife.

A husband's duty to provide maintenance to his wife after their marriage has been consummated is made clear both in Article 23, which maintains the husband as the head of the household, and in Article 38 of the PSC. Article 39 would seem to offer him some reprieve, stating that a husband who is poor does not owe maintenance. However, the duty is absolute in that this article allows the judge to pronounce a divorce if the husband is unable to fulfil his duty for more than two months. The implication here is that a wife is materially dependent on her husband and should be freed to remarry if her husband fails to provide for her basic needs.

Various procedures are in place to ensure that a wife who is denied this vital living allowance can make a claim rapidly to the court to force him to provide for her. These cases take between two weeks and three months to reach a judgement.

Such cases are heard in the cantonal court, selected due to its accessibility for litigants; as a local court, the procedures are deemed easier, their cost is low and no lawyer is required. A case may be launched by the wife making a simple verbal complaint to the cantonal judge that she lacks maintenance, and showing her marriage contract to prove that she is married.

How does the court ascertain whether a husband is failing in his duty to provide maintenance? It begins with the presumption that if a wife comes to ask for maintenance, then he is not providing for her. Her words are backed up by two procedures, although the burden of proof remains on the husband to demonstrate that he does pay. First, the cantonal judge can ask a social worker to visit the marital home and to provide what the judge called 'real information'. Second, the husband will be summoned to a meeting with the judge, where he may also bring his pay slips or any other evidence of his financial resources such as tax returns, a second home or a pension. Some of these documents may prove elusive; for instance, many men are self-employed and would not receive an official payslip. An absence of official documentation to prove the husband's income is a frequent difficulty for these men and for the judge, who must take a decision about the appropriate level of maintenance payments the husband will be required to pay.

As another judge put it:

> The woman has all the rights. There is a presumption that he is guilty and he must prove the contrary. As for the wife, it is something negative – how could she prove he does not do something? She cannot prove that he does not pay. So a *nafaqa* case is easy for a woman. There is a 90 per cent guaranteed result.

Naturally, many of the women who initiate these cases are in genuine need. However, an awareness of the relative ease with which they can succeed in court, and the fact that such a judgement can be used as evidence in divorce cases, leads some women to take out a maintenance case and store the judgement 'just in case', to use as a weapon to pressurise their husband or to file for divorce in the future. Conversely, some women in genuine need refrain from taking their impoverished husbands to court.

What if the husband does not pay the amount awarded by the judge as maintenance?

Once a wife has a *nafaqa* judgement in her hands, there are various procedures available to enforce the sentence. The one relevant here, evidence of which is present in several of the divorce files, is the penal sanction, which men are subject to if they fail to pay maintenance for more than one month.[30] Repaying the debt to his wife releases a husband from his prison sentence, which may range from three months to a year. Crucial to the current argument, once a husband is in prison for failing in what could be seen as the ultimate male duty, various documents (judgement for *nafaqa*, judgement for failure to pay *nafaqa*) will have been produced that, stamped with the seal of the court and his colleague's approval and prior investigation, speak very loudly indeed to the divorce judge.

In the Files: The Wife's Initiation of Divorce for Harm

Failure to pay *nafaqa* could be seen as directly or indirectly related to all the cases of divorce for harm in my sample.

It is no coincidence that all the 13 successful cases of divorce for harm initiated by women included evidence of at least one other court case. Nine of these fulfilled the ideal of including a final judgement. In five cases the husband was in prison at the time of the divorce. A further husband would have been in prison for not paying *nafaqa* had he not been living in the USA. Three husbands were in prison for crimes related to their wives – adultery, violence and failure to pay *nafaqa*. Four were in prison for crimes unrelated to their wives – sexual abuse of a minor, drugs-related offences, bank robbery. The husband involved in the last of these attempted to defend himself by claiming that the bank had been harmed and not his wife, but the court was apparently unconvinced. In any case, an imprisoned husband is necessarily failing in his duty to provide *nafaqa*, itself grounds for divorce.

The remaining three successful cases included other cases which were still in process. Strikingly, all these cases involved domestic violence. In one instance, the husband, who a medical certificate stated was mentally ill, had allegedly attacked his wife with a knife. In allowing the divorce in the absence of a final judgement, my sense is that the court acted to remove these wives from immediate danger.

In all eight unsuccessful cases for harm initiated by wives, final judgements, or evidence of any other court judgement, were notably absent. Several of these used medical certificates as evidence of domestic violence; sadly, it is simply not the role of the divorce judge to rule on what would be a penal matter.

This picture of which pieces of evidence speak convincingly of a bad husband is in harmony with that painted by Naima, a female lawyer experienced in defending battered wives. Although the legal procedures are available to prove domestic violence, they are not always accessible or desirable. She was often forced to ask clients whether they preferred a long period of uncertainty with a violent husband or whether they would prefer to file for divorce quickly without grounds, at the risk of having to pay their husband damages. Divorce without grounds is often the default divorce option in the absence of evidence. As taking the husband to court for violence could take between three and nine months, many wives opt for the quicker option. This lawyer explained to me that the procedures could be drawn out even longer if the husband was tried in his absence, entitling him to five years in which to appeal. Only after this could she use the judgement as evidence. While we have seen, in the above cases related to domestic violence where no final judgement was present, that the court can be sympathetic, we do not know whether those decisions were later reversed in the Court of Appeal.

Saida (4)

Part of her arsenal of evidence against her husband, Saida also has a judgement against him. However, she talks about this more in terms of her relief that he is now forced to pay her and her son nafaqa, *her only stable source of income, rather than the role this may play in her divorce case.*

At roughly the same time as she filed for divorce for harm, her husband had initiated a case for divorce without grounds. Since dropping his previous case for divorce without grounds, he had found another woman and wanted to be free to pursue this relationship. In addition, he had 'sold' his business, which enabled him to claim that he was a simple employee earning a modest salary and thus would have fewer financial resources against which Saida could claim in her nafaqa *case or in the divorce settlement.*

It was suggested to Saida that she should just drop her case for harm; the uncertainties surrounding evidence mean that these cases are all too often rejected by the court. In any event, if he divorces her without grounds she will be entitled to moral and material damages, just as she would if she divorced for harm.

Nadia was also in the midst of a divorce when I met her. Herself a lawyer, she was very aware of the problems related to divorce for harm, and although she had gained a judgement against her husband for domestic violence, she did everything possible to push him to divorce her without grounds. This released her from the burden of proof, merely requiring her to attend court and claim she wanted to remain in her miserable, violent marriage for the sake of their baby daughter; if she had shown her desire to divorce, the couple would have divorced by mutual consent and she would lose her rights. Her plan apparently worked in her favour. However, as I was leaving, she was taking the divorce settlement to appeal; the damages awarded to her could not compensate for all she had suffered during her marriage. Although she was relieved to be free, justice remained elusive. Saida resisted resorting to this strategy of divorce without grounds, even where evidence seemed to be present. She was anxious, having been hurt by her previous experience; her husband had already dropped one case for divorce without grounds to avoid paying damages to her, and could easily do so again. The most certain path appeared to be to pursue her own divorce case, on the strength of the evidence that would surely speak in her favour.

Making Bad Wives: A Wife's Duty to 'Cohabit'

'The counterpart of maintenance is the wife's cohabitation' (a judge during an interview).

Marriage is premised on the reciprocity of rights and duties. Although the legal code refers to the consummation of the marriage as the condition for the wife to receive *nafaqa*,[31] current legal practice is represented by the judge quoted above, who sees cohabitation as its counterpart. Cohabitation should not be interpreted restrictively: a wife cannot fulfil her socially understood marital duties, such as housework, caring for the children and the couple's sexual relationship, if she is absent from home.

As a consequence, a wife's failure to cohabit releases her husband from his duty of maintaining her. This duty gains its legal validation via jurisprudence and Article 2, and (unlike *nafaqa*) has no specific backing elsewhere in the PSC. The Court of Cassation has repeatedly ruled that if a wife remains away from home and refuses to return, she is said to be failing to respect Article 23, which states that she must not cause harm to her spouse.[32]

Jurisprudence, however, also underlines that the wife can only be accused of abandoning the marital home if she has left with no justification, and that the court must therefore examine the reasons why she left.[33] The Family Judge told me that he would always look at such 'reasons' why she left home. For him to accept the case, her absence must be proven and 'without justification'; only then is a wife deemed guilty of this *'nushuz'* – a notion entirely restricted to women.[34]

It is this latter point that makes the difficult procedures of proving *nushuz* close to impossible. There are, nonetheless, some legal means available to a husband whose wife has abandoned the marital home. The husband may make an official demand for her to return, via a notary. In this, the wife is informed that if she fails to return she will be guilty of *nushuz*, and her husband will be entitled to divorce for harm. A notary may also be brought to the marital home to certify the wife's absence. As one judge told me, however, he would only accept a divorce case based on *nushuz* if the wife told him herself that she had left home for no reason, even if a notary's report had witnessed her absence. This approach is a reaction to the potential for abuse in the production of this kind of evidence. The notary may visit the marital home when the wife is absent for legitimate reasons such as shopping, working or visiting her family; and an unscrupulous husband may deliberately arrange for the notary to visit during such justified absence. Crucially, however, even supposing proof of her absence was accepted, the notary cannot attest to the reasons for it. Many wives are compelled to leave the marital home by domestic violence or by their husband's failure to provide maintenance, or they may have been forced by him to leave the house. In nearly all the cases I observed, the wife did not appear to be required to back up her justification with evidence; the benefit of the doubt seems to rest with her.

Although many documents are produced via these procedures (a notarised request to return to the marital home, the wife's notarised response to this request), they fail to speak of the all-important lack of justification for the wife's absence, and consequently, at best, whisper softly in the ear of the divorce judge. In the words of a former litigant, whose ex-wife had sent him to prison for failing to pay *nafaqa*: 'There should be a law to send wives to prison if they do not do their duty... The law seems to believe the words of women, more than the words of men.'

In the files: divorce for harm initiated by the husband

Testimony to these ambiguities and the potential for manipulation is the fact that there were only three successful cases of divorce for harm initiated by husbands. In contrast, nine other such cases were rejected by the court; six of these were based on *nushuz*.

All three successful cases were also based on the wife having abandoned the marital home. It is notable that in two of these cases the wives were entirely absent and did not communicate with the court at all during the case. In one case, the husband claimed that not even her parents knew where she was. In the other, she had allegedly left home only ten days after the marriage was consummated.

The judgement of the third successful case surprised me, in that its evidence and arguments echoed those found in those which had been rejected. The next section will explore this case in more detail in order to elucidate how different litigants may formulate different strategies based on the same evidence, with very different outcomes.

Part 4
A Tale of Two Contrasting Cases Based on *Nushuz*

Mohammed and Leila: Divorce for Harm Initiated by the Husband

Mohammed had filed for divorce for harm and argued, via his lawyer, that his wife Leila was failing in her duty to cohabit with him, as underlined in Article 23 PSC. As evidence, he provided a report prepared by the two notaries who went to see Leila in her father's house and transmitted his request for her to return to the marital home. Their report also recorded Leila's response to this; she stated that she had left as she was sworn at and beaten by her husband. In total, two such 'demands to return to the marital home' were included in the file.

Leila's lawyer asked the court to reject the request for divorce; there was no harm, given that Leila had left the marital home under duress and not of her own accord. As evidence, she drew on a statement Leila had made to the judge to that effect during the reconciliation session and which he had recorded. Rather, it was she who had suffered harm, as evidenced by two cases filed against her husband for violence, but which she had subsequently dropped. She had decided to tolerate this treatment to protect their young family. In spite of doubts over the wife's motives for leaving the marital home, the court decided to approve the divorce. That Mohammed had only claimed a symbolic millime in compensation from his wife may have helped to convince the court to allow the divorce in this case.

Ali and Souhayr: Divorce Without Grounds Initiated By the Husband

Ali also supported his divorce case by using two 'demands to return to the marital home'. However, unlike Mohammed he had decided to file for divorce without grounds. The judge cannot refuse this kind of divorce; what is at stake here is how much compensation Ali would have to pay his wife. His case was unusual in making explicit the suspicions and manipulations that implicitly underlie so many divorce cases, adding to the general atmosphere of anxiety surrounding them. His strategy aimed to reduce to a minimum the compensation he would have to pay, and to weave his somewhat shaky evidence into an eloquent narrative in order to convince the judge.

Ali's lawyer made it clear to the court that he was asking for a divorce without grounds in the best interests of his children and 'in respect for family relations', and not because he lacked the evidence he would need to ask for divorce for harm. As well as the 'demands to return to the marital home', he also referred to statements made by his wife to the judge during their reconciliation sessions and to the cantonal judge during a case she had brought against him for *nafaqa*, but later dropped. In these, she had allegedly confessed to leaving the marital home of her own accord.

In addition, he levelled a further accusation against her, which has legal consequences. She violated his right to visit his children by taking them away from their usual address on the day of *'Ayd al-Kabir* (a Muslim celebration). He provided a notary's report witnessing their absence from her father's address, which, in the words of the lawyer, 'shows the wife's intention to punish the husband and prevent him from seeing his children by misleading him that they were at the house they were usually staying in'.

The lawyer acting for Souhayr, his wife, shed a different light on this evidence, describing how Souhayr's hopes for a happy marriage had been dashed as her husband pressurised her, humiliated her and subjected her to continued aggression. First, her alleged confession that she had left the marital home was made under pressure from her husband and in a desire to continue married life (for social and financial reasons); and she dropped her *nafaqa* case because he promised to drop his divorce case if she did so. This left her in a precarious position, living in her parent's house with her three children and with no income of her own, supported only by her father's old age pension.

Her lawyer concluded that, as the husband's request for a divorce was not justified, there is no *nushuz* and Souhayr should be entitled to generous compensation.

Second, concerning the allegation regarding the children, the lawyer had the following to say:

> The wife contacted her husband by phone to inform him that they would be spending the holiday in her father's house in Tozeur,[35] taking the children with her. He gave his permission for this, as he could then weaken her by filing a complaint against her later on. He is the one who really humiliated his wife. It should be clear to the judge that the husband did not really want to reconcile with his wife, but more than this he wanted to send her to prison so that custody of the children would be taken away from her. All this means that our [...] demands should be granted to my client.

It is of note that it would be in her husband's best interest to gain custody of the children. This would allow him to break any remaining financial ties with his wife, as he would no longer have to provide her with their *nafaqa* or housing. In this case, as he had moved away from the capital, the incentive seems stronger still.

The court did grant quite generous compensation to the wife, who was awarded 5000 dinars in moral damages – 10 times her husband's monthly salary – and a monthly pension of 100 dinars following the divorce.

Souhayr and her lawyer succeeded in making Ali appear dishonest. From that point onwards, his evidence was silenced; this was possible *because* that evidence was of a kind that did not require the judge to listen and be tied to a particular decision. She seemed like the 'good' wife and he the 'bad' husband, and the court ruled in her favour.

Conclusion

Mohammed and Ali's divorce cases sum up the ways in which 'formal orders are incapable of *determining* the actual course and outcomes' even if they are 'nonetheless *practically* relevant to their conduct.'[36] Each litigant (and their spouse) chose a different strategy – with more or less success – yet in both cases this was shaped by the presence and quality of the documentary evidence available. These documents do not seem so boring after all.

Final judgements, dressed in their official garb, shout loudly and clearly. Demands to return to the marital home whisper softly at best and, like wolves in sheep's clothing, are likely to be treated with a great deal of suspicion. 'Facts do not speak for themselves'; some translate better than others via the procedures available – and in the light of the manipulation demonstrated above, not all documents are able to speak for them with the same conviction.

The documents thus enable different types of agency, allow different strategies to be followed, and frame – but do not determine – the choices litigants make during their divorce cases. The spaces opened up are like a stage on which litigants attempt to demonstrate perform their trustworthiness. In the absence of incontrovertible evidence, elaborate personal narratives and tragic sagas may seem compelling to the judge. As such, they also simultaneously expand or restrict the his flexibility to take decisions *within* the law, as in the contradicting cases highlighted above. The outcome is rarely predetermined in advance. This degree of interpretation, this uncertainty, is a breeding ground for anxiety, shared among litigants, and sometimes also by the judge.

The construction of evidence, like these personal narratives, is woven around the legal expectations of husbands and wives which are, in practice, found to be gendered; particular male and female subjectivities are called into play in the court as litigants strive to turn their spouse into a 'bad' husband or wife in the eyes of the judge. *Nafaqa* leads more readily to legally authoritative evidence than *nushuz* does, making opportunities to divorce for harm more readily available to wives than to husbands. Whilst the case material suggests this is also true in practice as well as in theory, the canvas against which these family sagas play out cannot be forgotten. As has been seen, various social and material constraints play their own role in a litigant's ability to follow the necessary procedures in producing certain pieces of evidence. On this level too, litigants' experiences of divorce bifurcate along gendered lines. In these spaces created by silences in the law, not only is a great deal of uncertainty produced – categories of 'good' and 'bad' husbands and wives are also created, with all the implications this can have in a divorce court.

Saida (5)

What of Saida? Although the gendered structure of divorce would seem to play in her favour, my concerns for her grew with our friendship. The strength of the evidence (maktub), *on which her desire to divorce for harm was pinned, was unclear. Nonetheless she clung to her documents, sometimes literally, carrying with her the copies she had obsessively made each time she went to court. I left before her judgement and do not know whether she found the justice she was looking for. At our last meeting, I found her anxious and tense, and sensed that her hopes of finding justice through the legal system were fading. 'In any case,' she sighed, comforting herself that her fate lay in the hands of a greater, benevolent power, 'it is all* maktub *{pre-destined, written by God}.'*

Notes

* Fieldwork for this chapter was carried out in the Personal Status Office of the Court of First Instance and in the lower-middle-class neighbourhood of Ben Arous between May 2007 and December 2008. Field research was partially funded by a Sutasoma Award from the RAI. All names and some identifying details have been changed. This chapter, and earlier drafts, have benefited from comments by my supervisors and from my writing-up seminar at the London School of Economics, from participation in the 2010 World Congress for Middle Eastern Studies (WOCMES) panel on 'Family Law in the MENA', and in particular, from the help of Maaike and Arzoo. My thanks as ever to my parents for editorial (and countless other forms of) support.

1. This question is a nod to Latour's work on a very different legal system in his 2010 study, of which Ch. 2 is entitled 'How to make a file ripe for use'.
2. Latour 2010: 26.
3. There are both male and female judges in Tunisia; however, to ease readability I will use the words 'he', 'him' and 'his' throughout the text.
4. Riles 2006.
5. See Kelly 2006; Messick 1989.
6. Riles 2006: 21 (emphasis added).
7. Messick 1989: 27.
8. Ibid: 36.
9. For a detailed exploration of the representational – and hence fallible – nature of documents, see Messick 1989.
10. Pottage 2004: 21.
11. Latour 2004: 82.
12. Kelly 2006: 90.
13. Ibid: 103–4.
14. Tunisian Constitution, Article 6 'Equality: All citizens have the same rights and the same duties. They are equal before the law.'
15. Article 29, Personal Status Code (hereafter PSC).
16. See at <www.tunisie.com/femmes>, accessed 26 November 2010.
17. Under the French protectorate, before independence, family-law matters were left to the jurisdiction of the religious courts. As a result, Muslim men and women had very different rights to divorce: husbands could repudiate their wives with no justification, and without paying compensation, while options for wives were far more restricted. A wife could divorce unilaterally (*khul'*), but her husband's consent was required, and she had to pay him compensation, forfeit her dower and lose any financial rights he had owed to her. She could also divorce her husband if he reneged on a clause that had been negotiated in the marriage contract, the most common being that he had agreed to allow her a divorce if he took a second wife. In all cases a divorce initiated by a woman was sanctioned by a male authority – either the judge or her husband, with the latter either consenting to *khul'* or having signed his consent

in the marriage contract. Only women were required to go to court and bear the burden of proof if their husband did not agree to a divorce. See Hafsia 2005; Blili Temime 1999 for more detail on the situation before 1956.
18 Article 30, PSC.
19 Article 31, PSC
20 Méziou 1984: 256.
21 See Welchman 2007 for a comparative perspective on how the structure of compensation payments in divorce law varies across the region.
22 I made it an ethical rule never to consult the files of people known to me; once no longer anonymous, I wished to leave my informants in control of what I knew about them.
23 It is not compulsory to use a lawyer in divorce cases. However, given the difficulties of evidence described in this chapter, lawyers are frequently used, in particular for the more complex cases where evidence was presented.
24 Messick 1989: 34.
25 See ibid, for a fuller discussion of the use of notaries and of written vs oral evidence in Islamic legal traditions.
26 See Charfi 1997: 252–6, for a more detailed and extensive discussion of the use of evidence in civil law cases.
27 Of the remainder, six couples agreed to divorce by consent, six litigants changed the type of their divorce to divorce without grounds and three couples reconciled. My sense is that these last three most likely reconciled because the litigants, like Rachida's husband, were unwilling to change their demand to one for divorce for caprice (at the risk of paying their spouse damages), and because they were unable to agree to divorce by mutual consent. It would not be surprising if, like Saida and her husband, these couples returned to the divorce court in the future.
28 See Voorhoeve, this volume, for greater detail on the judge's decision-making processes.
29 Article 218, Penal Code.
30 Article 53 *bis*, PSC.
31 Article 38, PSC. Interestingly, it is the consummation of the marriage and not the legal act of marriage (signing the marriage contract) that counts.
32 See for instance decision no. 2422, 4 February 1998.
33 Decision no. 20425, 7 December 1988.
34 Whilst *nushuz* may have a broader meaning historically and elsewhere in the Muslim world (for instance, the Hans Wehr Dictionary of Modern Arabic refers to it as 'violation of marital duties on the part of either husband or wife, specifically recalcitrance of the woman toward her husband and brutal treatment of the wife by the husband (Islamic Law)'), my use of it here to mean the wife having abandoned the marital home reflects the current juridical practice I was exposed to in the case files studied in Ben Arous.
35 A town in Southern Tunisia around seven hours' drive from the capital.
36 Lynch and Bogen 1996: 121.

References

Blili Temime, Leila, *Histoire de Familles: Mariages, Répudiations et Vie Quotidienne à Tunis, 1875–1930* (Tunis, 1999).

Charfi, Mohammed, *Introduction à l'Etude du Droit* (Tunis, 3rd edn. 1997).

Hafsia, Nazli, *Le Contrat de Mariage en Tunisie jusqu'en 1956* (Tunis, 2005).

Kelly, Tobias, 'Documented lives: fear and uncertainties of law during the second Palestinian *intifada*', *Journal of the Royal Anthropological Institute*, xii/1 (2006), pp. 89–107.

Latour, Bruno, 'Scientific objects and legal objectivity'. In Pottage, A. and M. Mundy (eds.), *Law, Anthropology and the Constitution of the Social: Making Persons and Things* (Cambridge, 2004).

—— *The Making of Law: An Ethnography of the Conseil d'État* (Cambridge, 2010).

Lynch, Michael, and David Bogen, *The Spectacle of History: Speech, Text and Memory at the Iran-Contra Hearings* (Durham and London, 1996).

Messick, Brinkley, 'Just writing: paradox and political economy in Yemeni legal documents', *Cultural Anthropology*, 4/1 (1989), pp. 26–50.

Méziou, Kalthoum, 'Féminisme et Islam dans la réforme du Code du Statut Personnel du 18 février 1981', *Revue Tunisienne de Droit*, 1984, pp. 253–82.

Pottage, Alain, 'Introduction: the fabrication of persons and things'. In Pottage and Mundy (eds.), *Law, Anthropology and the Constitution of the Social*.

Riles, Annelise, 'Introduction: in response'. In Annelise Riles (ed.), *Documents: Artefacts of Modern Knowledge* (Ann Arbor, MI, 2006).

Welchman, Lynn, *Women and Muslim Family Laws in Arab States* (Amsterdam, 2007).

8

JUDICIAL DISCRETION IN TUNISIAN PERSONAL STATUS LAW*

Maaike Voorhoeve

Tunisian personal status law is known for its 'progressive' character, shown for example by its prohibition of polygamy. Charfi writes: 'The Tunisian personal status code is much talked about, both in Tunisia and outside. Abroad, the code is often presented as a model of adaptation of Islamic law to the realities of the 20th century. It is in fact due to this code, that Tunisia is known as a modern state [...] Within the country, people are proud of the code, as people consider it one of the most important achievements of the nation, and maybe even the most precious one.'[1]

Nonetheless, Tunisian legislation contains many lacunae that allow for 'non-progressive' interpretations. This chapter examines what factors curtail the judicial interpretation of these lacunae judicial in the field of Tunisian personal status law. Part 1 addresses the concept of lacunae and judicial discretion, both in codifications in general and in Tunisian personal status law in particular. Part 2 describes how, in some delicate areas of law, this discretion leads to uniformity in judicial practices, but how in other areas such practices are characterised by diversity, and examines what factors lead to these different outcomes. I start with an outline of the methodology used in my research.

Methodology

The material for this chapter was collected during field work conducted between July 2008 and September 2009, in the context of a doctoral dissertation on the judicial interpretation of legislative lacunae in what I call 'delicate fields of law': those fields of law that are particularly sensitive as they concern topics related to a fundamental 'symbolic order' (Héritier 1996).

In this chapter I make use of field-work material concerning, first, divorce for harm; second, paternity of children born out of wedlock; and third, mixed marriages (specifically cases concerning marriage between a Muslim woman and a non-Muslim man, inter-religious succession, and custody by a non-Muslim mother after divorce).

The material for this chapter consists of recent court decisions, interviews and observations of reconciliation sessions in divorce cases. The larger part of it was collected at the Court of First Instance in Tunis (hereafter CFI Tunis), and dates from the years 2008–09. It includes court decisions issued by the two Family Chambers in this court; interviews conducted with both Family Judges, who are the *vice-présidents*, each presiding over one of the Family Chambers; and observations of reconciliation sessions presided over by the two Family Judges and other *vice-présidents* appointed to conduct such sessions. I also conducted field work at the CFIs in Sousse, Sfax, Gafsa and Le Kef, which resulted in a small collection of recent court decisions, interviews and observations. Finally, I collected published and unpublished decisions of the Court of Cassation, from the period 1996–2008. I also obtained one entire case file regarding a divorce for harm on the grounds of adultery.

In order to examine what factors curtail judicial discretion, I make use of ethnomethodology, which is an epistemological approach to the treatment of empirical data. It emerged in the 1960s as a critique of the dominant theories in the social sciences.[2] It is a sociological method of studying a variety of social practices, including the study of law.³ However, the ethnomethodological study of legal practice in the MENA remains uncommon.⁴

Ethnomethodology 'does not pursue the development of typologies or other analytic constructs'.⁵ It describes the acts in themselves, without explaining them on the basis of an underlying structure.⁶ In traditional sociology acts are often interpreted from a predefined theory. For example, Weber studied his data from the *ex ante* presumption of modernisation, Durkheim on the presumption that it reflected society, and Marx from the viewpoint of power relations.⁷ This is problematic as it can lead to what Garfinkel calls 'fact production': if a certain fact does not fit in with the theory, it is manipulated to make it do so. This risk is removed if the study is confined to what actors say.

Furthermore, ethnomethodology focuses on the social construction of reality, and examines how actors organise their everyday activities, what rules they apply. For this, ethnomethodology follows the *actor's account*. Garfinkel argues that actors apply certain rules to organise their everyday activities, and themselves try to understand what these rules are: they make 'inquiries to accomplish rational accountability'. Garfinkel underlines that the way in which actors understand their own acting, and their accounts of it, are reliable, or 'accountable'.⁸ In this way, ethnomethodology differs from other approaches in sociology and anthropology that presume a gap between actors' accounts of why they act in a certain way, and the 'truth'; this is known as the 'ironic' approach.⁹

This study examines how Tunisian judges organise their everyday activities, namely the application of the law: what factors do they employ to curtail their interpretational freedom? This is answered by following the judges' own accounts. Therefore judicial practices are not *ex ante* related to some underlying structure, such as Sharia. The academic value of an ethnomethodological study of judicial decision-making lies in the fact that law in action is a matter of constructing reality. One cannot obtain insights into judicial practice without considering the judge's account of this activity.¹⁰ The social importance of an ethnomethodological study of legal practice in the MENA is related to the current polarised social, political and academic climate. Following the judges' account of judicial interpretation forms a counter-argument to the many culturalist and orientalist studies that explain everything *ex ante* from the Sharia.

Part 1
Judicial Discretion

The existence of judicial discretion is not limited to Tunisian law: the phenomenon is universal and therefore judicial discretion is a crucial topic in legal theory (see for instance Kelsen 2002; Knight 2002; Hart 1994; Dworkin 1977; Kennedy 1997; Troper et al 2005). In the case of an open norm (e.g. 'equity'), the legislation is extremely vague and indeterminate, leaving much discretion to judges. For example, Tunisian personal status law grants child custody in accordance with 'the best interests of the child', which is a typical open norm.

But provisions that seem clear and determinate at first sight, can appear in specific cases to be *in*determinate. Hart calls these 'borderline cases' – those that are not regulated by the legislature, deliberately or because they are unforeseen. One cause of this indeterminacy is the open texture of language.[11] Hart gives the example of the rule 'No vehicles in the park'.[12] If a car enters the park, this clearly entails a violation of the rule; but if a cyclist or roller-skater does so, it is not clear whether this actually violates the rule. Here, the open texture of language ('vehicle') leaves interpretational freedom to the judge. Another reason for indeterminacy can be the legislature's desire to leave judges able to adapt the decision to the circumstances of the case. A third reason for lack of regulation is the wish to refrain from giving final answers to specific delicate questions.[13] By contenting themselves with providing open norms, the legislature leaves it to the judge to regulate certain sensitive matters. It has been argued that for this reason Tunisian personal status law is indeterminate on many matters.[14]

It should be noted that there is a large amount of theoretical literature on the question of whether judges do indeed have discretionary powers in hard cases, or whether they are bound by specific factors, such as jurisprudence (Hart 1994), principles underlying the legislation (Dworkin 1977), political preferences (critical legal studies), or other legal constraints (Troper et al 2005).

An example of the Tunisian legislature's desire to refrain from regulating sensitive matters concerns provisions in the field of mixed marriages. Tunisian legislation does not explicitly discriminate against inter-religious marriages, but at the same time it does not explicitly allow such marriages either – the relevant provisions are clearly ambiguous. Thus the article with regard to marriage impediments makes no reference to religion (a Muslim woman cannot marry a non-Muslim man), but the general article regarding marriage provides that a marriage should not violate the *mawani' shar'iyya*, a term that can be translated as 'legal impediments' or 'Sharia impediments'.[15] Likewise, the article regarding impediments for succession does not provide that a non-Muslim cannot inherit from a Muslim, but it prescribes that homicide is *one of* the impediments to succession (*min al-mawani'*); this implies that other impediments may exist which are not mentioned. Similarly, the law does not provide that a mother, to obtain custody rights after divorce, must be a Muslim; on the contrary, it provides that a non-Muslim cannot act as custodian to a Muslim child *unless* she is the mother.[16] But at the same time the law prescribes that the judge assign custody after divorce 'in the best interests of the child'.[17] The effect of these lacunae is to allow discrimination against mixed marriages.

Levels of Discretion

Tunisian personal status law is laid down in a variety of laws. Substantive law is codified in the Personal Status Code (PSC)[18] and additional laws. The PSC dates from 1956 and was amended several times (especially in 1981 and 1993).[19] Additional legislation includes the law legalising adoption (1957),[20] that addressing the question of the fund to secure the payment of maintenance after divorce (1993),[21] that relating to the community of goods within marriage (1995)[22], and that concerning children born out of wedlock (1998).[23] Other legislation applicable in personal status cases consists of the Civil Code (CC), the Penal Code (PC) and the Constitution (1957). Procedural law in the field of personal status consists of the Code of Civil Procedure (CCP), the Code of Civil Status (CCS, 1957) and the Code of International Private Law (CIPL, 1998).

Tunisian substantive law in the field of personal status contains many lacunae, but this is only one level of judicial discretion, which also exists on three other levels: the qualification of the facts, the requirements regarding evidence and the financial amounts awarded (in cases of maintenance or damages in divorce cases). An example of personal status law that contains these four instances of discretion is divorce for harm (*darar*).

In Tunisia the law provides that both spouses can file for divorce on three different grounds: by mutual consent (*bi-ttaradi*), without grounds (*insha'an*) or for harm (*darar*).[24] In the case of divorce without grounds, the spouse who initiates the divorce is liable to paying damages (*ta'wid*). For this reason, divorce for harm is financially a more attractive option, as in this latter case it is the *defendant* who must pay damages.[25]

However, the law does not define the term 'harm' in any way – its meaning is left vague, and judges are thus free to interpret this term.[26] This is the first instance of judicial discretion, namely at the level of substantive law. On the basis of court decisions, I concluded that judges generally award divorce for harm in cases of domestic violence, adultery or 'disloyalty', non-payment of maintenance and the wife's refusal to cohabit.[27]

To take the example of domestic violence, judicial discretion is not extinguished with the assertion that 'harm' is interpreted as embracing acts of violence. Three questions remain open to judicial interpretation: which acts qualify as 'violence', how the violence should be proven and what amount of compensation should be awarded.

The first question – which acts are to be treated as violence and which acts are not – concerns the manner in which the facts of the case are qualified.[28] For example, the Court of Cassation was repeatedly confronted with the question whether one act of violence sufficed to qualify a situation as domestic violence, or whether the violence needed to be repetitive.[29]

The second instance of discretion concerning the evidence that is required to prove violence is also open to judicial interpretation. Judges have discretionary powers here as the legislation is vague on the topic: the provision regarding evidence provides that 'No specific form is required for the evidence of an obligation, unless the law prescribes otherwise.'[30] I concluded elsewhere that Tunisian judges treat evidence of domestic violence in divorce cases cautiously, as they harbour suspicions about various kinds of fraud. For this reason, judges require either a confession, or the declaration of two witnesses who actually *saw* the act of violence, or a previous penal conviction for violence. Thus a medical certificate together with a police *procès-verbal*[31] is insufficient.[32]

The third instance of discretion concerns the amount of damages the defendant should pay. The claimant has a right to moral damages and, if the claimant is the wife, a sum in compensation for material harm. The legislation provides for indicators to calculate the reparation of material harm (*niveau de vie* and the costs of housing). However, the law is silent on the question of how the amount of moral damages should be calculated. In the decisions issued by the CFI in Tunis between 2008 and 2009, cases for divorce for domestic violence were either dismissed or changed during the process. Thus I cannot provide estimates illustrating the range of the sums decided upon for moral damages. But it is clear that, in the absence of indicators, there is much room for discretion.

Part 2
Uniformity and Diversity in the Application of Tunisian Personal Status Law

One would expect that with so many lacunae in both substantive and procedural law, Tunisian judicial practice would be characterised by a good deal of casuistry, i.e. diversity in the way different judges apply the law. But in fact this is not entirely the case: many provisions are applied in the same way by judges from Le Kef to Mednin to Tunis. This can be explained by several factors that curtail discretionary powers. Section one below enumerates the factors that limit judicial discretion, such as the intention of the legislature, precedents, doctrine, judges' training and procedural law.

But while a range of factors curtail discretionary powers, some questions do remain open to judicial discretion, resulting in a degree of diversity (casuistry) in the application of the law. Section two below elaborates on this issue.

Section One – Uniformity

Article 532 CC prescribes that 'when applying the law, it cannot be given another meaning than the one resulting from its expressions, its grammatical order, its usual significance and the intention of the legislature.' In this way, the legislation provides that discretionary powers should be curtailed by the preparatory work that accompanies legislation ('the intention of the legislature'). However, the PSC, which contains the bulk of Tunisian personal status law, was issued directly after independence and before the installation of parliament. Thus, in many cases such preparatory work did not take place.

Considering this situation, judges might look elsewhere for the intention of the legislature, such as in public communications by the President of the Republic or the Minister of Justice. Indeed, President Bourguiba publicly denied a break with Sharia when he stressed that all developments were accomplished 'in accordance with the teachings of the Holy Book'.[33] Similarly, Minister of Justice Mestiri pointed out that: 'The Tunisian legislature is inspired directly by the precepts of Sharia as they are enounced in the Quran, the *hadiths*, jurisprudence and doctrine, following a new conception of *ijtihad*'.[34]

But judges can also look into the exact wording of the legislation to discover the intention of the legislature. For example, in a case concerning inter-religious succession the Court of Appeal argued that as the legislature explicitly mentioned that homicide excludes a person from succession, this means that the intention was to exclude all other succession impediments, such as difference of religion (a non-Muslim cannot inherit from a Muslim).[35] This is in fact an interpretation method, based on reasoning *a contrario*.

Precedents

As Tunisia has a Civil Law system, the legislation does not provide that precedents are a source of law. Thus, judges are not officially bound by decisions of the highest court – the Court of Cassation – but in practice they tend to follow those decisions, simply because they do not wish to see their own contrary decision annulled on appeal. They learn about the Court of Cassation's decisions through a bulletin, the *nashriyat mahkamat al-taʿqib*.

Of those decisions containing reference to precedents, most did so in relation to *fiqh al-qada'* (jurisprudence) in general, without mentioning a specific decision. For example, the Court of Cassation argued in a paternity case that the paternity of a child born out of wedlock could not be established as 'the jurisprudence of the Court of Cassation (*fiqh qada' mahkamat al-taʿqib*) has confirmed that illegitimate relations cannot bring about paternity'.[36]

I came across one decision that explicitly referred to a particular judgment. The wife had obtained a maintenance decision (*hukm nafaqa*) from the Cantonal Court, but the husband went to appeal, arguing that the wife had no right to maintenance as she had left the marital home. The Family Judge annulled the maintenance decision, arguing that this was in accordance with 'the Cassation decisions (*aqrar taʿqibiyya*) of 13 November 1985, 13411, and 23 May 1989, 22664'.[37] (Ironically, this practice had already been abandoned by the Court of Cassation – see below.)

Despite these examples of reference to jurisprudence, I noticed regularly that Family Judges were not aware of certain positions taken by the highest Court, although the judges at the CFI Tunis assured me that they read the relevant bulletin every week-end.[38]

Doctrine

Another source of law that might curtail judicial discretion is doctrine. Law professors as well as practitioners publish articles, notably in three legal journals: *Revue tunisienne de droit*, *Revue de jurisprudence et de legislation* and *Actualités juridiques tunisiennes*. Similarly, edited volumes appear with contributions from a range of law professors, such as *Mouvement du droit contemporain. Mélanges offerts au professeur Sassi Ben Halima*.[39] Also, the former president of the Court of Cassation, Mohammed Lajmi, has published a book on the application of Tunisian personal status law, entitled *Qanun al-usra* (family law).[40] Copies of this were distributed among the two Family Chambers by the president of the CFI Tunis.

I came across only one decision in which reference was made to doctrine. In a case concerning divorce on the grounds that the wife had abandoned the marital home, the Court of Cassation argued that 'according to doctrine, marriage is a contract that involves duties for both husband and wife, namely that they live under one roof in order to give each other affection and to have sexual relations [...]'.[41]

Apart from this one example, I did not come across references to doctrine in court decisions or interviews. This seems to indicate that judges do not follow doctrine, and thus that doctrine does not significantly curtail judicial discretion. This suspicion is corroborated by the fact that judicial practice in the field of paternity flagrantly contradicts doctrine. Numerous articles have appeared, notably from Ali Mezghani and Sassi Ben Halima, on the question of the paternity of children born out of wedlock, where it is argued that judges should apply the relevant provision in the sense that it allows (full) paternity outside marriage.[42] Nevertheless, judges systematically refuse to interpret the law in this way. Similarly, many other articles appeared, notably this time by Sana and Souhayma Ben Achour, on jurisprudential developments concerning mixed marriages.[43] Nonetheless, judges at the CFI Tunis continue to follow the former practice (see below).

Custom and Habit

Some decisions in cases concerning divorce for harm on the basis of the wife's refusal to cohabit refer to custom and habit, *al-'urf wa-l-'ada,* as a factor that curtails judicial discretion.

The law does not explicitly prescribe that the wife should cohabit with her husband, so to justify the opinion that she in fact is so obliged, judges refer to the provision describing the reciprocal rights and duties within marriage (Article 23 PSC). This article provides that 'the spouses should fulfil their marital duties in accordance with custom and habit'. In some decisions, it is stressed that custom and habit prescribe that the wife cohabits with her husband, and that by violating this duty, the wife harms her husband.

Good Morals

Some decisions make reference to good morals as curtailing discretionary powers. For example, in a case concerning a child born out of wedlock, the Court of Cassation decided that recognition by the father (*iqrar*) could not effect legal paternity, as this would be contrary to good morals because the child was born out of illicit sexual relations.[44] In this way, the decision referred to Article 439 CC, which provides that recognition does not provide evidence if it is contrary to good morals.

Sharia

Some decisions refer to Sharia as a factor curtailing discretionary powers. This is done by mentioning *al-shar'ia, al-fiqh al-islami*, a specific *hadith* or a legal term originating in Islamic law (*nushuz, zina*).

That decisions mention Sharia is interesting, as the law does not *explicitly* provide for it to be a source of law. In this sense, the use of Sharia as a factor curtailing judicial discretion is different from the use of custom and habit (mentioned in Article 23 PSC) and good morals (Article 439 CC). The personal status code does not provide that in case of lacunae, the judge should have recourse to the Maliki *fiqh*, which is the case in Morocco.[45] Similarly, the Tunisian constitution does not provide that Sharia is a source of law, as the Egyptian constitution does.[46] However, the constitution does provide that the state religion is Islam (Article 1).

Tunisian judges are not trained in Islamic law: even if they wished to apply the *fiqh*, they in principle do not know what it consists of. This is because neither law school nor the *École Supérieure de la Magistrature* (ESM) pays attention to the *fiqh*, apart from a small introductory course in the first year of law school and some general outlines on the *fiqh* in the third-year family-law course.

However, reference to Sharia is made, for example, in decisions relating to mixed marriage. Here, the motivation consists of the argument that, as the legislation is unclear, recourse should be had to Islamic law, which (according to these decisions) prohibits marriage between a Muslim woman and a non-Muslim man, and inter-religious succession.

Another occasion on which reference was made to Sharia was in a 2007 decision of the Court of Cassation.[47] The case concerned divorce for harm on the grounds that the husband moved house and the wife refused to follow him. The family, who lived in Mednin, moved to Tunis for the husband, who suffered from epilepsy, to have medical treatment. After living in Tunis for some two years, the husband was cured, and decided to move back to Mednin. However, his wife refused to follow him, staying in Tunis with their children. The husband sought divorce for harm, on the grounds that the wife refused to cohabit with him. The Court of Cassation granted his claim, arguing that 'Amongst her basic duties according to Sharia and to the legislation (*shar'an wa qanunan*), on the basis of Article 23 PSC, are cohabitation and [sexual] relations (*musakina wa mu'ashara*) with her husband [...]' Thus, the Court of Cassation argued that Sharia prescribes that the wife should cohabit, and that by violating this duty, she harms her husband.

Some decisions refer to Sharia in more implicit ways. This is true for many cases dealing with paternity outside marriage. In some cases, the Court of Cassation cites the *hadith* that provides that 'the child belongs to the marital bed and the adulterer belongs to the stone'.[48] In other cases, the decision makes reference to the *fiqh*. For example, the court once argued that 'in case of vagueness in the legislation, the judge should have recourse to the sources of the law, namely the Islamic *fiqh*'.[49] Again, in other cases, the reference to Islamic law consists of using a term to denote a certain act that seems to be derived directly from that law. For example, in cases concerning divorce for harm on the basis of the wife's refusal to cohabit, decisions often use the term *nushuz*. As these decisions do not refer explicitly to 'Sharia', 'the *fiqh*' or a specific *hadith*, it is not clear whether in these cases judicial discretion is actually being curtailed by such sources. However, in employing these terms, the argument is already directed towards a certain decision. In this way, by qualifying behaviour as *nushuz* or *zina*, the judge in question certainly limits the possible outcomes of the case at hand.[50]

The Constitution and International Conventions

In some cases, reference is made to the Tunisian constitution and/or international conventions. References to the constitution concern the articles protecting the principle of equality before the law and of freedom of religion (Articles 5 and 6). References to international conventions concern the ICCPR, CEDAW and CRC.[51]

In the Tunisian legal system, the constitution prevails over national legislation, and international conventions over national law (Article 32 Constitution). Thus, the law cannot formally be interpreted in a way that contradict these two sources. Before their issuance, the *Conseil Constitutionnel* checks the conformity of laws with the constitution and with international conventions[52] and, after implementation, both lower Courts and the Court of Cassation check their compatibility with these sources (note that Tunisia, unlike Egypt, does not have a Constitutional Court).

Since 1999, an increasing proportion of decisions in the field of mixed marriages contain reference to the constitution or international conventions. There is an increasing practice among the courts to argue that as the legislation is not unclear on the matter, and as the constitution and international conventions prohibit discrimination and protect freedom of religion, the legislation should be interpreted in a way that allows the marriage between a Muslim woman and a non-Muslim man, inter-religious succession and the recognition of a foreign decision that attributes custody over a Tunisian child to a foreign, non-Muslim mother.[53]

Another instance where an established judicial practice was contradicted with reference to the constitution and to international conventions concerns a unique paternity case. In 2004, the CFI La Manouba decided on the paternity of a child born out of wedlock. The law prescribes that paternity can be established by marriage, recognition or a declaration by two or more witnesses.[54] As a rule, judges refuse to bring about paternity when a child is born out of wedlock,[55] but in the Manouba case paternity was nonetheless established. The court decided that the relevant provision is indeterminate and that on the basis of the constitution and of the CRC discrimination between legitimate and illegitimate children cannot be accepted, and therefore established the paternity relationship between the biological father and his child born out of wedlock.[56]

Training

Another factor that curtails judges' discretionary powers is their training. During their education in law school and at the *École Supérieure de la Magistrature* (ESM) – which provides a two-year training course for law-school graduates – future judges learn about how the law should be applied. This is done on the basis of two general introductory works on Tunisian law and legal interpretation[57], as well as important decisions of the Court of Cassation and doctrine. At the ESM, professors lecture on how the law should be applied. For example, Professor Sassi Ben Halima gave a lecture in 2008 on how the article with regard to paternity should be applied.[58] This seemingly enhances uniformity in the interpretation of the law, especially among those who graduated from law school and/or the ESM during the same period. For example, the two Family Judges at the CFI Tunis, who graduated from the same university at around the same time, cited the famous 'Hurriyya' case when asked about the application of the law concerning mixed marriages.[59] On the basis of this decision, dating from 1966, they argued that marriage between a Muslim woman and a non-Muslim man is null and void, and that a non-Muslim cannot inherit from a Muslim.[60] They continue to maintain this despite the fact that the Court of Cassation abandoned the practice.

Constant Deliberation Between Judges

The fourth factor that curtails judicial discretion is constant deliberation between judges on how the law should be applied. Once a year the ISM (*Institut Supérieur de la Magistrature*) organises a seminar for all the country's Family Judges, where they all give presentations on the interpretation of the law. Although these lectures do not have any binding force, they do enhance uniformity. Topics addressed here, for example, include proceedings and the provisional measures in reconciliation sessions, the calculation of maintenance, and the attribution of post-divorce custody.[61]

Another instance of judicial deliberation occurs during the monthly gatherings of the two Family Judges at the CFI Tunis. In order to prevent the two Family Chambers from interpreting the law differently, the president of the court invites the two Family Judges to his office every month. During this session, they go over a range of decisions taken during that period, selected by the president. One question to be addressed is for example the amount of damage awarded in divorce cases.[62] (Note – this is the only CFI in Tunisia that has two Family Chambers.)

The Case File

Another factor that curtails judicial discretion is the case file. The file of a case at the CFI Tunis serves as an example; it concerned the husband's suit for divorce for harm on the grounds of abandonment of the marital home and adultery.[63]

In the case in question, the wife had been sentenced by the penal judge to eight months' imprisonment for adultery, both in first instance and on appeal (adultery is punishable by up to five years' imprisonment).[64]

The relevant documents in the file were the following: first, documents relating to the penal case for adultery, consisting of the *procès-verbaux* of the police hearings of the husband, the wife and her lover, as well as two men who declared that she had proposed having sexual relations with each of them; a list of the telephone numbers dialled by the wife; and the decisions of the penal judge in first instance and on appeal;[65] second, documents relating to the divorce case: the birth certificates of the husband, the wife and their two children; the marriage contract; a *procès-verbal* of a bailiff declaring that on a certain day the wife was not at home, seeking to prove that she had abandoned the marital home; the claim for divorce for harm on the grounds of abandonment of the marital home; the pleas of the husband's and the wife's respective lawyers in the divorce case in first instance and on appeal; and the *procès-verbaux* of the reconciliation sessions in the divorce case.

As all these documents tended to confirm the adultery, the file pointed the judge in a certain direction and limited the possibility for him of refusing the suit for divorce for harm.

It should be underlined here that the members of the judicial corpus (both the police and the reconciliation judge) have a great deal of influence on the composition of the evidence, and thus on the contents of the case file, as the *procès-verbaux* are non-verbatim records of the litigants' statements. An example of the reconciliation judge's influence on the contents of the *procès-verbal*, and therefore on the file, and therefore on the outcome of the case, was demonstrated in a divorce case for domestic violence. During the reconciliation session I attended, the husband confessed that he had attacked his wife with a chair. As the judge did not make a note of this, the confession was not entered in the file. As a consequence, the wife's case was most probably dismissed, as she had no other evidence of violence.[66]

Procedural Law and Judges' Orientation Towards Procedural Correctness

In his praxiological analysis of an Egyptian personal status case, Dupret argues that judicial discretion is limited by the orientation of judges and other legal practitioners towards procedural correctness.[67] This not only concerns the anticipation of having a decision annulled on appeal on the basis of the interpretation of substantive law (see the discussion of precedents above). It also regards all those facets of a court case that are constrained by procedural law. This begins at the moment when a plaintiff submits a petition to the court: from this moment on 'the judge's work is, at least formally, constrained by the many stipulations of [the relevant] statutory provision. A sequential process is initiated in which the case follows a series of successive steps before reaching the stage of the judge's decision.'[68]

In divorce cases, the legislation provides that the claim should be addressed to the court and that the defendant must be summoned. The court then sets a date for the reconciliation session, and both parties are summoned to attend. At this session, presided over by a reconciliation judge, the judge attempts to reconcile the couple and provisional measures are taken. The session is recorded in a *procès-verbal*, and is followed by two more sessions – unless in case of divorce by mutual consent, or if no children are involved – after which a date is set for the court hearing. At this hearing, the parties or their lawyers have the opportunity to present documents containing evidence, after which both parties or their lawyers have the opportunity to respond to one another's documents. At the court hearing, a date is set for the final decision.

If one of these (or any other) procedural prescriptions has been violated, the decision risks annulment on appeal. The sequence is therefore recorded in the decision to make public that the necessary steps were taken. Decisions follow a format:

> The plaintiff addressed a claim to the Court and to the defendant, providing that [...]. For this reason, the Court set a date for a reconciliation session, which was attended by [...]. During the reconciliation session, the parties claimed that [...]. Then the following provisional measures were taken and the court hearing was set for [...]. At the court hearing, the parties/lawyers claimed that [...]. Then a date was set for the final decision. The final decision is that given the fact that [...] and that [...], the Court decides that [...].'

The procedure delimits judicial discretion in different ways. For example, the legislation requires that in divorce cases the defendant is properly summoned to attend the reconciliation session and the court hearing. If the plaintiff cannot establish that this requirement was properly met, then the case is dismissed.[69] This procedural prescription was addressed in a large part of the reconciliation sessions I attended; it curtails judicial discretion in the sense that the judge cannot neglect the existence of the second party – in principle, both parties have to be heard.

Another example concerns the question of which party sues for divorce first. In one case, the husband sued for divorce for harm, consisting of an online love affair between the wife and her childhood lover, the evidence for which was a report containing every message sent on the internet between them. The Family Judge in question told me that, much as she wished to grant the husband divorce for harm, she could not, as the wife's suit for divorce without grounds (*insha'an*) predated the husband's suit for divorce for harm. Therefore, the husband's suit was dismissed.[70]

Section Two – Casuistry

Although to a large extent Tunisian judicial practice is characterised by uniformity, some is casuistic. This is true for the four levels of discretionary powers: the award of an amount of maintenance or damages, requirements regarding evidence, the qualification of the facts and the interpretation of the law. As causes for casuistry I came across the following.

Lack of Knowledge of Certain Precedents

As stated above, I did not come across many decisions that mentioned precedents, and I often noticed that the Family Judges at the CFI Tunis were not aware of certain positions taken by the highest court. The case of illegitimate children can serve as an example.

In 1998, the Tunisian legislature introduced a revolutionary law, entitled 'Law concerning the attribution of a father's name to abandoned children and children of unknown descent.'[71] This law provides that the court can grant the father's family name to children born out of wedlock. This has important consequences, both financial and social: financial, as the attribution of the father's name obliges him to pay maintenance;[72] social, as children born out of wedlock do not have a surname at all (they cannot obtain their mother's family name), or a fictional one. Without any last name, they cannot obtain an ID-card, which in turn prevents them from obtaining formal employment, and this is the reason why some illegitimate children are adopted by a family member.[73] When the Public Guardian (*tuteur publique*) assigns a family name to an illegitimate child, this does not necessarily protect against stigmatisation, as the family name is often recognisable as one belonging to a child born out of wedlock. For example, a child born in Gafsa will be called 'Gafsi', a family name that does not exist in Tunisia. Previously, these children would obtain President Bourguiba's last name ('the children of Bourguiba') and were recognisable as such.

In order to apply the 1998 law, biological paternity should be proven. This can be done through recognition by the biological father, or through a declaration by two witnesses that the child is the biological child of a certain man, or through a DNA test proving biological paternity.[74] However, many men refuse to co-operate with a DNA test, which leaves the child without any evidence. To solve this problem, the Court of Cassation decided repeatedly since 2000 that the man's refusal to co-operate constitutes evidence that he is the biological father of the child.[75] In this way, the family name can be attributed to the child without performing a DNA test.

In 2009, nine years after the Court of Cassation had taken its position on the issue, a Family Judge told me about the yearly training for Family Judges he had recently attended. He said: 'I have learned such an interesting thing: the Court of Cassation decided that if a man refuses to co-operate with a DNA test, the court can nevertheless grant the illegitimate child the father's name.'[76] This remark shows that this judge had failed to apply the 1998 law in all those instances in which the man refused to undergo a DNA test, with all the negative financial and social consequences for the children in question, simply because he was unaware of the ruling.

Diversity in the Assessment of Evidence

Differences in the assessment of evidence is the cause of many annulments on appeal. This seems self-evident, as the appreciation of evidence can be very delicate. For example, if a wife states consistently during three reconciliation sessions that she is mistreated by her husband, judges can decide differently on the question of whether the *procès-verbaux* of these sessions contain sufficient evidence of domestic violence to have legal consequences. This question was the subject of a difference of opinion between the two Family Judges at the CFI Tunis, in a case concerning a couple involved in both a maintenance and a divorce case.

The two cases were each brought before one of the two Family Chambers/Family Judges at the CFI Tunis. In the first case, the husband sued for divorce for harm on the basis of the wife's abandonment of the marital home. The second case concerned the wife's maintenance claim.[77]

The two cases were heard in the same period of time, and both judges based their decisions on what had been said during the reconciliation sessions in the divorce case. But the judges viewed the *procès-verbaux* of these sessions in two diametrically opposite ways.

The first chamber dismissed the husband's suit for divorce for harm because the wife had established that her abandonment was justified. In this case, the *procès-verbaux* of the reconciliation sessions were held to be sufficient evidence for the alleged violence.[78] The second Family Judge, on the other hand, dismissed the wife's claim for maintenance, arguing that the wife had no right to maintenance, since her leaving the marital home was in fact without such justification.[79] This demonstrates that the second judge did not consider the *procès-verbaux* to be sufficient evidence of domestic violence.

Development in the Interpretation of Open Norms in Substantive Law

An example of casuistry that is currently much-discussed in Tunisian legal circles concerns decisions in the field of mixed marriages. As stated above, the Tunisian personal status code does not explicitly discriminate against mixed marriages: it does make explicit that the marriage between a Muslim woman and a non-Muslim man is null and void, it does not explicitly prohibit inter-religious inheritance and it does not explicitly prevent a non-Muslim mother obtaining custody of her child. Nevertheless, the courts have applied the law in a 'discriminatory' way. In a famous case, known as 'Hurriyya', the Court of Cassation decided that the marriage between a Muslim woman (Hurriyya) and her non-Muslim husband was null and void.[80] The court argued that: 'It is incontestable that the woman who marries a non-Muslim commits a sin, and that Islamic law declares such a marriage null and void.' This decision was in line with a *circulaire* issued in 1962 prohibiting public officers from registering a mixed marriage.[81]

'Hurriyya' set a precedent for a judicial practice.[82] The invocation of the religious impediment was not limited to marriage, but extended to inheritance and custody. In fact, the original 'Hurriyya' case actually concerned an inheritance issue. Because Hurriyya's marriage had made her an 'apostate', the court decided that she could not inherit from her Muslim mother. Similarly, in custody cases the courts refused recognition of any foreign decision attributing child custody to a non-Muslim mother. They argued that if a child is a Tunisian Muslim, it is not in its best interests to be brought up in a non-Muslim country by a non-Muslim mother.[83]

It is only recently that more and more judges underline that the legislature has not pronounced on inter-religious issues, and that judges are therefore free to allow mixed marriages, inter-religious succession, and custody by non-Muslim mothers. With regard to the validity of mixed marriages, it was the decision of the CFI Tunis in 1999 that constituted a break with the practice,[84] the new interpretation being confirmed by the Court of Appeal of Tunis[85] and finally by the Court of Cassation in 2004.[86] Similarly, the practice of not recognising a foreign custody decision was revoked in 2001, when a Belgian woman sought recognition of a Belgian decision concerning her custody.[87] The Court of Cassation decided the child's Muslim Tunisian identity did not provide sufficient grounds to deny the non-Muslim mother her custody rights. But a breakthrough in the field of inter-religious inheritance took longer.[88] Although the Court of Appeal of Tunis had already affirmed that nothing impeded inter-religious inheritance,[89] it was not until February 2009 that the Court of Cassation accepted this position.[90]

Although the Court of Cassation has pronounced on these three issues, casuistry remains. This became clear during my fieldwork, in that the Cantonal Court in Tunis follows the reformed practice, whereas the CFI Tunis does not.

Regarding inheritance, the Cantonal Court is competent to draw up the list of heirs, after which the notary divides the inheritance on the basis of the legislation. Following the new practice, the Cantonal Court in Tunis includes the non-Muslim heirs, despite possible objections from the other heirs. But in cases regarding the validity of mixed marriages and the recognition of foreign custody decisions, it is the CFI Tunis which is competent. In interviews, both Family Judges at the CFI Tunis affirmed that marriage between a Muslim woman and a non-Muslim man is null and void unless the husband proves that he is a Muslim, which can be done with a *shahada* from the State Mufti.

Similarly, during observation of a session with the Children's Judge (a separate post within the Family and Children Division of the Court), it became clear that she does not follow the new practice regarding custody cases. In one case concerning a 13-year-old girl named Fathiyya, the facts were as follows: the girl was born and raised in Paris by her French mother and her father, who was of Tunisian origin but had dual French/Tunisian nationality. Every summer, the family went on holiday to Tunisia to visit the father's family. A similar arrangement continued after the parents' divorce (when they continued to live in Paris but in separate homes), and when Fathiyya was 12 she spent the summer with her father in his family's home in Zarzis, a small provincial town in southern Tunisia. At the end of the holiday, her father left for France and took Fathiyya's passport with him. Fathiyya stayed in Zarzis for another five months until her mother came to fetch her. Finally, her mother decided to move to Tunisia, and fetched her child from Zarzis to live with her in Tunis. Throughout all this time, Fathiyya's father was living in France.

At the hearing I attended, Fathiyya's mother requested an emergency measure, consisting of a temporary (24-hour) suspension of the travel interdiction which her ex-husband had obtained in respect of Fathiyya from the President of the CFI Tunis (to legitimise the fact that he had taken Fathiyya's passport away). The Children's Judge, as well as the delegate from the Child Protection Brigade, responded by saying that this would be unlawful as the mother would take the child to France, which would result in a violation of the law regarding custody.

Diversity in the Use of Manoeuvres to Circumvent the Law

An instance where the interpretation of the substantive law differs from one judge to another concerns paternity cases, although it should be made clear that this difference became less significant with the introduction of the law regarding the attribution of the father's name. In fact, the diversity among judgements concerning paternity outside marriage does not so much concern the interpretation of substantive law: all judges seemingly agree that the law does not allow the establishment of paternity for children born out of wedlock. Thus judicial decisions that do establish paternity out of wedlock remain silent on the subject of whether a child is in fact illegitimate. Instead, the diversity rests in a willingness to use manoeuvres to circumvent this interdiction, and to summon the Registrar to write the father's name on the child's birth certificate despite the lack of a marriage. This is feasible because the Registrar does not require evidence of marriage when a child is registered under the father's name. That there is diversity in the willingness to apply manoeuvres became evident in interviews with the Family Judges in Tunis (the two Family Judges), Sousse, Sfax, Gafsa and Le Kef. The diversity can be described as follows.

Two Family Judges, namely one at the CFI Tunis and the one in Le Kef, assured me that in order to establish legal paternity the claimant had to prove, by producing a marriage certificate, that the child was born within marriage.[91] The second Family Judge in Tunis, as well as the one in Sousse, confided to me that if a couple get married after the birth of a child, these judges will pretend that the child was born within marriage and will summon the Registrar to register the child under the biological father's name.[92] The judge in Sfax confessed that he allows the paternity claim if the biological father recognises the child, i.e. when he acknowledges that he is the biological father.[93] The judge in Gafsa, finally, told me that he also establishes legal paternity if the father recognises the child; but he goes further: when the man denies paternity, this judge grants the demand if the wife establishes that she had a relationship with the man at the time of conception. In this case, the relationship is qualified as an 'informal marriage', which is null and void, but according to the law does have legal consequences for paternity.[94]

Corruption

Some casuistry may be explained by corruption. For instance, if a wife sues for divorce for harm on the grounds of domestic violence, the case might be rejected despite the evidence of an eyewitness's report, perhaps because of personal relations between the litigant and the judge, or in exchange for money or for a favour.

The concept of corruption is often mentioned by litigants, but I have never witnessed it. Many litigants had stories about documents missing from their file, but they are often so much persuaded of their own rightness that they cannot imagine that the case was actually dismissed on legal grounds. For example, one informant told me about her divorce case, which was dismissed. She was sure that the reason for this outcome was that the scribe had removed the evidence from the file. However, the documents in question, a medical certificate and a police *procès-verbal*, are in any case insufficient for divorce for harm.

I did observe (attempts at) clientelism, in the sense that judges were visited or called by friends, or friends of friends, who had a favour to ask: 'Could the judge make sure that [...]?', was an often-repeated question. Requests could be as 'innocent' as talking to the judge handling the case, but some might have been rather decisive for its outcome – but I have no information on the results of such attempts.

Conclusion

This chapter has aimed to make three points. The key argument is that the 'progressive' character of Tunisian personal status law is only relative, as the legislation leaves much room for judicial interpretation. Judicial discretion exists on four levels: the interpretation of substantive law, the qualification of the facts, the requirements relating to and the appreciation of evidence, and discretion regarding financial awards. While due to the vagueness of the law, there is much diversity in its application, at the same time there is also a degree of uniformity. I have attempted to outline the factors that explain this uniformity, namely those that curtail judicial discretion, mentioning that judges have recourse to the intentions of the legislature, to precedents, to doctrine, to Sharia, to good morals, to custom and habit, and to the constitution and international conventions. Likewise, judges' training, and the continuous deliberation between them, the contents of the case file and the requirements of procedural correctness all curtail judicial discretion. However, despite these limiting factors a degree of casuistry remains. This is partly due to the limited knowledge judges have of precedents, to corruption, to the personal willingness of a specific judge to apply a certain manoeuvre to circumvent the law and to an (as yet ongoing and incomplete) development in the application of the law, where some judges follow a new practice whereas others choose not to do so.

Bernard-Maugiron writes: 'Under the guise of neutrality [...] judicial decisions hide many things.' One of the hidden aspects of judicial decision-making is the extent to which the decision is the result of judicial discretion. This 'fades before the abstract nature of legal jargon, [but a] careful reading of [a] decision [...] shows how the court first proceeded to a construction of the facts in the affair, before constructing the law to be applied and interpreting it'.[95] A careful study of the process of judicial decision-making reveals its hidden aspects; knowledge of how much judicial discretion judges enjoy, as well as of the factors that curtail or enhance this discretion, enables the person studying such decisions to understand their provenance.

Notes

* This chapter could not have been written without the co-operation of the Family Judges and the help of Baudouin Dupret, Jessica Carlisle, Dorien Pessers, Sarah Vincent and Sarah's parents.

1 Charfi 1973 : 11.
2 Garfinkel 1967 and Schütz 1987.
3 Travers and Manzo 1994
4 Dupret 2006a.
5 Manzo 1994 : 6.
6 Idem 1994.
7 Ibid.
8 Garfinkel 1967.
9 Dupret 1998.
10 Manzo 1994 : 10.
11 Bix 1991.
12 Hart 1994.
13 Maris 1996 : 3.
14 Méziou 1992 : 251.
15 Articles 5 and 14 PSC.
16 Article 59 PSC.
17 Article 67 para. 3 PSC.
18 *Majallat al-ahwal al-shakhsiyya*, 28 December 1956.
19 Law no. 81-7, 18 February 1981, and Law no. 93-74, 12 July 1993.

20 Law no. 1958–27, 4 March 1958, amended by Law no. 58–69, 19 June 1959.
21 Law no. 1993–65, 5 July 1993, amended by Decree no. 1993–1655, 9 August 1993.
22 Law no. 98–91, 9 November 1998.
23 Law no. 98–75, 28 October 1998, amended by Law no. 2003–51, 7 July 2003.
24 Article 31 PSC.
25 Ibid.
26 The Court of Cassation decided that the interpretation of *darar* is open to the discretion (*ijtihad*) of the judge. Court of Cassation 12 December 1989, 23643.
27 See for example: domestic violence – CFI Tunis 5 May 2008, 66970; adultery – CFI Tunis 26 February 2008, 63237; 'disloyalty' – CFI Tunis 21 April 2008, 61660; non-payment of maintenance– CFI Tunis 12 January 2009, 69314; wife's refusal to cohabit – CFI Tunis 5 January 2009, 67836.
28 Dupret 1998.
29 Interview with the head Public Prosecutor (*Procureur de la République*), CFI Tunis, 16 February 2009.
30 Article 422 CC.
31 An official record.
32 Voorhoeve 2010.
33 Speech 1966: 'Discours prononcé à l'occasion du mouled' ; see Tessler et al 1978: 147.
34 Mestiri 1966. See Ben Achour, Y. 2005–06: 58–9.
35 Court of Appeal 14 June 2002, 82861, in *Revue de jurisprudence et de législation*, (December 2002), pp. 85–6 (French), 75–85 (Arabic).
36 Court of Cassation 13 May 1997, 56315.
37 CFI Tunis 4 November 2008, 13465.
38 Interviews on 8 and 12 July 2010.
39 Tunis, 2005.
40 Lajmi, 2008.
41 Court of Cassation 7 June 2007, 12678.
42 Ben Halima 1975, Mezghani 2005.
43 Ben Achour, S. 2000: 403; 2003: 1203; Ben Achour, Y. 2005.
44 Court of Cassation 31 December 1963, 2183.
45 Article 400, *Mudawwanat al-usra*.
46 Egyptian Constitution, Article 2. Article 1 of the Tunisian Constitution provides that Islam is the state religion, and Article 38 that the President must be a Muslim.
47 Court of Cassation 6 December 2007, 15116.
48 *Al-walad li-l-firash wa-l-'ahir li-l-hajar*; see Court of Cassation 7 May 1996, 49089; 18 October 1996, 43354; 13 May 1997, 56315.

49 Court of Cassation 26 November 1996, 51346.
50 'To say of someone that he gives himself up to sexual perversion means providing an anticipatory justification to his condemnation as a debauchee. It means that typifying someone as perverse serves as a scheme underlying the interpretation of facts and purporting to give them a legal value' (Dupret 2008: 293).
51 International Covenant on Civil and Political Rights; Convention on the Elimination of all Forms of Discrimination against Women; Convention on the Rights of the Child.
52 Article 72 Constitution.
53 Marriage – Court of Cassation 2 March 2001, 7286–2000, *Revue de jurisprudence et de législation* (January 2002), pp. 87–8, 183–95; inheritance – Court of Cassation 5 February 2009, 31115, *Revue de jurisprudence et de législation* (March 2009), pp. 93–4; Custody – Court of Cassation, 20 December 2004.
54 Article 68 PSC.
55 This practice was set by Court of Cassation 31 December 1963, 2183; for a more recent decision, see Court of Cassation 18 October 1996, 43354.
56 CFI La Manouba 2 December 2003, 16189/53.
57 Charfi 1997; Ben Achour, Y. 2005.
58 Ben Halima, 24 October 2008.
59 de Lagrange 1968.
60 See for example interview with one of the two Family Judges at the CFI Tunis on 8 July 2010.
61 *Al-yawm al-dirasi al-takwin li-qudah al-usra, yawm al-jum'a, 29 fifri 2008*, 2007–2008.
62 Interview with the president of the CFI Tunis, 11 July 2010.
63 CFI Tunis 21 April 2008, 61660.
64 Article 236 PC.
65 CFI Tunis 12 September 2006, 27753; Court of Appeal Tunis 30 October 2006, 14264.
66 Reconciliation session headed by one of the Family Judges at the CFI Tunis, 19 January 2009.
67 Dupret 2006b.
68 Ibid
69 Article 5 CCP.
70 Interview with one of the Family Judges at the CFI Tunis, 9 February 2009, 65920.
71 Law no, 98–75, 28 October 1998, amended by Law no. 2003–51, 7 July 2003.
72 Article 3 *bis* of the Law concerning the father's name.
73 I witnessed this situation at an adoption session at the Cantonal Court Tunis, 27 August 2009.
74 Article 3 *bis* of the Law concerning the father's name.

75 Court of Cassation 16 November 2000, 4182; 12 October 2001, 10020; 2 March 2006, 7799.
76 To prevent any possible repercussions for this particular judge, I do not specify here at which Court this judge works, nor the date of the interview.
77 Here, the Family Judge (note, not the Family Chamber) at the Court of First Instance is competent in appeal of decisions taken by the maintenance judge of the Cantonal Court. In first instance, the wife had demanded a maintenance decision (*hukm nafaqa*), arguing that the husband did not pay any maintenance. This would constitute a violation of the personal status code, which prescribes that the husband should maintain his wife and children during marriage. The Cantonal judge awarded an amount of maintenance, to be paid monthly by the husband. The husband went to appeal, arguing that his wife had no right to maintenance since she had left the marital home.
78 CFI Tunis 20 October 2008, 66798.
79 CFI Tunis 4 November 2008, 13465.
80 de Lagrange 1968.
81 *Circulaire du Secrétariat de l'État du 17 mars 1962*, followed by a *Circulaire* issued by the Ministry of Justice, 5 November 1973. See Ben Achour, S. 2003: 1203.
82 Ben Achour, S. 2005: 827; Ltaief 2005; Ben Halima 2005: 134–5.
83 Court of Cassation 3 June 1982, 7422 and Court of Cassation 19 October 1985, 14220..
84 CFI Tunis, 29 June 1999, *Revue tunisienne de droit,* 2000, p. 403, annotated by Souhaima Ben Achour
85 Court of Appeal Tunis, 14 June 2002, 82861; 4 May 2004, 3351; 6 January 2004, 120; see Ben Achour, S. 2003: 1207
86 Court of Cassation, 20 December 2004.
87 CC 2 March 2001, 7286–2000, *Revue de jurisprudence et de législation* (January 2002), pp. 87–8, 183–95.
88 CFI 1 November 1994, 8179 regarding inheritance. See Ben Achour, S. 2003: 1205 ; CFI Tunis, 18 May 2000, *Revue tunisienne de droit* (2000), p. 247, annotated Ali Mezghani.
89 Court of Appeal Tunis, 6 January 2004; Ben Achour, S. 2003: 1208–12.
90 Court of Cassation 5 February 2009, 31115, annotated Malik Ghazouani
91 Interview with one of the Family Judges at the CFI Tunis, 9 February 2009; interview with the Family Judge, Le Kef, 4 February 2009.
92 Observation of a discussion between one of the two Family Judges and a lawyer on 10 June 2009, CFI Tunis; interview with the Family Judge, 27 January 2009, CFI Sousse.
93 CFI Sfax: interview with the Family Judge, 31 January 2009.
94 Article 22 PSC. interview with the Family Judge, CFI Gafsa, 2 February 2009.
95 Bernard-Maugiron 2008: 243.

References

Al-yawm al-dirasi al-takwin li-qudah al-usra, yawm al-jum'a, 29 fifri 2008 (2007–08).

Ben Achour, Rafaa, 'Le problème du contrôle de la constitutionnalité des lois par le juge ordinaire en Tunisie', *Revue tunisienne de droit* (1983), pp. 51–66.

Ben Achour, Sana, 'Le code tunisien du statut personnel, 50 ans après', *L'Année du Maghreb* (2005–06), pp. 55–74.

—— 'Figures de l'altérité. À propos de l'héritage du conjoint non-musulman'. In *Mouvements du droit contemporain. Mélanges offerts au Professeur Sassi Ben Halima* (Tunis, 2005), pp. 823–40.

Ben Achour, Souhayma, annotation of Court of First Instance, Tunis, 29 June 1999, *Revue tunisienne de droit* (2000), p. 403.

—— 'Tunisie', *Journal de droit international*, 4 (2003), pp. 1195–213.

Ben Achour, Yadh, *Introduction générale au droit* (Tunis, 2005).

Ben Ammou, Nadhir, 'Les revirements de jurisprudence'. In *Mouvements du droit contemporain. Mélanges offerts au Professeur Sassi Ben Halima* (Tunis, 2005), pp. 95–109.

Ben Halima, Sassi, annotation of CA Sfax, 20 April 1972, 575, *Revue tunisienne de droit*, (1975), pp. 143–61.

—— 'Religion et statut personnel en Tunisie'. In *Mouvements du droit contemporain. Mélanges offerts au Professeur Sassi Ben Halima* (Tunis, 2005), pp. 107–38.

—— 'Al-nasab w-al-ubuwa', lecture at the *École supérieure de la magistrature*, Tunis, 24 October 2008.

Ben Jemia, Mounia, 'L'exequatur des décisions étrangères en matière de statut personnel', *Revue tunisienne de droit*, (2000), pp. 139–57.

Ben Tardaiet Ghamersa, Monia, 'La preuve génétique de la paternité à travers la loi no. 98–75 du 28 octobre 1998 relative à l'attribution d'un nom patronymique aux enfants abandonnés ou d'une filiation inconnue telle que modifiée par la loi no 2003–51 du 7-7-2003', *Revue tunisienne de droit* (2004), pp. 157–204.

Bernard-Maugiron, Nathalie, 'The judicial construction of the facts and the law: the Egyptian Supreme Constitutional Court and the constitutionality of the law on *khul*''. In B. Dupret, B. Drieskens and A. Moors (eds.), *Narratives of Truth in Islamic Law* (London and New York, 2008), pp. 241–64.

Bix, Brian, 'H.L.A. Hart and the "open texture" of language', *Law and Philosophy*, x (1991), pp. 51–72.

Botiveau, Bernard, 'Le métier de juger. Constructions sociales et politiques de la figure du juge dans le monde arabe', *Droit et cultures*, 30 (1995), pp. 9–15.

Chalfouh, Imen, *La garde des enfants, issus de mariages mixtes, en cas de divorce*. Unpublished thesis, Faculté des sciences juridiques, politiques et sociales (Tunis II), 1994–95.

Charfi, Mohammed, 'Le droit tunisien de la famille entre l'islam et la modernité', *Revue tunisienne de droit*, (1973), pp. 11–37.
—— *Introduction à l'étude du droit* (Tunis, 3rd edn. 1997).
Djedidi, Narjes, 'L'article 32 de la constitution du 1er juin 1959 après la révision constitutionnelle du 1er juin 2002', *Revue tunisienne de droit* (2002), pp. 149–76.
Dupret, Baudouin, 'Entre le droit et la Loi. Le juge et le jeu de normalisation islamique du droit positif', *Droit et cultures*, 30 (1995), pp. 47–64.
—— 'Repères pour une praxéologie de l'activité juridique: le traitement de la moralité à partir d'un exemple égyptien', *Droits d'Egypte: histoire et sociologie*, 34 (1998), pp. 115–40.
—— *Droit et sciences sociales* (Paris, 2006a).
—— 'The practice of judging: the Egyptian judiciary at work in a personal status case'. In Masud, Kh.M., R. Peters and D.S. Powers (eds.), *Dispensing Justice in Islam: Qadis and Their Judgments* (Leiden, 2006b), pp. 143–68.
—— 'The categories of morality: homosexuality between perversion and debauchery'. In Dupret et al (eds.), *Narratives of Truth in Islamic Law*, pp. 289–324.
Dworkin, Ronald, *Taking Rights Seriously* (Cambridge, MA, 1977).
Garfinkel, Harold, *Studies in Ethnomethodology* (Englewood Cliffs, NJ, 1967).
Ghazouani, Malik, annotation of Court of Cassation, 5 February 2009, 31115, *Revue de jurisprudence et de législation* (March 2009), pp. 93–4.
Ghéraïri, Ghazi and D. Jaïbi, 'La constitution tunisienne et le droit international'. In Rafaa Ben Achour and S. Laghmani (eds.), *Droit international et droits internes: développements récents* (Paris, 1998), pp. 107–130.
Hart, Herbert L.A., *The Concept of Law* (Oxford, 2nd edn. 1994).
Héritier, Françoise, *Masculin/Féminin. La pensée de la différence* (Paris, 1996).
Jayussi, Lena, 'Values and moral judgment: communicative praxis as a moral order'. In Button, G. (ed.), *Ethnomethodology and the Human Sciences* (Cambridge, MA, 1991), pp. 227–51.
Kelsen, Hans, *The Pure Theory of Law*, trans. M. Knight (Union, NJ, 2002).
Kennedy, Duncan, *A Critique of Adjudication (fin de siècle)* (Cambridge, MA: 1997).
de Lagrange, Emérentienne, annotation of Court of Cassation, 31 January 1966, 3384, *Revue tunisienne de droit* (1968), pp. 114–20.
Lajmi, Mohammed, *Qanun al-usra* (Tunis, 2008).
Ltaief, Wassila, 'International law, mixed marriage, and the law of succession in North Africa: "... but some are more equal than others"', *International Social Science Journal*, lvii/184 (2005), pp. 331–50.
Manzo, John F., 'Ethnomethodology, conversation analysis, and the sociology of law'. In Travers, M. and J.F. Manzo (eds.), *Law in Action: Ethnomethodological and Conversation Analytic Approaches to Law* (Aldershot, 1994), pp. 1–15.

Maris, Cees W., 'Algemene inleiding'. In Maris, C.W. and F.C.L.M. Jacobs (eds.), *Rechtsvinding en de grondslagen van het recht* (Assen, 1996), pp. 1–37.

Mayer, Ann E., 'Law and religion in the Muslim Middle East', *American Journal of Comparative Law*, xxxv/1 (1987), pp. 127–84.

Mellouli, Slahhedine, 'Le juge et l'équité. Réflexions sur le recours à l'équité en droit privé interne', *Revue tunisienne de droit*, (1983), pp. 507–34.

Mezghani, Ali, annotation of CFI Tunis, 18 May 2000, *Revue tunisienne de droit* (2000), p. 247.

―― 'Le droit tunisien reconnaît ses enfants naturels. À propos de la loi no 98–75 du 28 octobre 1998 relative à l'attribution d'un nom patronymique aux enfants abandonnés ou de filiation inconnue'. In *Mouvements du droit contemporain. Mélanges offerts au Professeur Sassi Ben Halima* (Tunis, 2005), pp. 651–82.

Méziou, Kalthoum, 'Pérennité de l'islam dans le droit tunisien de la famille'. In Carlier, J.-Y. and M. Verwilghen (eds.), *Le Statut Personnel des Musulmans: droit comparé et droit international privé* (Brussels, 1992), pp. 247–74.

―― 'Approche iconoclaste du droit des successions'. In *Mouvements du droit contemporain. Mélanges offerts au Professeur Sassi Ben Halima* (Tunis, 2005), pp. 907–31.

Mhateli, Leila, 'Le conseil constitutionnel tunisien', *Revue juridique et politique*, 1 (2007), pp. 9–27.

Schütz, Alfred, *Le chercheur et le quotidien* (Paris, 1987).

Sghaier, Kaouther, *L'héritage de la non-musulmane devant les tribunaux tunisiens*. Unpublished master's thesis, Faculté des sciences juridiques, politiques et sociales, Tunis II, 2001–02.

Tessler, Mark A., J. Rogers and D. Schneider, 'Women's emancipation in Tunisia'. In Beck, L. and N. Keddie (eds.), *Women in the Muslim World* (Cambridge, MA, 1978), pp. 141–58.

Troper, Michel, V. Champeil-Desplats and Ch. Grzegorczyck (eds.), *Théorie des contraintes juridiques* (Paris, 2005).

Voorhoeve, Maaike, 'Divorce for prejudice on the ground of domestic violence: judicial practices in Tunisia'. Paper written for the eleventh Mediterranean Research Meeting, Florence and Montecatini Terme 24–27 March 2010, organised by the Mediterranean Programme of the Robert Schuman Centre for Advanced Studies at the European University Institute.

CONTRIBUTORS

Susanne Dahlgren is Senior Lecturer in University of Tampere. She did her postdoctorate at the Helsinki Collegium for Advanced Studies, served as the Academy of Finland research fellow in the University of Helsinki and acted as a Visiting Research Associate Professor in the National University of Singapore. Her book *Contesting Realities. The Public Sphere and Morality in Southern Yemen* was published in 2010 by Syracuse University Press. Her current research project *Politics of Islam, Post-Socialism and Modernization in the Arabian Peninsula* will lead to her second monograph and discusses, among others issues, the theme of moral conflicts over urban space in Yemen.

Baudouin Dupret is Directeur de Recherche at the French National Centre for Scientific Research (CNRS). He worked in Egypt (1995-2003), Syria (2003-2007), and he ran the Centre Jacques Berque in Morocco (2010-2015). He is based at the Ecole des Hautes Etudes en Sciences Sociales (EHESS), Paris. He is also guest lecturer at the University of Louvain and Assistant Professor at the Van Vollenhoven Institute of Leiden University. He has published extensively in the field of the sociology and anthropology of law, legislation and non-legal normativities, especially in the Middle East. Among his most recent publications are *Law at Work: Studies in Legal Ethnomethods* (with Michael Lynch and Tim Berard, Oxford University Press, 2015) and *La Charia. Des sources à la pratique, un concept pluriel* (La Découverte, 2014; English translation forthcoming with I.B. Tauris).

Esther van Eijk is a postdoctoral researcher working on projects on religion, marriage and divorce at Maastricht University, the Netherlands. Her PhD dissertation (Leiden University, 2013) focuses on the multireligious family law of Syria and will be published under the title *Family Law in Syria: Patriarchy, Pluralism and Personal Status Laws* (I.B. Tauris).

Sarah Grosso received her PhD in Anthropology from the London School of Economics. Her doctoral thesis entitled "Extraordinary ethics: an ethnographic study of marriage and divorce in Ben Ali's Tunisia" (2013) focused on the extent to which personal status laws supported or failed to support women's rights and gender equality. Currently she is working as Adjunct Professor in the Media Communications Department of Webster University in Geneva, having previously taught at the American University in Paris. She is also an independent consultant conducting research and evaluating projects for international organisations and NGOs.

Christine Hegel-Cantarella is Assistant Professor of Anthropology at Western Connecticut State University. She received her Ph.D. from CUNY Graduate Center and was affiliated with the Institute for Money, Technology, and Financial Inclusion (IMTFI) at UC Irvine. Her work has focused on questions of contemporary legal subjectivity in the Middle East, which she examined through ethnographic research on contracting and litigation in Egypt. This research has formed the basis of essays in *Anthropology of the Middle East and North Africa Into the New Millennium* (Indiana University Press) and *Law, Culture, and Humanities Journal*. Since 2011, Hegel-Cantarella has been collaborating with anthropologist George E. Marcus and designer Luke Cantarella on projects that explore intersections between design and ethnography.

Arzoo Osanloo is Associate Professor in the Law, Societies, and Justice Program at the University of Washington and also Director of the Middle East Center there. Professor Osanloo teaches courses on the intersection of law and culture, including human rights, women's rights in Muslim-majority societies, and refugee rights. She holds a PhD in Cultural Anthropology from Stanford University and a JD from American University, Washington College of Law. Her first book, *The Politics of Women's Rights in Iran* (2009), earned widespread praise. She is currently finishing a manuscript that considers the Muslim mandate of forgiveness in Iran's criminal justice system. Prior to entering academia, Professor Osanloo worked as a human rights lawyer in Washington, D.C. and San Francisco.

Massimo Di Ricco is lecturer at the Universidad del Norte (Colombia) and a research fellow attached to the UNESCO Chair for Mediterranean Intercultural Dialogue at the University of Tarragona, Spain, where he received his PhD with a dissertation entitled *Reclaiming the Community Public Sphere: Communal Individuals, Communities and the Lebanese System* (2008). He conducted fieldwork in Lebanon, and is currently involved in a project concerning sexual health and human rights in the MENA region. Areas of his research interest include minorities and communities in the Middle East and North Africa, the role of civil society and the status of individuals within it, examined from the perspective of 'personal rights'.

Nadia Sonneveld is a research fellow at the Centre for Migration Law at Radboud University, the Netherlands. She has conducted extensive research in Egypt and Morocco on the implementation of shari'a-based family law reforms.

Previously she was a guest scholar at the School of Oriental Studies (SOAS) in London and Al-Akhawayn University in Ifrane, Morocco. She is author of *Khul' Divorce in Egypt: Public Debates, Judicial Practices, and Everyday Life* (2012) and *Women Judges in the Muslim World: A Comparative Study of Discourse and Practice* (forthcoming in 2016, together with Monika Lindbekk).

Maaike Voorhoeve specializes in the socio-legal study of contemporary Tunisia. Her doctoral thesis on contemporary Tunisian judicial practice in the field of divorce was published with I.B. Tauris (*Gender and Divorce in North Africa*, 2014). Voorhoeve held post-doctoral positions and research fellowships at the Islamic Legal Studies Program of Harvard Law School, the Ecole des Hautes Etudes en Sciences Sociales, and the Forum Transregionale Studien of the Wissenschaftskolleg zu Berlin. She is currently a Humboldt Fellow at the Europe in the Middle East – The Middle East in Europe program at the Forum Transregionale Studien and at the Re-configurations Programme of the Philipps Universität Marburg.

INDEX

Abaza, Mona 84, 97
Abduh, Muhammad 92
Abu Hamdan, May 39–40
Adeni Women's Union (AWU) 19, 22
adultery 177, 183–184, 187, 200, 204, 213 *see also zina*
Ahmadinejad, Mahmoud 53, 64–65, 67
Alawi 151, 164n
Alexandria 143n
alimony 40, 113, 127, 129–130, 143n, 161 *see also nafaqa* (maintenance)
America-Mideast Educational and Training Services (AMIDEAST) 120–121
amin al-sirr (bailiff) 125
Anderson, J. and Norman, D. 148
apostasy 150, 218
Arab Association for Supporting Women's and Juvenile Issues (AAFSWJI) 20
Arabi, Oussama 94
Armenian communities 151, 152, 166n
al-Ashtal, Amal 28
al-Assad, Bashar 149

bailiff, *see amin al-sirr*
Bangladesh 86
bayt al-taʿa (house of obedience) 26
Ben Achour, Sana 208
Ben Achour, Souhayma 208

Ben Halima, Sassi 208
Berger, Maurits S. 148
Bernard-Maugiron, Nathalie 223
Bible 158
Bin Buraik, Abdul Aziz 23
Bogen, David 173
Bourdieu, Pierre 117
Bourguiba, Habib (President) 206, 216
Brown, Nathan 125

Cardinal, Monique C. 150, 151
Carlisle, Jessica 163
Catholic 33, 147, 148, 150, 151, 152–157, 159, 163, 166n, 167n
children 20, 23, 31, 85, 91, 118, 127, 184, 210
  adoption of 152, 203, 216
  custody 34, 40, 56, 72, 84, 124, 202–203, 211, 218–220
  and divorce 39, 88–89, 148, 157, 160, 163, 165n, 192–193, 213–214
  and *fiqh* 210
  and inheritance 41
  maintenance of 83, 96, 150, 189 *see also nafaqa*
  paternity 200, 207–209, 211, 216–217, 221 *see also* paternity
  and polygamy 94
  rights 35

Index

children – *continued*
  right to nurse (*hadana*) 148 *see also* nursing
  right to visit 192
  unborn 78
Chodosh, Hiram E. 122, 123
Christian 130
  activists 44
  communities 33, 46n, 147–148, 151
  courts 33, 153, 155–156, 164
  marriage 155–156
  and personal status law 150–152, 166n
civil law
  in Iran 60, 64
  in Syria 150
  in Tunisia 206
Congregation for Reform (Islah) party) 18, 20, 26, 27
Convention on the Elimination of Discrimination Against Women (CEDAW) 62, 149, 211
Convention on the Rights of the Child 67, 211
Copt 130
Cottam, Richard 59
Cuno, Kenneth 90

El-Dean, Bahaa Ali 124, 125
divorce
  and children, *see* children and divorce
  forms of
    bi-ttaradi (mutual consent) 176, 204
    insha'an (divorce without grounds) 176, 204, 215
    khul' 79, 85, 88–89, 102n, 119–120, 196n
    mukhala'a (wife-initiated or mutual consent) 159–163, 168n

    tafriq (judicial divorce) 160, 162, 168n
    talaq (repudiation) 16, 22, 36, 88, 156, 160–162, 196n
    for harm (*darar*) 119, 128, 161, 172, 175–183, 187–192, 195, 200, 204–205, 208, 210, 213, 215, 217–218, 221–222, 224n
  in Egypt 79, 82, 88–91, 92, 102n, 119–120, 128
  in Iran 65, 140
  in Lebanon 34, 35–36, 39–40
  in Syria 147–150, 153, 163, 165n, 168n
  in Tunisia 171–195, 196n, 203, 204–205, 208, 210, 213–216, 217–218, 221–222
  in Yemen 26, 37
dower, *see mahr*
Drieskens, Barbara 98
Druze 31–32
  Community Council (*al-majlis al-madhhabi l-al taifa al-durziyya*) 31, 37–38, 44, 47n
  courts 35, 166n
  faith 46n
  in Lebanon 34, 36
  and polygamy 150
  shaykh al-'Aql 37, 38, 42, 44, 46n, 47n
  shaykh al-Masheikh 37
  Supreme Council 35
  in Syria 147–148, 150, 151, 164n
Durkheim, Émile 201
Dworkin, Ronald 202

Egypt
  Administration of Justice Support (AOJS) 120–123, 140, 142n

Egypt – *continued*
  Cairo 77, 78, 80, 84, 91,
    104n, 118, 119, 120, 132,
    135, 143n
  Central Agency for Public
    Mobilisation and
    Statistics 87
  cost of marriage 83, 85, 100–101
  court 112–114, 117–118, 120,
    123, 125, 211
  Family Justice Project 118–120,
    123
  High Constitutional Court 99
  Law no. 1/2000 82, 102n, 161
  legal system 112
  Maglis al-Dawla 84
  Ministry of Justice 113, 118,
    120–121, 124–125, 129, 134
  National Center for Judicial Studies 120
  National Centre for Sociological
    and Criminological Research
    (NCSCR) 90–91
  National Council for Childhood and Motherhood
    (NCCM) 118
  National Lawyer's Syndicate 128
  Office of Experts (*maktab khubara'*) 113, 125, 127,
    131, 134, 137–139, 140
  second marriage 88–91
  unmarried women 87
  women's right 79
Egyptian Feminist Union 92
endogamy 34
Engel, David M. 116
Evangelicals (Protestants) 151, 152

family
  concept and perception in
    Iran 52–53, 67, 70
Fargues, Philippe 87, 90
fatwa 18, 85, 93–94, 96,
    102n, 104n

fiqh (Islamic jurisprudence) 1, 6,
    21, 62, 69, 147, 148, 155,
    164n, 207, 209–210
al-Fishawi, Ahmad 83, 84

Garfinkel, Harold 201
gender
  culture 24, 121
  and divorce 175, 182, 185, 195
  equality 33, 41, 43, 48n,
    174, 176
  roles and relations 36, 59,
    80–81, 175
General Union of Yemeni Women
    (GYUW) 15, 16
Ghalib, Taha 22
Greek Orthodox 151, 166n
guardianship *see also wali* (male
    guardian)
  of children 40
  in Druze family law in Lebanon 34, 36
  in Egypt (*wali*) 94, 99, 102n
  Public Guardian in Tunisia 216
  in Syria 148–149, 165n
  in Yemen 16, 21, 26

hadana, see children and right to
    nurse
hadith 20–21, 24, 159, 206,
    209–210
halal 95
Hanafi law
  in Egypt 80, 85
  in Lebanon 33, 35, 39, 40, 41
  in Syria 147, 148–149, 164n
Hariri, Rafik 36, 37, 46
Hariz, Noed 35
harm
  meaning and concept of 114–116,
    139, 182, 188 *see also* divorce
    for harm (*darar*)
Hart, Herbert L.A. 202
Hassan, Naim (Shaykh) 37–38

INDEX

Hasso, Frances S. 86, 97
Heidegger, M. 116
Herzfeld, Michael 115
hijab 23
al-Hinnawi, Hind 83, 84
honour
  women's and family 23, 46n,
    53, 78 *see* women's honour
    (*sharaf*)
house of obedience, *see bayt al-ta'a*

Ibn Baz, Abd al-Aziz 93, 96
ijab (marital proposal) 93
ijtihad' 206, 224n *see also* judges
  subjectivity and discretion
inheritance
  and children, *see* children and
    inheritance
  in Egypt 113, 127, 134
  and equality 44, 152
  inter-religious 218–219
  in Lebanon 33, 39, 41, 44, 47n
  in Syria 148, 151, 152
  in Tunisia 218–219
International Covenant on Civil
  and Political Rights
  (ICCPR) 211
Iran
  Centre for Women and Family
    Affairs 53, 62, 65–67
  Centre for Women's
    Participation 53, 62–64
  Family Protection Act and
    Bill 56, 68–70, 72,
    73n, 75n
  legal system 60
  Ministry of Justice 52
  revolution 52, 55–61
  struggle of power 53
  Supreme Council of the
    Cultural Revolution
    (SCCR) 62, 74n
  Veiling Act 56–57
  women's rights 53, 54, 62–64, 72

Islam
  and customs 21
  and women's rights 7, 13, 16,
    20–22, 24, 25, 29n, 58
Islamic feminism 58
Islamic government 73
Islamic jurisprudence, *see fiqh*
Islamic law 1–3, 15, 18, 55,
  102n, 149, 197n, 199,
  209–210, 218
Islamic republic 8, 52–54, 55, 57,
  58–60, 62, 72, 73, 74n
Islamic state 16, 52–53
Islamisation
  in Yemen 19
Ismaili 151

Jaafari law 33, 151
jabr (compulsion in marriage) 21
al-Jazeera 94, 96, 104n
Jewish communities
  in Lebanon 33
  in Syria 147, 148, 150, 151,
    164n, 166n
John Paul II (Pope) 152, 166n
Jordan 83, 85
judges
  subjectivity and discretion 60,
    117, 127, 183, 199, 200,
    202–205, 207–210,
    212–215, 216, 222–223,
    224n *see also ijtihad'*
Jumblatt, Walid 36–37

kafa'a (suitability of the groom)
  in Egypt 80, 85, 87, 98,
    100, 102n
Kelly, Tobias 183, 184
Kelsen, Hans 202
Kennedy, Duncan 202
Khatami, Mohammad 53, 54, 55,
  61, 62–64, 67, 75n
Khomeini, Ruhollah (Ayatollah)
  59–60, 61, 74n

Lajmi, Mohammed 207
Latour, Bruno 172, 173, 175
Lebanon 35, 152
  Beirut 31, 38, 40, 42, 152
  and citizenship 45
  French High Commissioner 33–34, 166n
  state and constitution 31, 32–33, 44, 46n
Lynch, Michael 173

ma'dhun (civil registrar)
  in Egypt 82, 91, 103n
mahr (dower)
  in Egypt 80, 84, 87
  as financial rights 160
  in Iran 52, 73n, 124
  in Syria 149, 160–161
  and taxes 52
  and temporary marriage 84
  in Yemen 16
maintenance, *see nafaqa*
Maliki law 180, 209
marriage
  minimum age 27, 30n, 40
  of a minor 26
  misyar (unregistered marriages)
    in Egypt 82, 85–86, 93, 95–96, 97
    in Saudi Arabia 86, 93–97
  mixed 200, 203, 209, 211, 218–219
  second 52, 68–69, 72, 80–81, 88–93, 94–95, 103n, 128, 196n
  temporary
    in Iran (*sigheh* or *mut'a*) 51–52, 70–72, 103n, 104n
    in Lebanon 103n
    in Yemen 18–19
  'urfi (informal or temporary marriage)
    in Egypt 79–80, 81, 83–84, 85–86, 89, 91, 97, 100
    in Tunisia 221

Marx, Karl 201
Masfar, Sa'id (Shaykh) 28
al-Mashtud, Abu Bakr 28
Memoirs of a Teenage Girl 77, 79
Messick, Brinkley 179
Mezghani, Ali 208
Millet, Kate 56
Mir-Hosseini, Ziba 123
modernisation 8, 16, 21, 28, 117, 201
modernity 13–14, 17, 24, 28, 54, 116–117
Moghaizel, Laure 44
morality
  in Iran 65
  in Yemen 13–14, 19, 27, 28
Morocco 115, 123, 209
Moustafa, Tamir 140
Muhammad Saif 'Abdallah Khalid al-'Adani 20–21
al-Muhayisni, Muhammad (Shaykh) 28
muhdir (process-server) 125
Munn, Nancy D. 117
musalaha (reconciliation) 155–157

nafaqa (maintenance) *see also* alimony
  children, *see* children and maintenance
  and cohabitation 189
  in Egypt 80, 83, 85, 92–94, 96, 98–99, 100–101, 119, 128, 143n
  and enforcement of the sentence 186
  failure to pay 187, 190, 226n
  as gendered duty 185
  in Iran 123–124
  in Lebanon 34
  lose the right of 157, 161, 207
  and *misyar* marriage 94
  in Saudi Arabia 102n
  and second marriage 93
  in Syria 149, 157, 161, 162, 168n

INDEX 239

nafaqa – continued
  in Tunisia 178, 185–187,
    188, 189–190, 192–195,
    203–204, 207, 212, 216,
    217–218, 226n
  and *'urfi* marriage 85
al-Najjar, Anissa 31, 34, 42–43, 44
National Centre for Sociological and Criminological Research (NCSCR) 90
National Women's Committee 27
nursing 148–150 *see also* children and right to nurse *(hadana)*
nushuz (rebellion/disobedience by the wife)
  in Tunisia 190, 191–194,
    197n, 209–210
  in Yemen 25

Orthodox 4
  groups 151–152, 166n
Ottoman Empire 23–24, 34, 46n, 81, 164n

Palestine 154, 174
paternity 34, 84, 148, 151, 184, 212, 220
  children, *see* children paternity and DNA test 184, 216–217
People's Democratic Republic of Yemen (PDRY) 15, 17, 19, 24
People's General Congress (PGC) 20
Personal Status Law
  in Egypt 79–80, 81–82, 86, 92, 97, 99, 100, 102n, 161
  in Iran 51–52
  in Lebanon 33–36
  in Syria 147, 148–152, 155, 159–160, 161, 163, 164n
  in Tunisia 174, 175–176, 179, 183, 185, 189, 191, 199, 203, 206, 207, 208–209, 222
  in Yemen 21, 25

polygamy
  abolition/ban of 36, 92, 175, 199
  and children, *see* children and polygamy
  and consent 92
  in Egypt 81, 82, 86, 88, 90–93, 94, 95, 97, 100–101
  and informal marriage 101
  in Iran 52, 75n
  in Lebanon 36
  limits of 16, 22
  and *misyar* 94
  in Saudi Arabia 94
  in Syria 149–150
  in Tunisia 175, 199
  in Yemen 16, 22, 24
Port Said 111, 113, 118, 122, 126, 127–129, 132–135, 141n, 142n
Pottage, Alain 173
pregnancy
  and adultery 184
  as shame 79
  and temporary marriages 84, 92
  unwanted 78
premarital sex 83, 100, 103n

al-Qadsi, Su'ad 21
al-Qaradawi, Yusuf 94–97, 98
Qasim, Amin 92
qubul (marital acceptance)
  in Egypt 93
Quran 20–21, 24–26, 60, 73, 149, 167n, 206

Rafsanjani, Hashemi (Ayatollah) 62
Rahimi, Amin Hossein 68–72
rape 79
Riles, Annelise 172
Rome 152–153
Rosen, Lawrence 115, 123, 124
Rozario, Santi 86
Rubaya 'Ali, Salim 15

Salafism
  in Yemen 18, 27
Salam, Nawaf 45
Salih, Ali Abdullah 26
al-Sana'ani, Salwa 23
al-Saqqaf, Abu Bakr 25–26
Saudi Arabia 19, 20, 27, 86, 93–96, 102n
al-Sayyid, Amir 34
sexual
  desire and fulfillment 84, 91, 92, 101, 104n
  intercourse 26, 30n, 91, 168n
  norms 84
  relations 19, 25, 189, 208–210, 213
  violence 79, 187
shabka (engagement presents)
  in Egypt 85
Sharia 1
  in Egypt 81–82, 84
  in Iran 53, 54–55, 60, 64, 69, 70, 71
  as Islamic law 4–6, 54
  perception of 4
  in Syria 150–151, 153–154, 155, 159–163, 164, 168n
  in Tunisia 201–202, 203, 206, 209–210, 222
  in Yemen 14, 20–21, 25–28
Shia 33, 52, 58, 74n, 103n, 151, 164n
Shojaee, Zahra 62
Singerman, Diane 85, 86
Sonbol, Amira El-Azhary 83
Sunna 26, 60
Sunni 21, 33, 104n, 151, 164n
Syria
  Court of Appeal 152
  Court of First Instance 156–157
  Damascus 47n, 103n, 148, 151, 152, 153–159, 160, 163, 166n, 168n
  French High Commissioner 166n

Law no. 98, 1961 166n
Law no. 18, 1975 149
Law no. 34, 1975 149
Law no. 31, 2006 152
Ministry of Justice 150
Syriac Orthodox 151, 166n

Tafsir (Quranic exegetics)
  in Yemen 21
Tanukhi, Emir 36, 46n
Troper, Michel 202
Tucker, Judith E. 154
Tunisia 92
  Cantonal
    court 185, 207, 219
    judge 185, 192, 226n
  Children's Judge 220
  constitution 174, 196n, 203, 210–211
  Court of Appeal 179, 188, 206, 219
  Court of Cassation 189, 200, 204, 206–212, 217–218, 219, 224n
  Court of First Instance 200, 205, 207–208, 211–213, 216–217, 219–221
  Decree no. 1993–1655, 1993 224n
  Family Chambers 200, 207, 212–213, 217
  Family Judge 179–181, 190, 200, 207, 212–213, 215, 216–217, 219, 221, 226n
  French protectorate 196n
  judges 201, 212, 222–223
  Law no. 1958-27, 1958 224n
  Law no. 58-69, 1959 224n
  Law no. 81-7, 1981 223n
  Law no. 93-74, 1993 223n
  Law no. 1993–65, 1993 224n
  Law no. 98-91, 1998 224n
  Law no. 98-75, 1998 224n, 225n

Tunisia – *continued*
  Law no. 2003–51, 2003
    224n, 225n
  maktub 171, 172, 179, 195
  Minister of Justice 204
  Tunis 178, 205, 210, 213, 221
Turkey 92, 103n

'ulama 20, 52, 58, 69, 71, 74n
United Arab Emirates 86, 102n
US Agency for International
    Development (USAID) 118,
    120–121, 142n

Vatican 33, 152, 153
violence
  domestic 157, 181–184,
    187–190, 204–205, 214,
    217, 218, 221

Wahhabism
  in Yemen 18
wakil al-'adl (church attorney)
    154, 167n
wali (male guardian) 94, 102n
  see also guardianship
waqf (religious endowment)
  in Lebanon 34, 37
Weber, Max 201
women's activism/group
  in Iran 52, 58, 67–68, 73
  in Lebanon 32, 38–43, 44
  in Syria 165n
  in Yemen 16, 19–21, 26, 28
women
  freedom to travel 79, 99, 220

honour (*sharaf*) *see* honour
  chastity (*'iffa*) 23–24
Women's Forum for Research and
    Training 21

Yazidi 164n
Yemen
  Aden 14, 18, 19, 24, 27, 29n
  constitution and laws 16, 17, 18,
    21, 29n
  Law no. 1, 1974 16
  Law no. 20, 1992 29n
  Law no. 30, 1992 14
  Southern
    laws 14, 25
    perception of Northerners
      19, 24
    women 13, 15, 17, 19, 22–23,
      26, 28
    women's rights 14–15, 21, 22, 24
Yemeni Women's Federation 19, 25
Yüksel, S. 99

zaffa (wedding party)
  in Yemen 26, 29n
Zammit, David 115
zawaj al-frind or *zawag al-frind*
    (friend for marriage) *see also*
    marriage, temporary
  in Egypt 85
  in Yemen 19
Zeisel, Hans 114
zina 209, 210 *see also* adultery
al-Zindani, Abdulmajid
    (Shaykh) 18–19, 27, 85
Zubaida, Sami 60, 74n